SACRAMENTO PUBLIC LIBRARY

SUPERMAN
ACTION COMICS
VOL. 1 INVISIBLE MAFIA

SUPERMAN
ACTION COMICS
VOL. 1 INVISIBLE MAFIA

BRIAN MICHAEL BENDIS
writer

RYAN SOOK
PATRICK GLEASON
YANICK PAQUETTE
WADE VON GRAWBADGER
artists

ALEJANDRO SANCHEZ
BRAD ANDERSON
NATHAN FAIRBAIRN
colorists

JOSH REED
letterer

RYAN SOOK
collection cover artist

PATRICK GLEASON and BRAD ANDERSON
RYAN SOOK
STEVE RUDE
original series covers

SUPERMAN created by **JERRY SIEGEL** and **JOE SHUSTER**
SUPERBOY created by **JERRY SIEGEL**
By special arrangement with the Jerry Siegel family

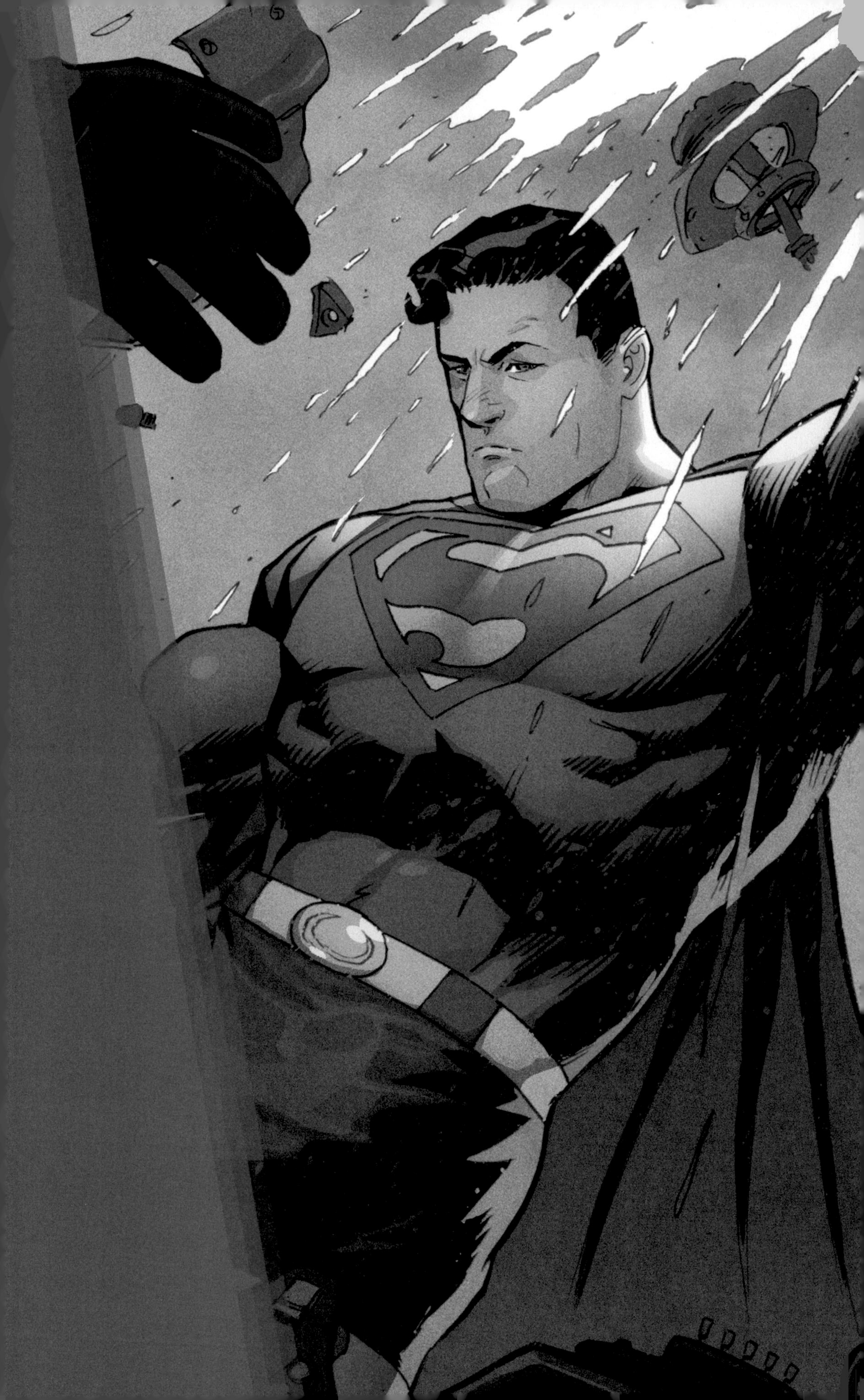

MIKE COTTON Editor – Original Series
JESSICA CHEN Associate Editor – Original Series
JEB WOODARD Group Editor – Collected Editions
SCOTT NYBAKKEN Editor – Collected Edition
STEVE COOK Design Director – Books
SHANNON STEWART Publication Design

BOB HARRAS Senior VP – Editor-in-Chief, DC Comics
PAT McCALLUM Executive Editor, DC Comics

DAN DiDIO Publisher
JIM LEE Publisher & Chief Creative Officer
AMIT DESAI Executive VP – Business & Marketing Strategy,
          Direct to Consumer & Global Franchise Management
BOBBIE CHASE VP & Executive Editor, Young Reader & Talent Development
MARK CHIARELLO Senior VP – Art, Design & Collected Editions
JOHN CUNNINGHAM Senior VP – Sales & Trade Marketing
BRIAR DARDEN VP – Business Affairs
ANNE DePIES Senior VP – Business Strategy, Finance & Administration
DON FALLETTI VP – Manufacturing Operations
LAWRENCE GANEM VP – Editorial Administration & Talent Relations
ALISON GILL Senior VP – Manufacturing & Operations
JASON GREENBERG VP – Business Strategy & Finance
HANK KANALZ Senior VP – Editorial Strategy & Administration
JAY KOGAN Senior VP – Legal Affairs
NICK J. NAPOLITANO VP – Manufacturing Administration
LISETTE OSTERLOH VP – Digital Marketing & Events
EDDIE SCANNELL VP – Consumer Marketing
COURTNEY SIMMONS Senior VP – Publicity & Communications
JIM (SKI) SOKOLOWSKI VP – Comic Book Specialty Sales & Trade Marketing
NANCY SPEARS VP – Mass, Book, Digital Sales & Trade Marketing
MICHELE R. WELLS VP – Content Strategy

SUPERMAN: ACTION COMICS VOL. 1: INVISIBLE MAFIA

Published by DC Comics. Compilation and all new material Copyright © 2019 DC Comics. All Rights Reserved.
Originally published in single magazine form in ACTION COMICS 1001-1006. Copyright © 2018 DC Comics.
All Rights Reserved. All characters, their distinctive likenesses and related elements featured in this
publication are trademarks of DC Comics. The stories, characters and incidents featured in this publication
are entirely fictional. DC Comics does not read or accept unsolicited submissions of ideas, stories or artwork.

DC Comics, 2900 West Alameda Ave., Burbank, CA 91505
Printed by LSC Communications, Owensville, MO, USA. 3/1/19. First Printing.
ISBN: 978-1-4012-8872-3

Library of Congress Cataloging-in-Publication Data is available.

PEFC Certified

This product is from
sustainably managed
forests and controlled
sources

PEFC
PEFC/29-31-337   www.pefc.org

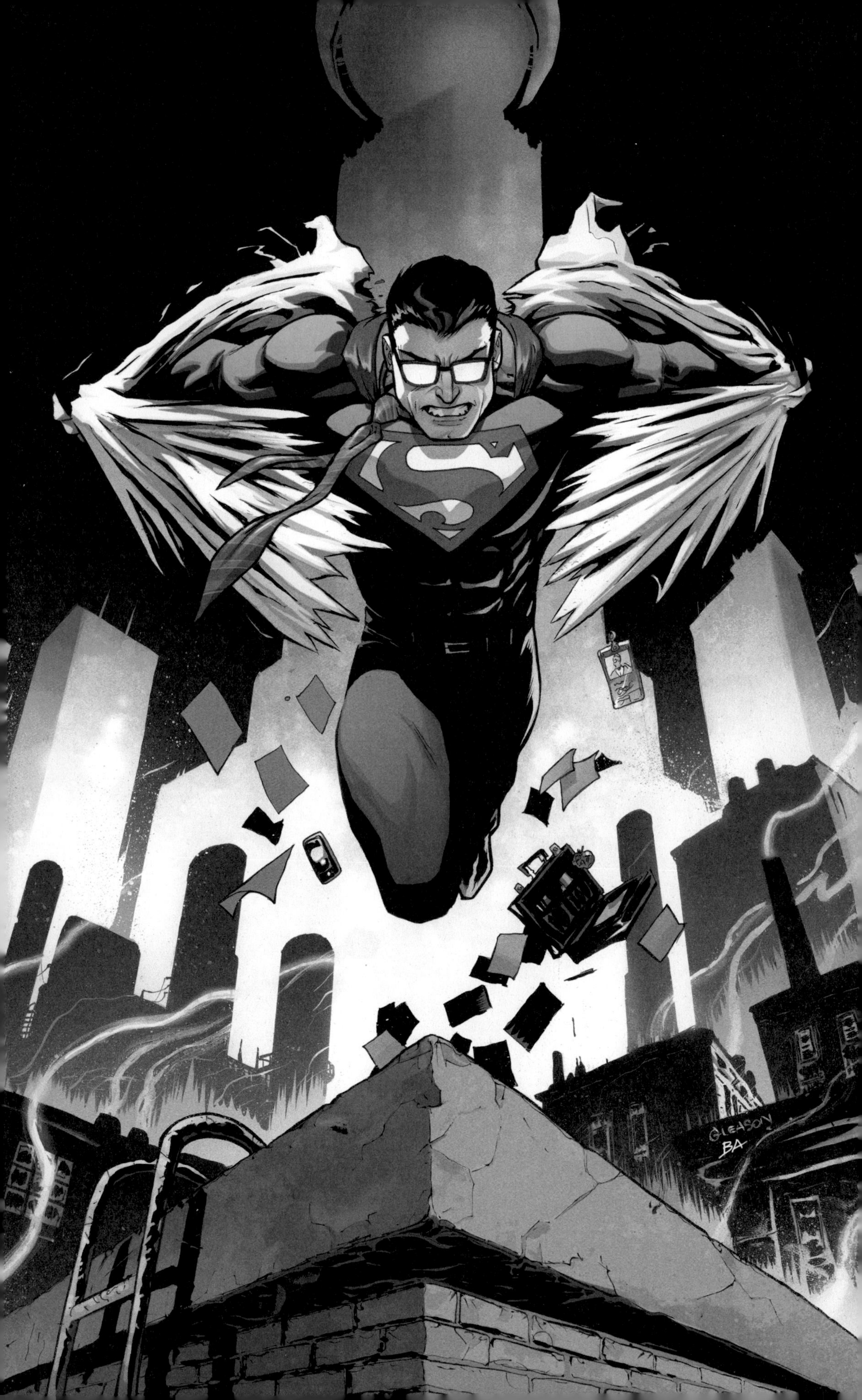
GLEASON
BA

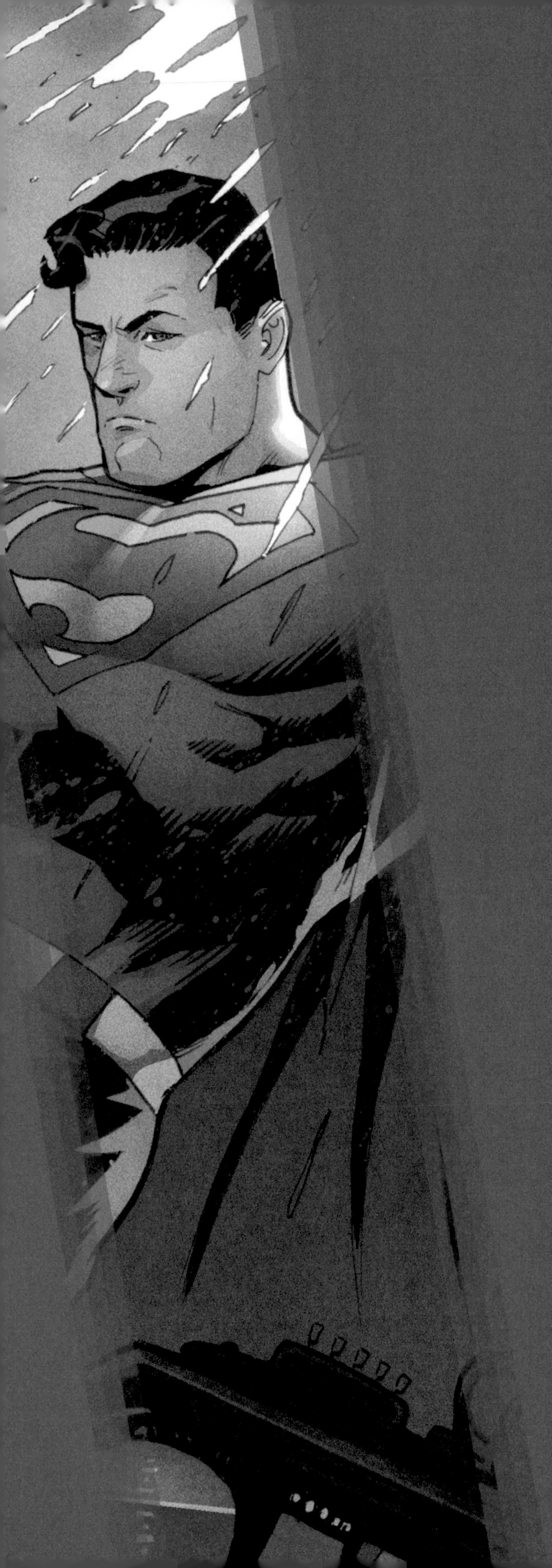

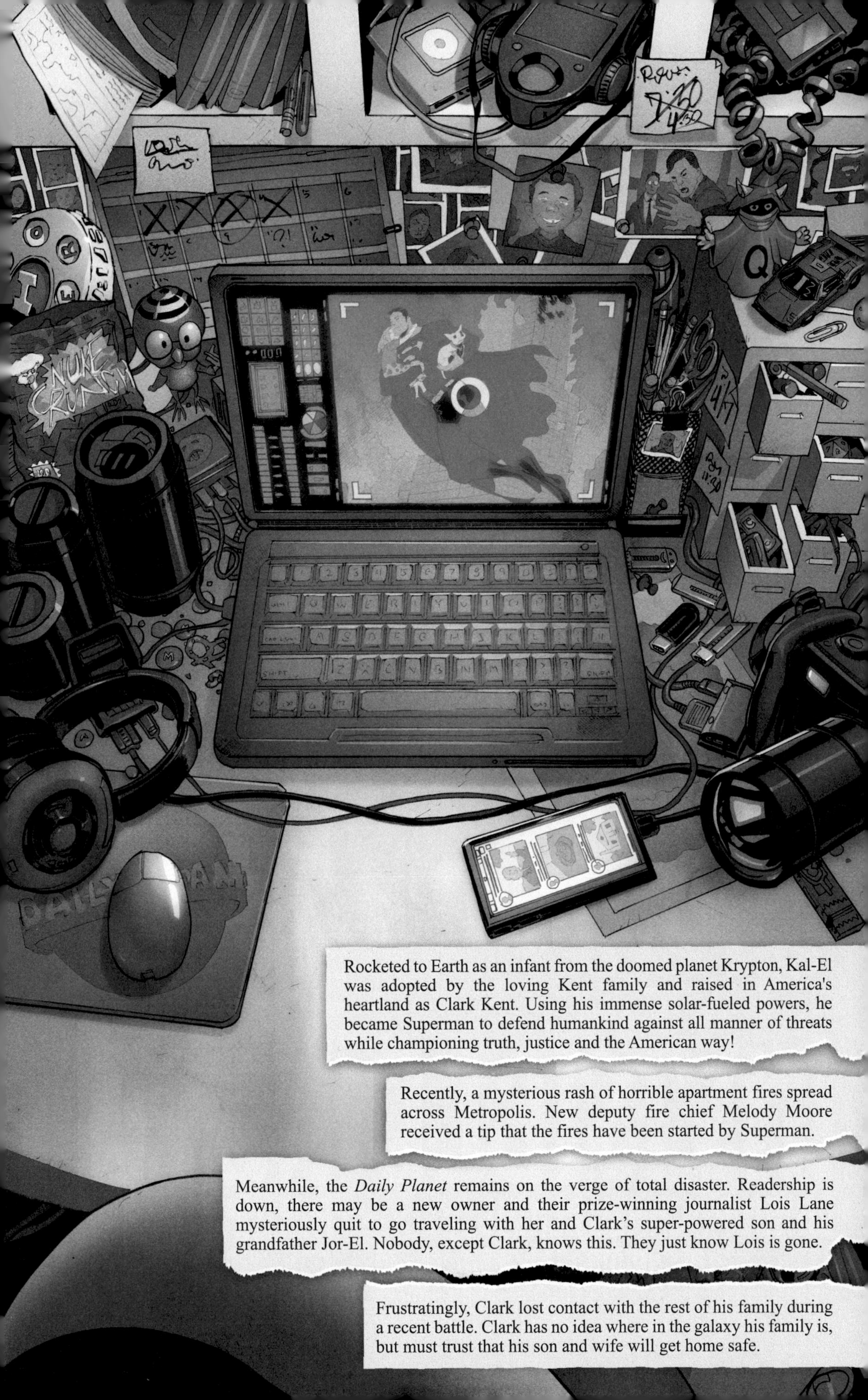
NUKE CRUNCH
Rocketed to Earth as an infant from the doomed planet Krypton, Kal-El was adopted by the loving Kent family and raised in America's heartland as Clark Kent. Using his immense solar-fueled powers, he became Superman to defend humankind against all manner of threats while championing truth, justice and the American way!
Recently, a mysterious rash of horrible apartment fires spread across Metropolis. New deputy fire chief Melody Moore received a tip that the fires have been started by Superman.
Meanwhile, the *Daily Planet* remains on the verge of total disaster. Readership is down, there may be a new owner and their prize-winning journalist Lois Lane mysteriously quit to go traveling with her and Clark's super-powered son and his grandfather Jor-El. Nobody, except Clark, knows this. They just know Lois is gone.
Frustratingly, Clark lost contact with the rest of his family during a recent battle. Clark has no idea where in the galaxy his family is, but must trust that his son and wife will get home safe.

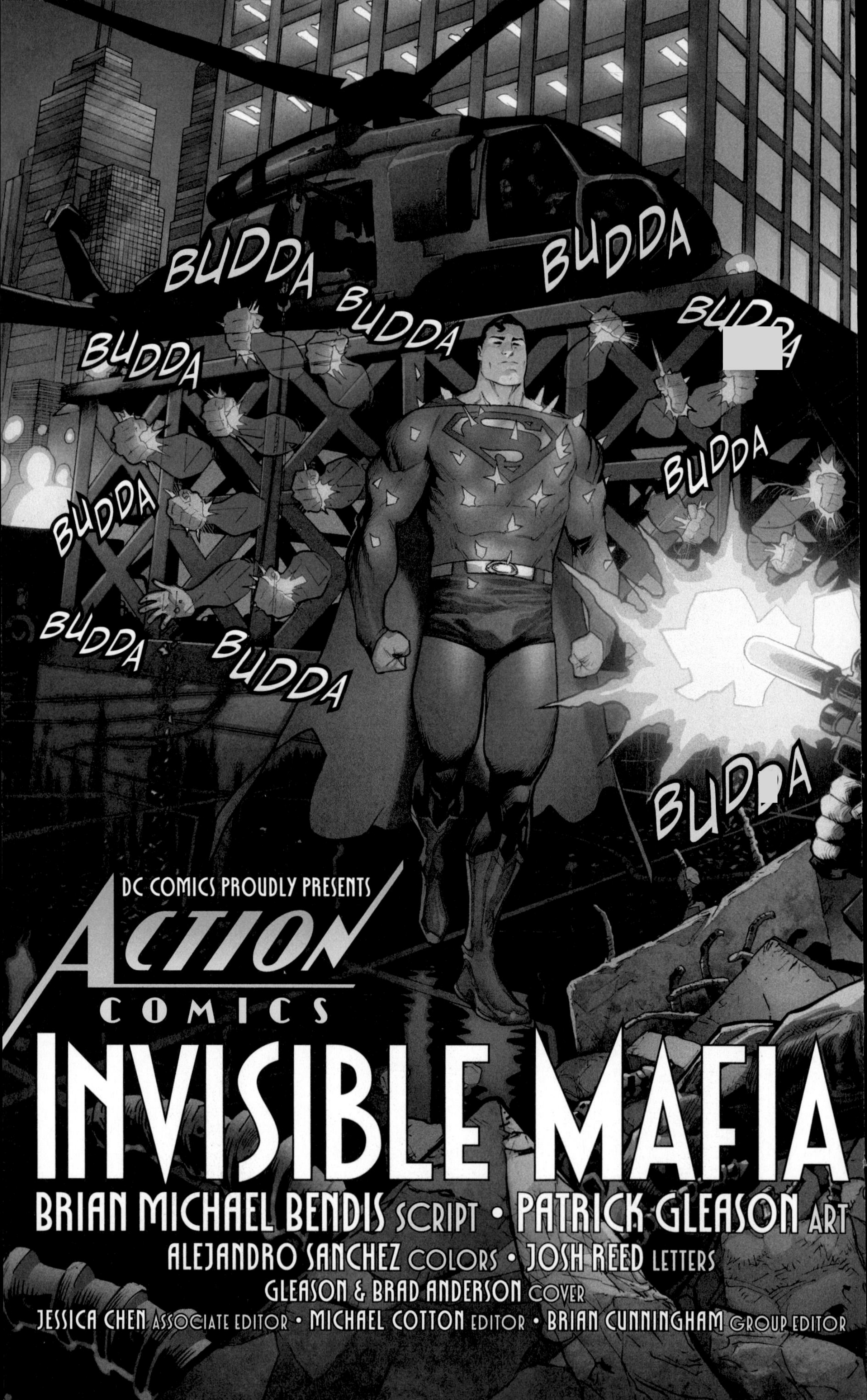

BUDDA
BUDDA
BUDDA
BUDDA
BUD
BUDDA
BUDDA
BUDDA
BUDDA
BU
DC COMICS PROUDLY PRESENTS
ACTION COMICS
INVISIBLE MAFIA
BRIAN MICHAEL BENDIS SCRIPT • PATRICK GLEASON ART
ALEJANDRO SANCHEZ COLORS • JOSH REED LETTERS
GLEASON & BRAD ANDERSON COVER
JESSICA CHEN ASSOCIATE EDITOR • MICHAEL COTTON EDITOR • BRIAN CUNNINGHAM GROUP EDITOR

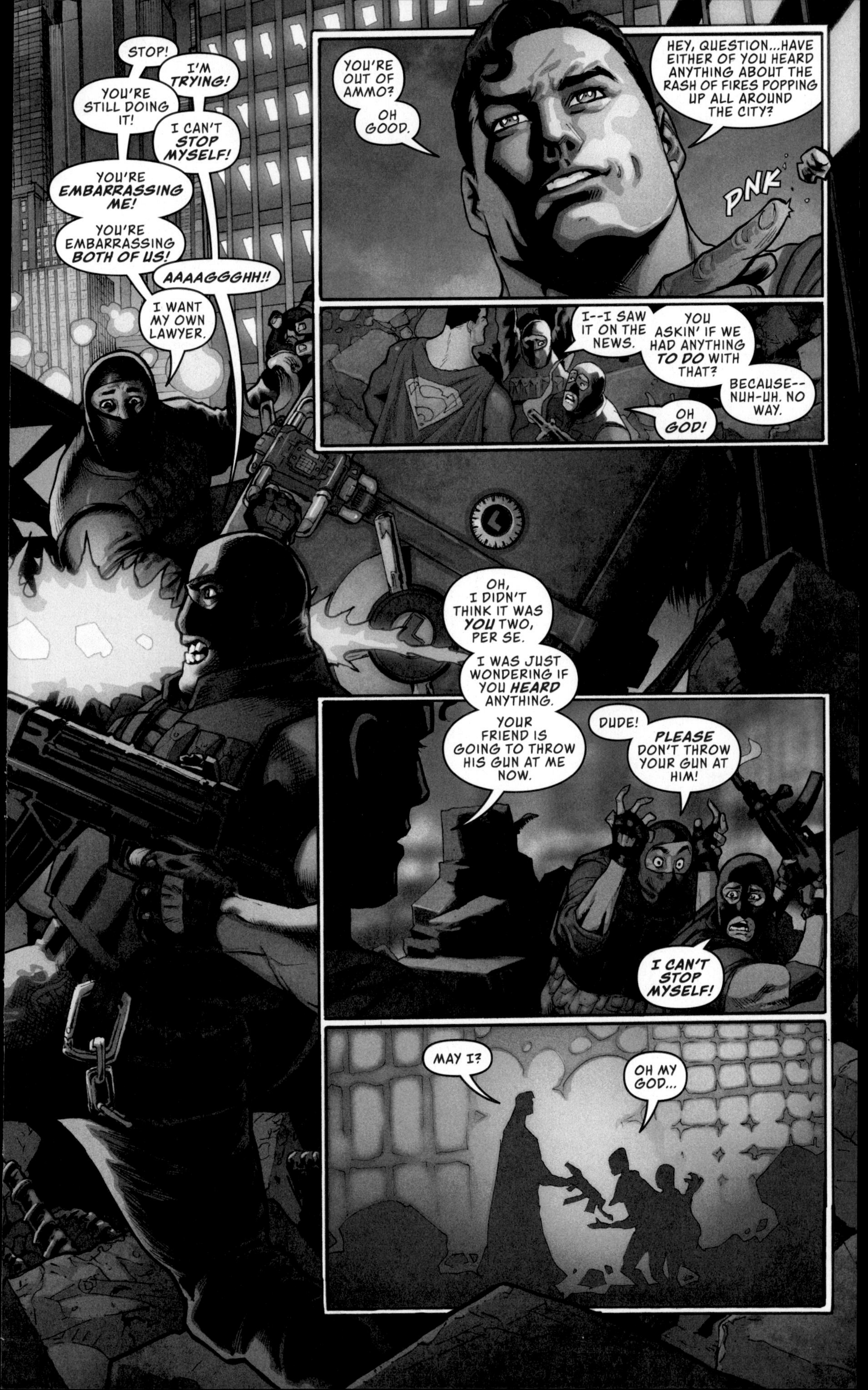
STOP!
I'M TRYING!
YOU'RE STILL DOING IT!
I CAN'T STOP MYSELF!
YOU'RE EMBARRASSING ME!
YOU'RE EMBARRASSING BOTH OF US!
AAAAGGGHH!!
I WANT MY OWN LAWYER.
YOU'RE OUT OF AMMO?
OH GOOD.
HEY, QUESTION...HAVE EITHER OF YOU HEARD ANYTHING ABOUT THE RASH OF FIRES POPPING UP ALL AROUND THE CITY?
PNK
I--I SAW IT ON THE NEWS.
YOU ASKIN' IF WE HAD ANYTHING TO DO WITH THAT?
BECAUSE-- NUH-UH. NO WAY.
OH GOD!
OH, I DIDN'T THINK IT WAS YOU TWO, PER SE.
I WAS JUST WONDERING IF YOU HEARD ANYTHING.
YOUR FRIEND IS GOING TO THROW HIS GUN AT ME NOW.
DUDE!
PLEASE DON'T THROW YOUR GUN AT HIM!
I CAN'T STOP MYSELF!
MAY I?
OH MY GOD...

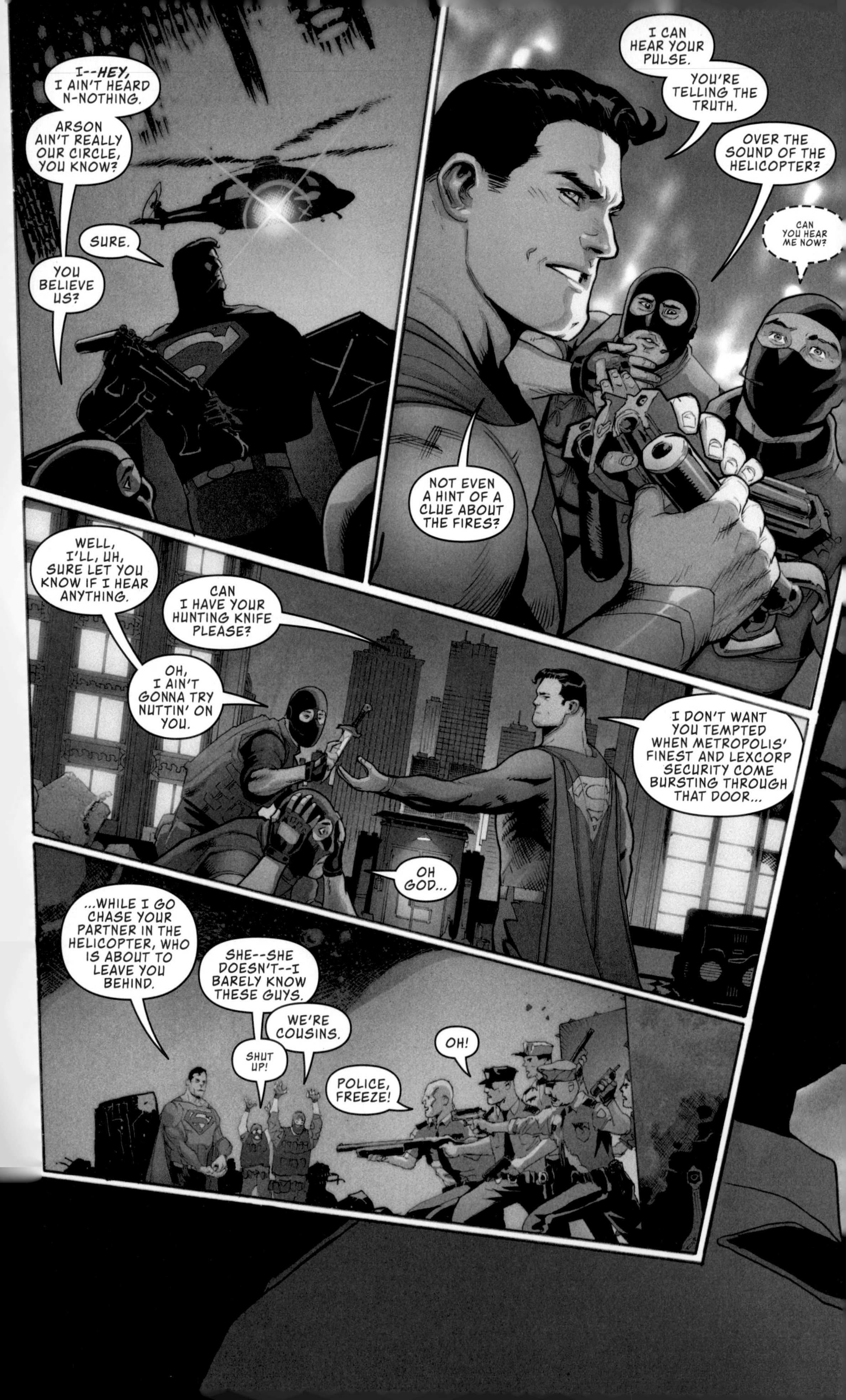
I--HEY, I AIN'T HEARD N-NOTHING.
ARSON AIN'T REALLY OUR CIRCLE, YOU KNOW?
SURE.
YOU BELIEVE US?
I CAN HEAR YOUR PULSE.
YOU'RE TELLING THE TRUTH.
OVER THE SOUND OF THE HELICOPTER?
CAN YOU HEAR ME NOW?
NOT EVEN A HINT OF A CLUE ABOUT THE FIRES?
WELL, I'LL, UH, SURE LET YOU KNOW IF I HEAR ANYTHING.
CAN I HAVE YOUR HUNTING KNIFE PLEASE?
OH, I AIN'T GONNA TRY NUTTIN' ON YOU.
I DON'T WANT YOU TEMPTED WHEN METROPOLIS' FINEST AND LEXCORP SECURITY COME BURSTING THROUGH THAT DOOR...
OH GOD...
...WHILE I GO CHASE YOUR PARTNER IN THE HELICOPTER, WHO IS ABOUT TO LEAVE YOU BEHIND.
SHE--SHE DOESN'T--I BARELY KNOW THESE GUYS.
WE'RE COUSINS.
SHUT UP!
OH!
POLICE, FREEZE!

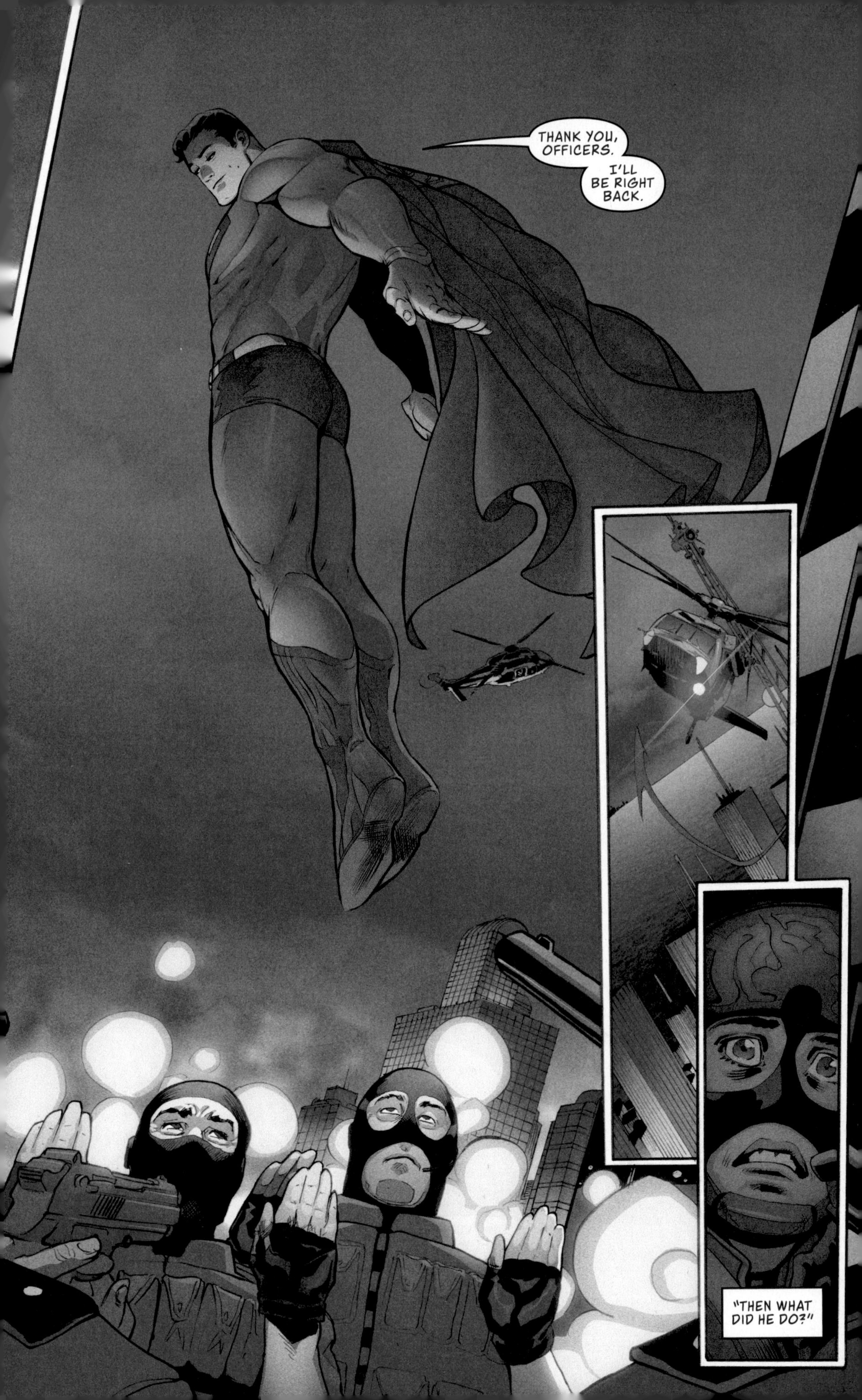
THANK YOU, OFFICERS.
I'LL BE RIGHT BACK.
"THEN WHAT DID HE DO?"

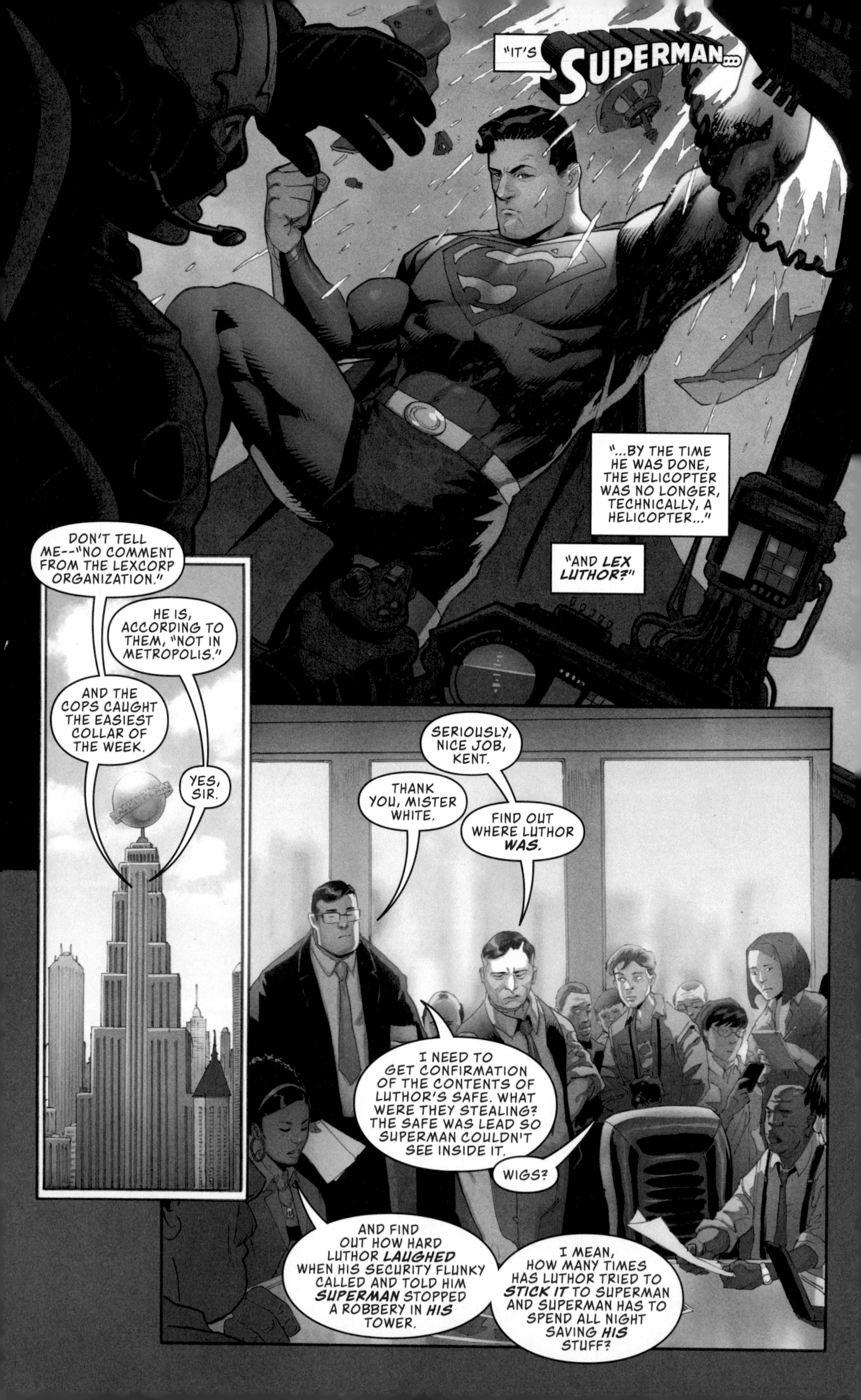
"IT'S
SUPERMAN...
"...BY THE TIME HE WAS DONE, THE HELICOPTER WAS NO LONGER, TECHNICALLY, A HELICOPTER..."
"AND LEX LUTHOR?"
DON'T TELL ME--"NO COMMENT FROM THE LEXCORP ORGANIZATION."
HE IS, ACCORDING TO THEM, "NOT IN METROPOLIS."
AND THE COPS CAUGHT THE EASIEST COLLAR OF THE WEEK.
YES, SIR.
SERIOUSLY, NICE JOB, KENT.
THANK YOU, MISTER WHITE.
FIND OUT WHERE LUTHOR WAS.
I NEED TO GET CONFIRMATION OF THE CONTENTS OF LUTHOR'S SAFE. WHAT WERE THEY STEALING? THE SAFE WAS LEAD SO SUPERMAN COULDN'T SEE INSIDE IT.
WIGS?
AND FIND OUT HOW HARD LUTHOR LAUGHED WHEN HIS SECURITY FLUNKY CALLED AND TOLD HIM SUPERMAN STOPPED A ROBBERY IN HIS TOWER.
I MEAN, HOW MANY TIMES HAS LUTHOR TRIED TO STICK IT TO SUPERMAN AND SUPERMAN HAS TO SPEND ALL NIGHT SAVING HIS STUFF?

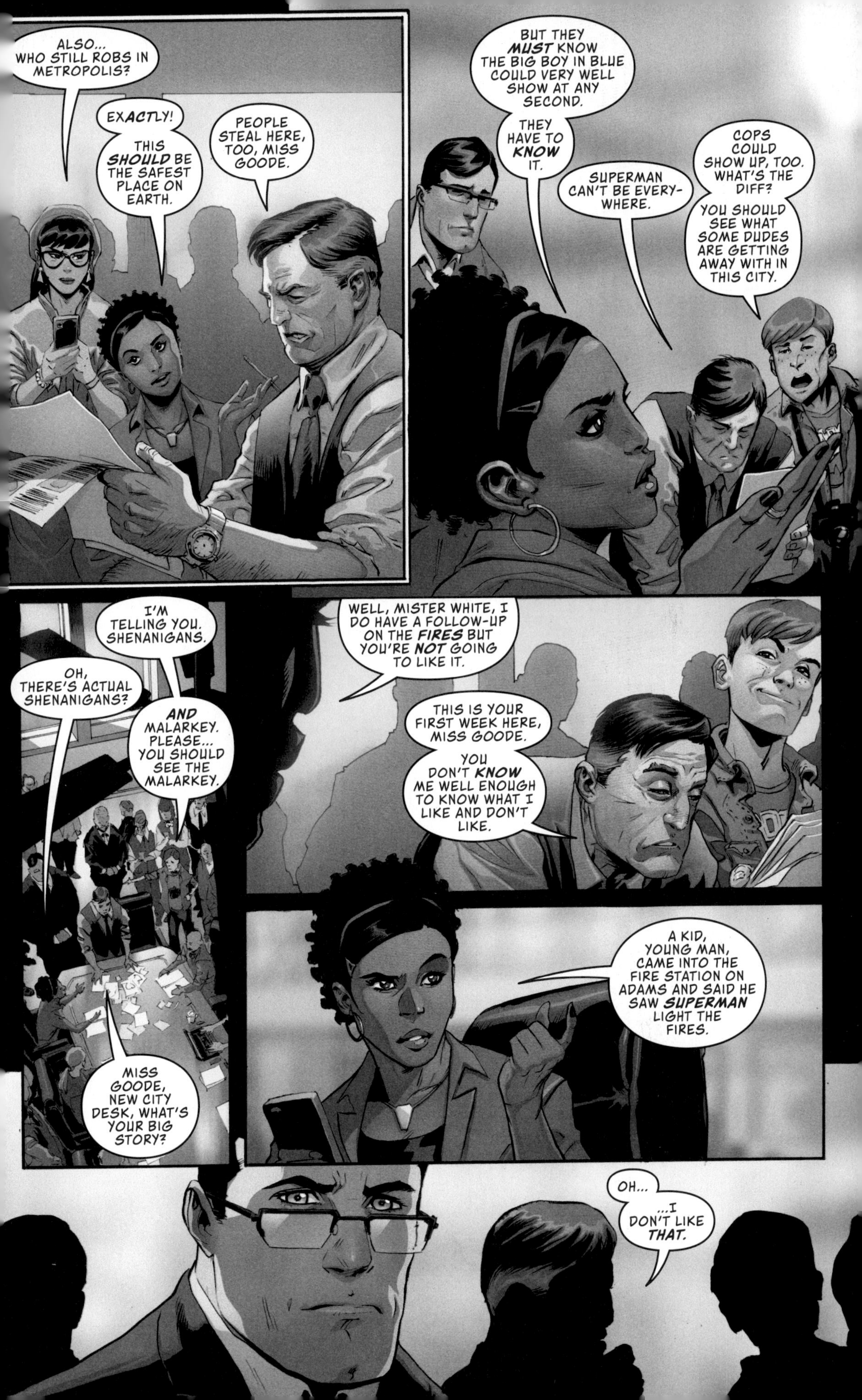
ALSO... WHO STILL ROBS IN METROPOLIS?
EXACTLY!
THIS SHOULD BE THE SAFEST PLACE ON EARTH.
PEOPLE STEAL HERE, TOO, MISS GOODE.
BUT THEY MUST KNOW THE BIG BOY IN BLUE COULD VERY WELL SHOW AT ANY SECOND.
THEY HAVE TO KNOW IT.
SUPERMAN CAN'T BE EVERY-WHERE.
COPS COULD SHOW UP, TOO. WHAT'S THE DIFF?
YOU SHOULD SEE WHAT SOME DUDES ARE GETTING AWAY WITH IN THIS CITY.
I'M TELLING YOU. SHENANIGANS.
OH, THERE'S ACTUAL SHENANIGANS?
AND MALARKEY. PLEASE... YOU SHOULD SEE THE MALARKEY.
MISS GOODE, NEW CITY DESK, WHAT'S YOUR BIG STORY?
WELL, MISTER WHITE, I DO HAVE A FOLLOW-UP ON THE FIRES BUT YOU'RE NOT GOING TO LIKE IT.
THIS IS YOUR FIRST WEEK HERE, MISS GOODE.
YOU DON'T KNOW ME WELL ENOUGH TO KNOW WHAT I LIKE AND DON'T LIKE.
A KID, YOUNG MAN, CAME INTO THE FIRE STATION ON ADAMS AND SAID HE SAW SUPERMAN LIGHT THE FIRES.
OH...
...I DON'T LIKE THAT.

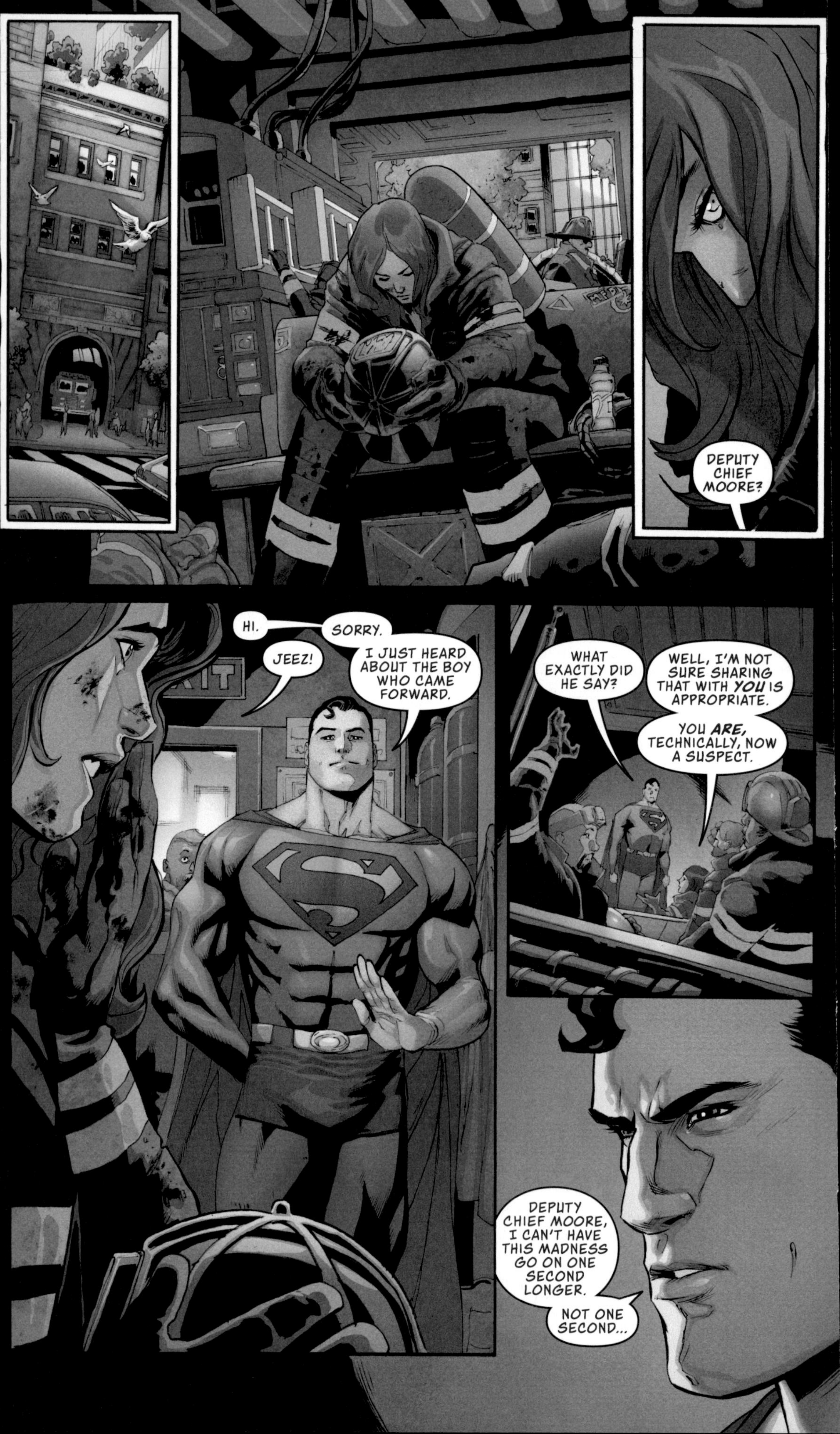
DEPUTY CHIEF MOORE?
HI.
SORRY.
JEEZ!
I JUST HEARD ABOUT THE BOY WHO CAME FORWARD.
WHAT EXACTLY DID HE SAY?
WELL, I'M NOT SURE SHARING THAT WITH *YOU* IS APPROPRIATE.
YOU *ARE,* TECHNICALLY, NOW A SUSPECT.
DEPUTY CHIEF MOORE, I CAN'T HAVE THIS MADNESS GO ON ONE SECOND LONGER.
NOT ONE SECOND...

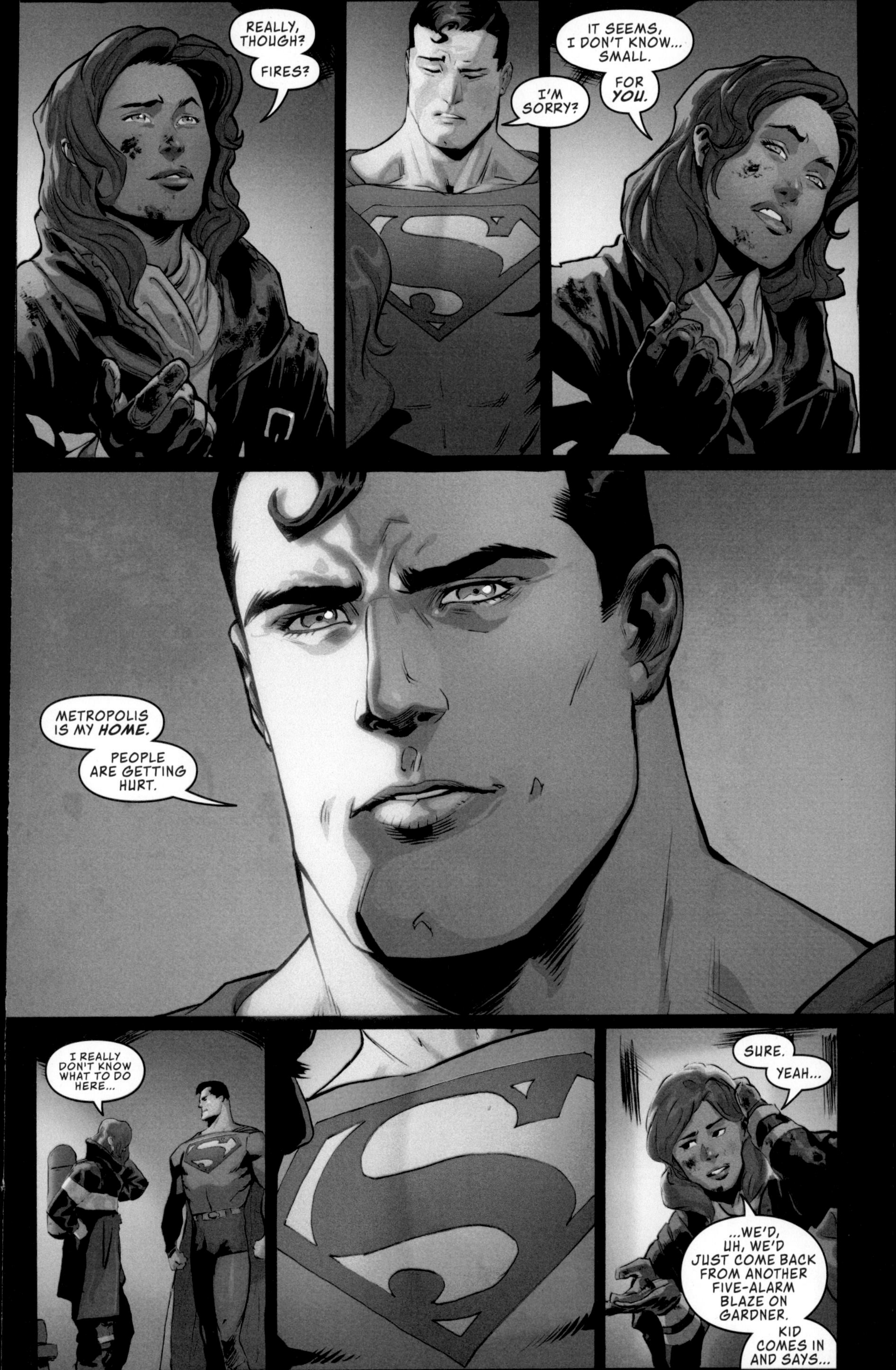
REALLY, THOUGH?
FIRES?
I'M SORRY?
IT SEEMS, I DON'T KNOW... SMALL.
FOR YOU.
METROPOLIS IS MY HOME.
PEOPLE ARE GETTING HURT.
I REALLY DON'T KNOW WHAT TO DO HERE...
SURE.
YEAH...
...WE'D, UH, WE'D JUST COME BACK FROM ANOTHER FIVE-ALARM BLAZE ON GARDNER.
KID COMES IN AND SAYS...

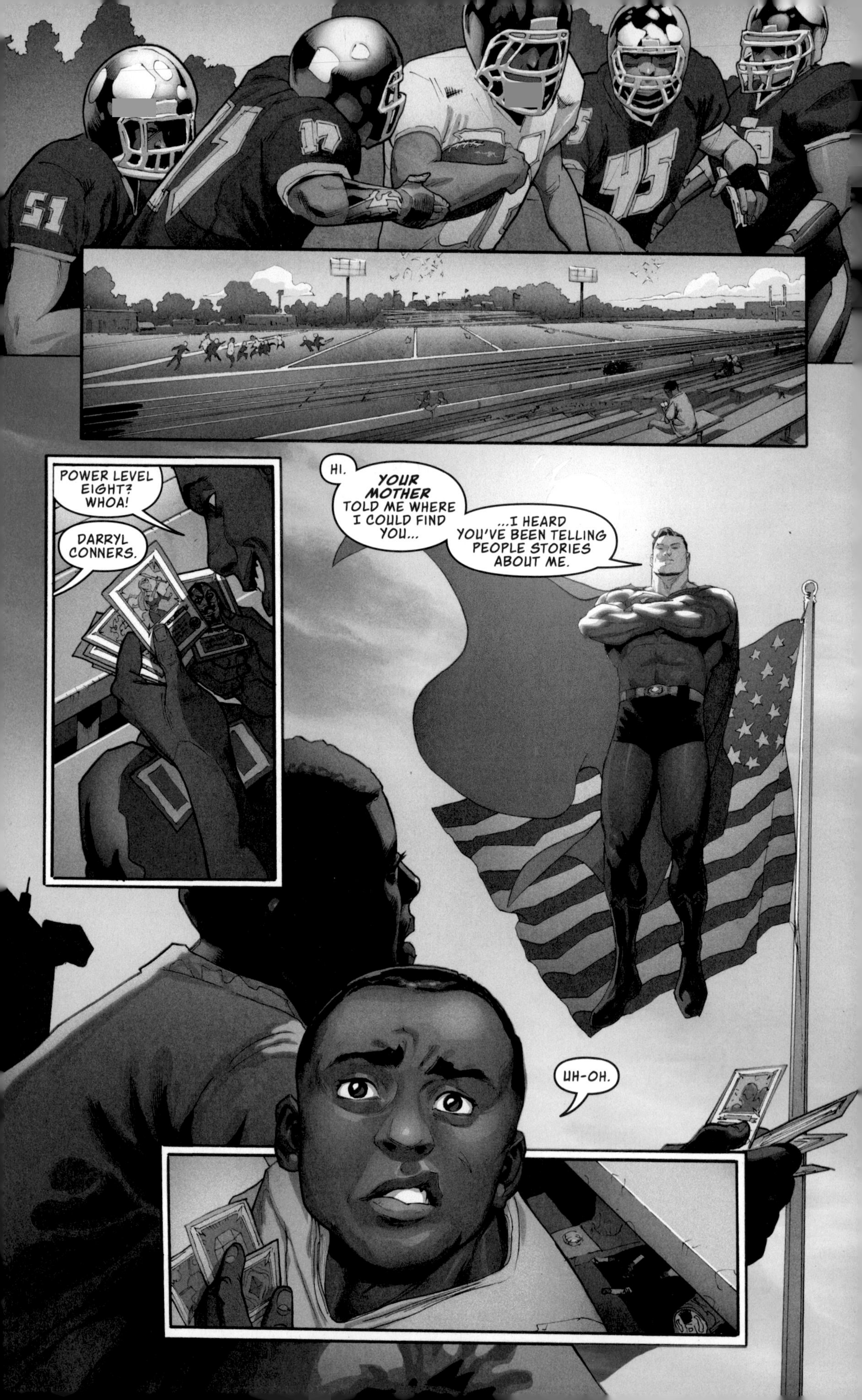
POWER LEVEL EIGHT? WHOA!
DARRYL CONNERS.
HI.
YOUR MOTHER TOLD ME WHERE I COULD FIND YOU...
...I HEARD YOU'VE BEEN TELLING PEOPLE STORIES ABOUT ME.
UH-OH.

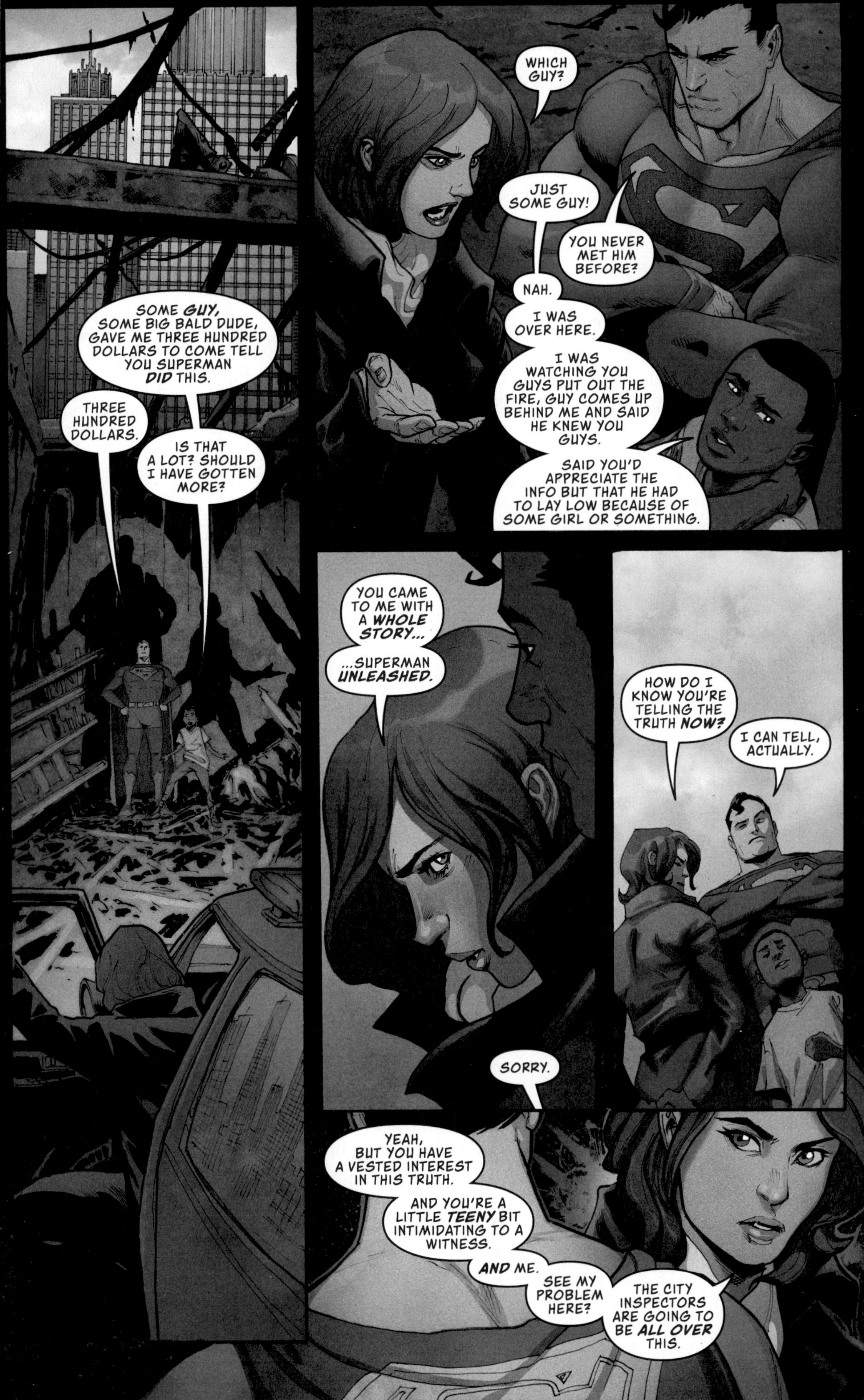
SOME GUY, SOME BIG BALD DUDE, GAVE ME THREE HUNDRED DOLLARS TO COME TELL YOU SUPERMAN DID THIS.
THREE HUNDRED DOLLARS.
IS THAT A LOT? SHOULD I HAVE GOTTEN MORE?
WHICH GUY?
JUST SOME GUY!
YOU NEVER MET HIM BEFORE?
NAH.
I WAS OVER HERE.
I WAS WATCHING YOU GUYS PUT OUT THE FIRE, GUY COMES UP BEHIND ME AND SAID HE KNEW YOU GUYS.
SAID YOU'D APPRECIATE THE INFO BUT THAT HE HAD TO LAY LOW BECAUSE OF SOME GIRL OR SOMETHING.
YOU CAME TO ME WITH A WHOLE STORY...
...SUPERMAN UNLEASHED.
HOW DO I KNOW YOU'RE TELLING THE TRUTH NOW?
I CAN TELL, ACTUALLY.
SORRY.
YEAH, BUT YOU HAVE A VESTED INTEREST IN THIS TRUTH.
AND YOU'RE A LITTLE TEENY BIT INTIMIDATING TO A WITNESS.
AND ME.
SEE MY PROBLEM HERE?
THE CITY INSPECTORS ARE GOING TO BE ALL OVER THIS.

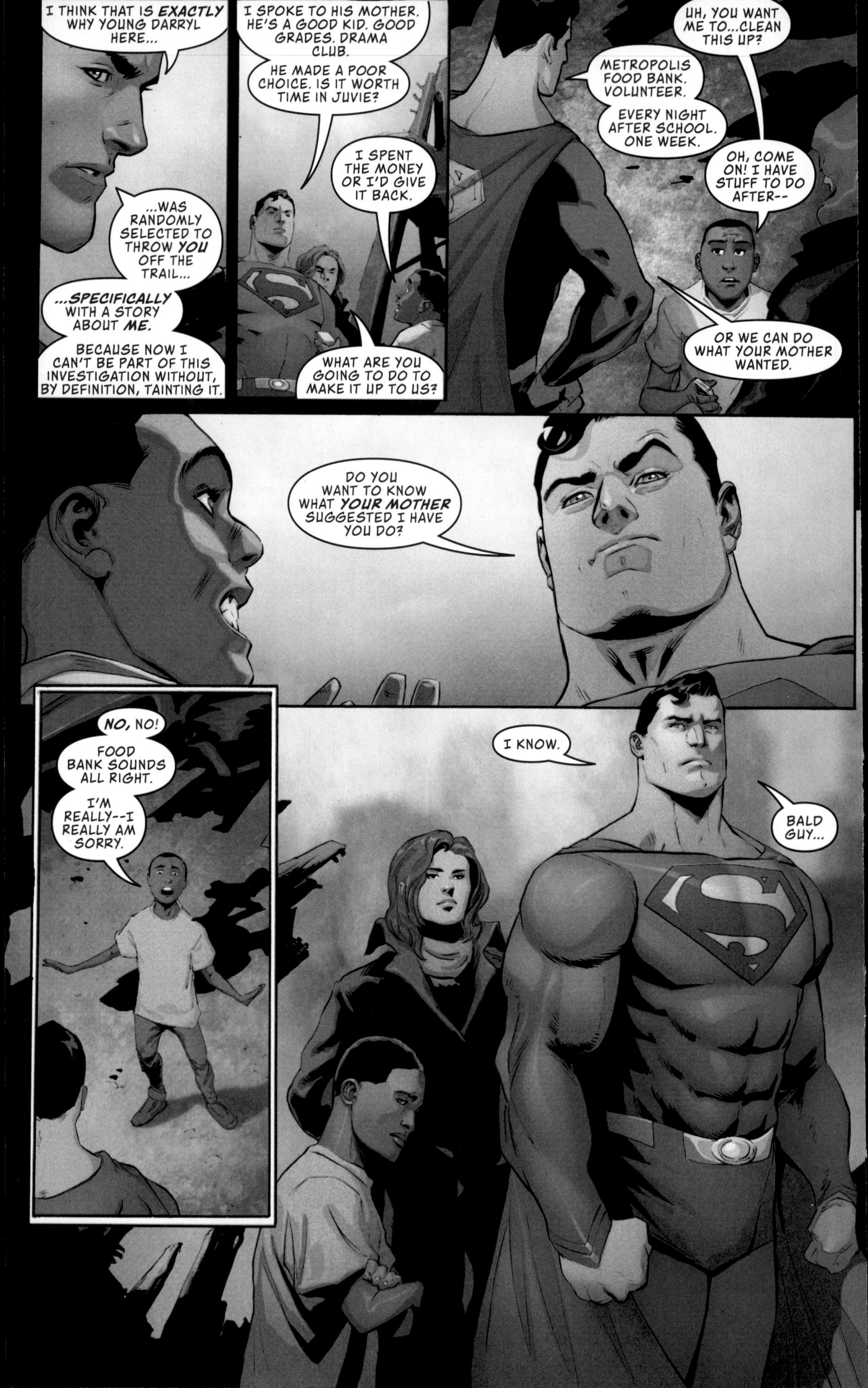
I THINK THAT IS EXACTLY WHY YOUNG DARRYL HERE...
...WAS RANDOMLY SELECTED TO THROW YOU OFF THE TRAIL...
...SPECIFICALLY WITH A STORY ABOUT ME.
BECAUSE NOW I CAN'T BE PART OF THIS INVESTIGATION WITHOUT, BY DEFINITION, TAINTING IT.
I SPOKE TO HIS MOTHER. HE'S A GOOD KID. GOOD GRADES. DRAMA CLUB.
HE MADE A POOR CHOICE. IS IT WORTH TIME IN JUVIE?
I SPENT THE MONEY OR I'D GIVE IT BACK.
WHAT ARE YOU GOING TO DO TO MAKE IT UP TO US?
METROPOLIS FOOD BANK. VOLUNTEER.
EVERY NIGHT AFTER SCHOOL. ONE WEEK.
UH, YOU WANT ME TO...CLEAN THIS UP?
OH, COME ON! I HAVE STUFF TO DO AFTER--
OR WE CAN DO WHAT YOUR MOTHER WANTED.
DO YOU WANT TO KNOW WHAT YOUR MOTHER SUGGESTED I HAVE YOU DO?
NO, NO!
FOOD BANK SOUNDS ALL RIGHT.
I'M REALLY--I REALLY AM SORRY.
I KNOW.
BALD GUY...

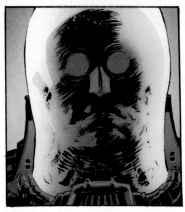

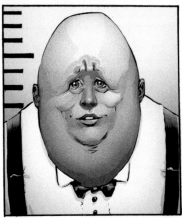

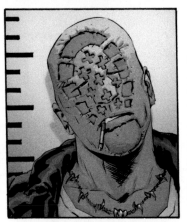

IS THIS YOUR DATING PROFILE?

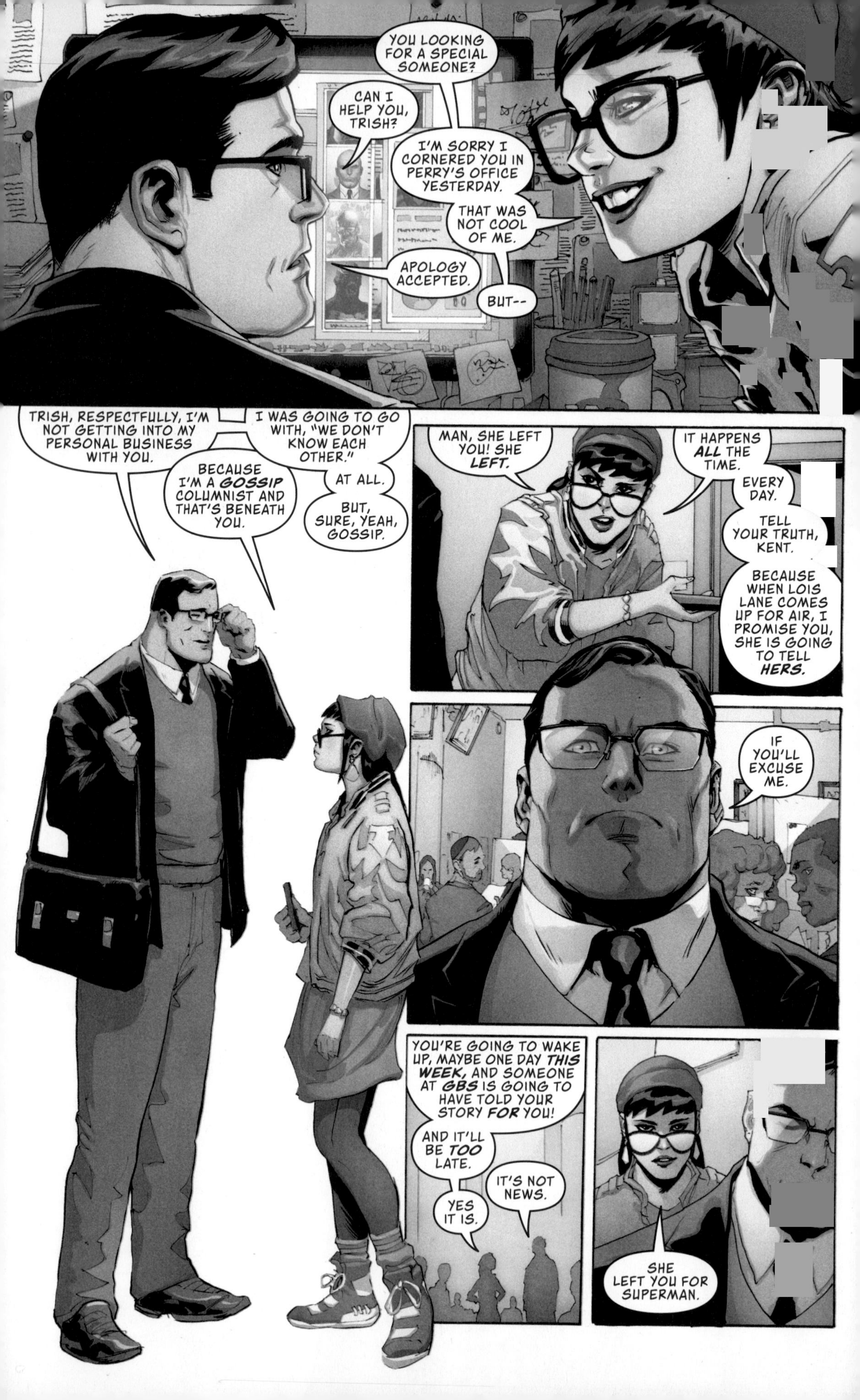
YOU LOOKING FOR A SPECIAL SOMEONE?
CAN I HELP YOU, TRISH?
I'M SORRY I CORNERED YOU IN PERRY'S OFFICE YESTERDAY.
THAT WAS NOT COOL OF ME.
APOLOGY ACCEPTED.
BUT--
TRISH, RESPECTFULLY, I'M NOT GETTING INTO MY PERSONAL BUSINESS WITH YOU.
BECAUSE I'M A GOSSIP COLUMNIST AND THAT'S BENEATH YOU.
I WAS GOING TO GO WITH, "WE DON'T KNOW EACH OTHER."
AT ALL.
BUT, SURE, YEAH, GOSSIP.
MAN, SHE LEFT YOU! SHE LEFT.
IT HAPPENS ALL THE TIME.
EVERY DAY.
TELL YOUR TRUTH, KENT.
BECAUSE WHEN LOIS LANE COMES UP FOR AIR, I PROMISE YOU, SHE IS GOING TO TELL HERS.
IF YOU'LL EXCUSE ME.
YOU'RE GOING TO WAKE UP, MAYBE ONE DAY THIS WEEK, AND SOMEONE AT GBS IS GOING TO HAVE TOLD YOUR STORY FOR YOU!
AND IT'LL BE TOO LATE.
IT'S NOT NEWS.
YES IT IS.
SHE LEFT YOU FOR SUPERMAN.

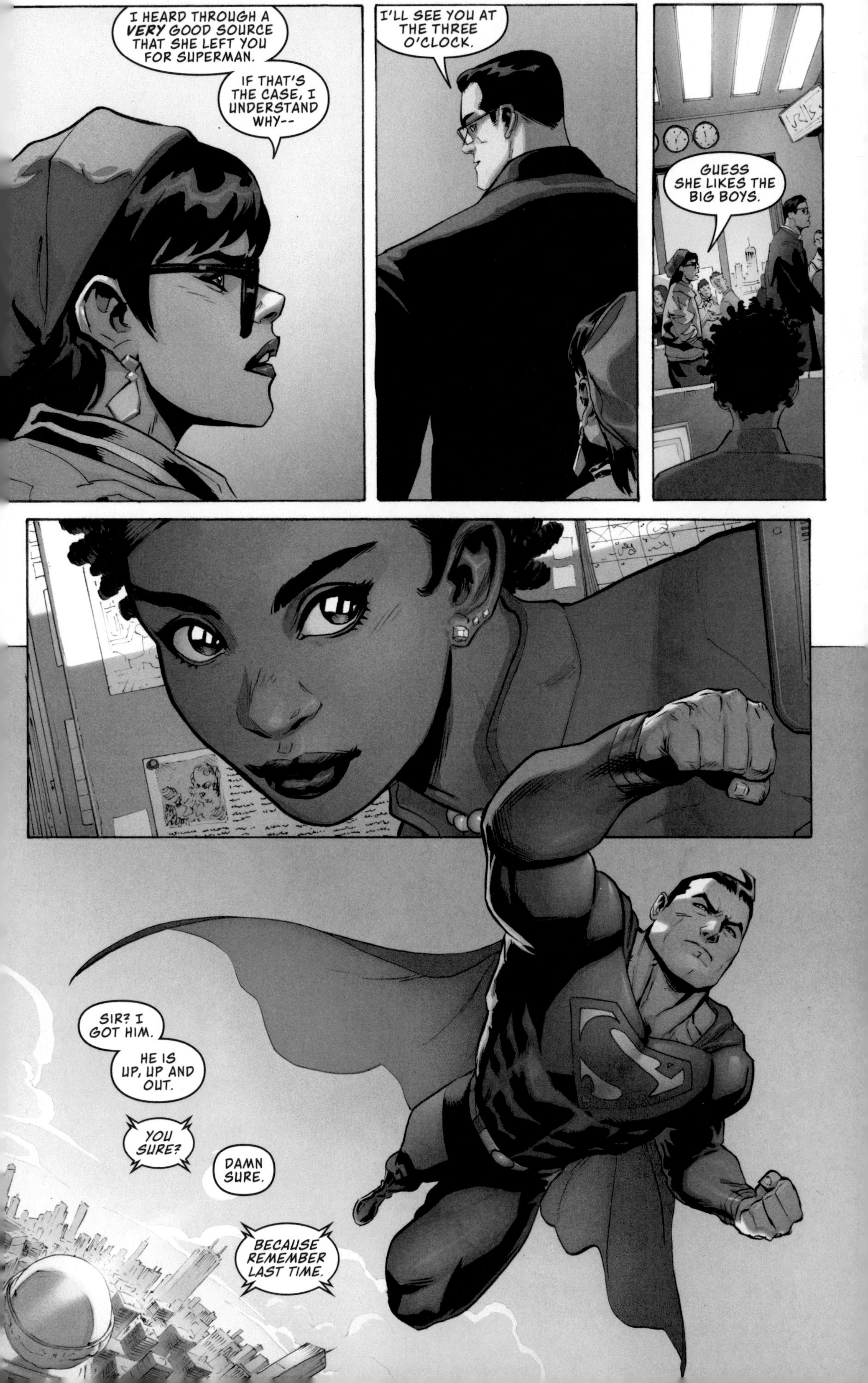
I HEARD THROUGH A VERY GOOD SOURCE THAT SHE LEFT YOU FOR SUPERMAN.
IF THAT'S THE CASE, I UNDERSTAND WHY--
I'LL SEE YOU AT THE THREE O'CLOCK.
GUESS SHE LIKES THE BIG BOYS.
SIR? I GOT HIM.
HE IS UP, UP AND OUT.
YOU SURE?
DAMN SURE.
BECAUSE REMEMBER LAST TIME.

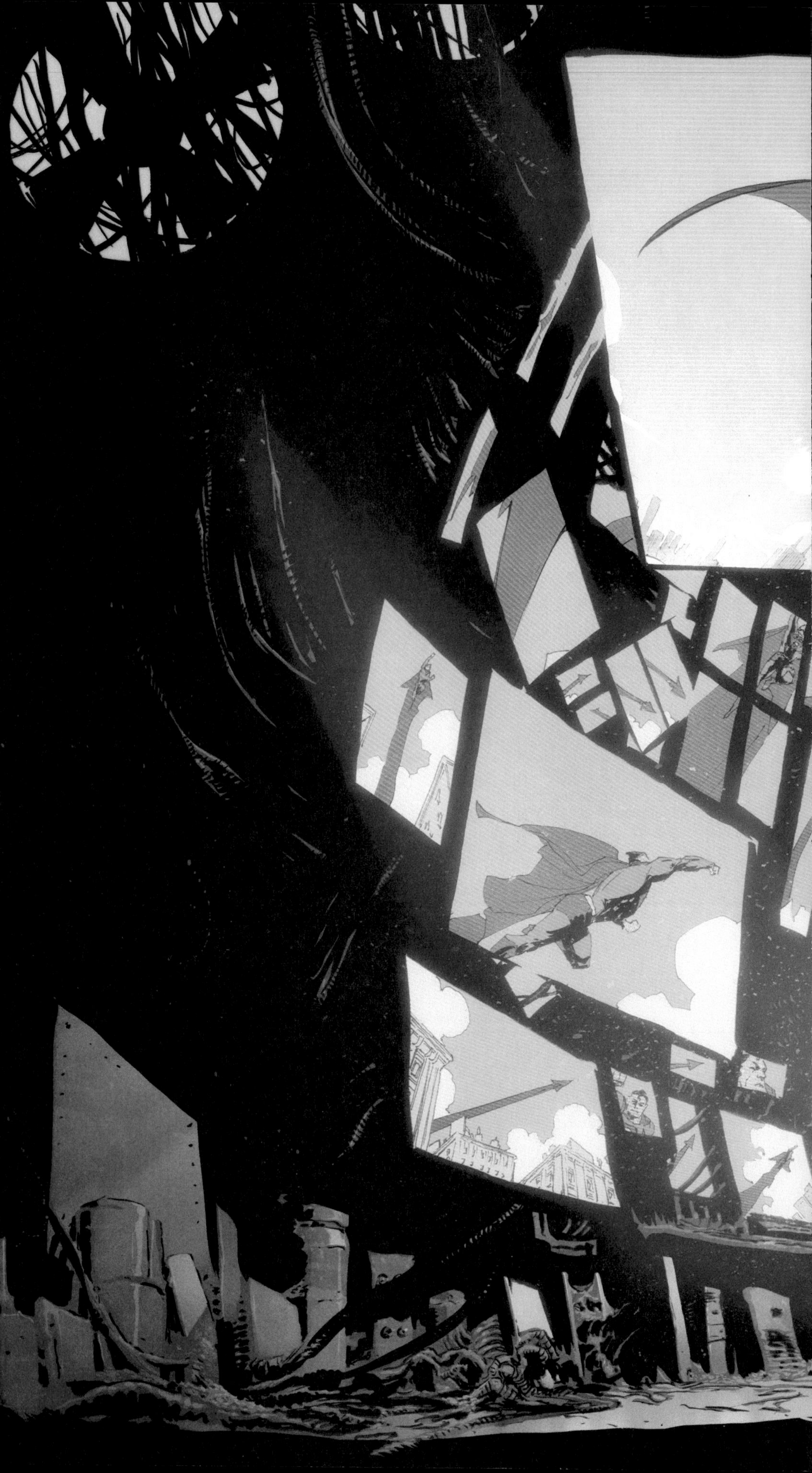

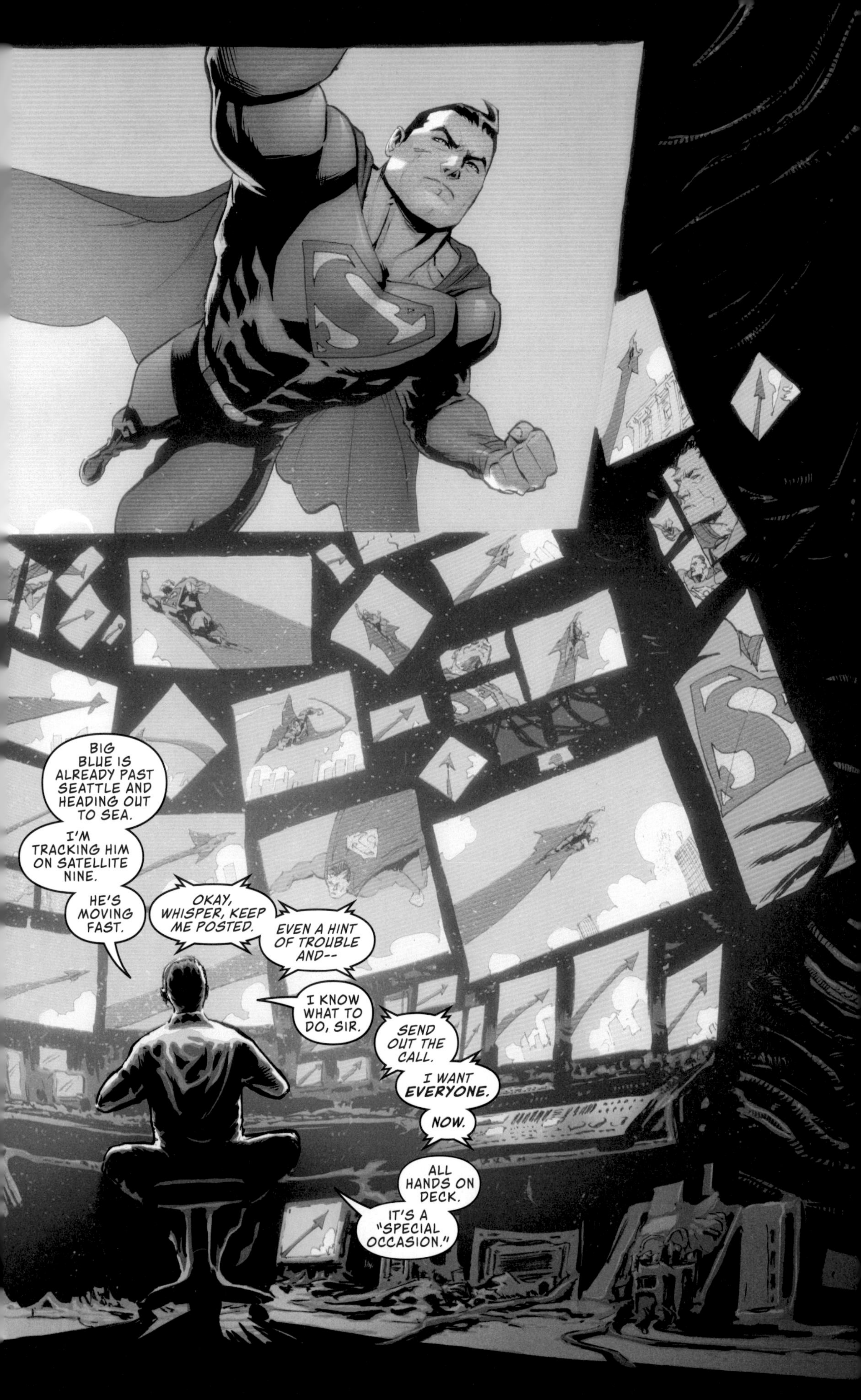
BIG BLUE IS ALREADY PAST SEATTLE AND HEADING OUT TO SEA.
I'M TRACKING HIM ON SATELLITE NINE.
HE'S MOVING FAST.
OKAY, WHISPER, KEEP ME POSTED.
EVEN A HINT OF TROUBLE AND--
I KNOW WHAT TO DO, SIR.
SEND OUT THE CALL.
I WANT EVERYONE.
NOW.
ALL HANDS ON DECK.
IT'S A "SPECIAL OCCASION."

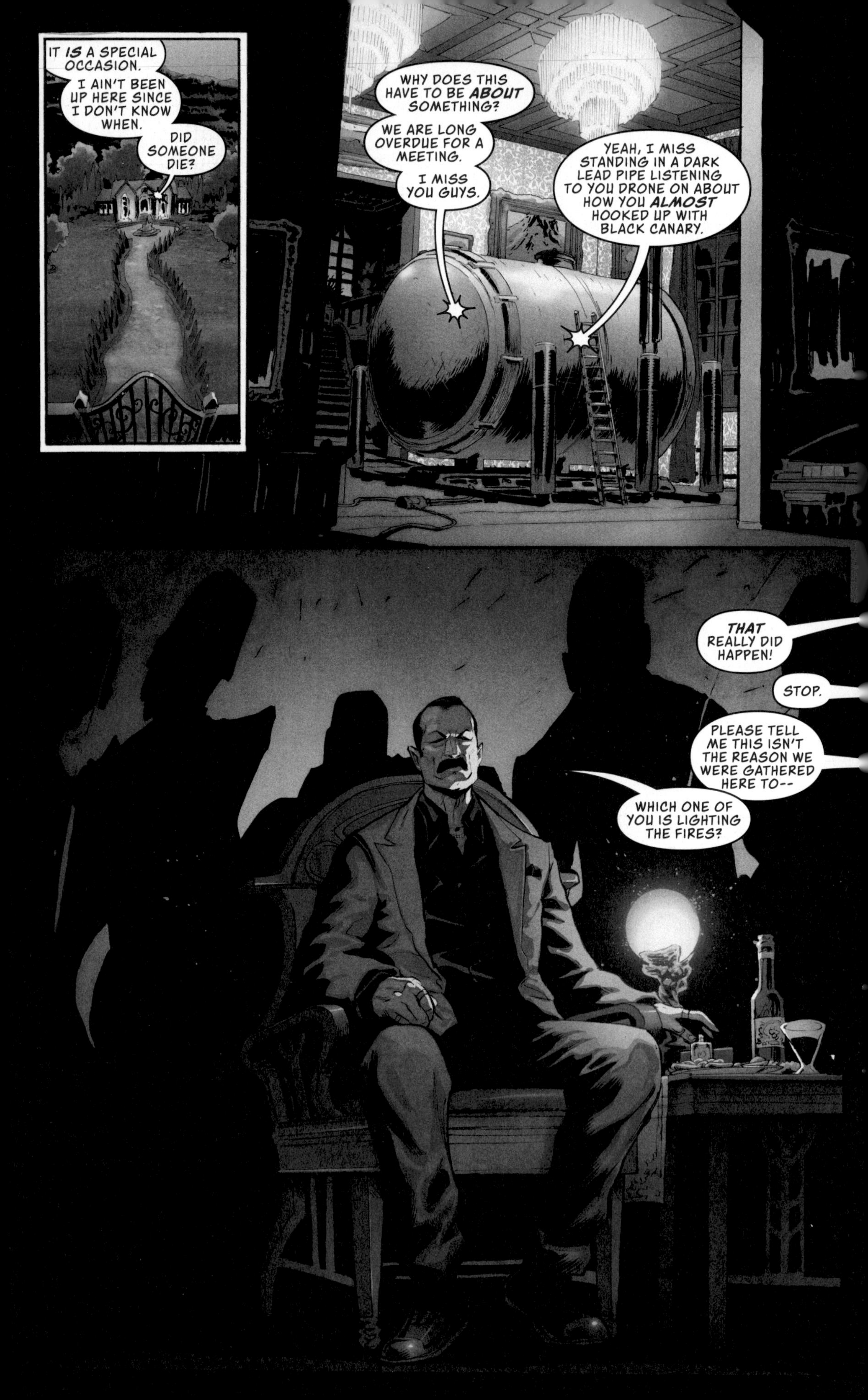
IT *IS* A SPECIAL OCCASION.
I AIN'T BEEN UP HERE SINCE I DON'T KNOW WHEN.
DID SOMEONE DIE?
WHY DOES THIS HAVE TO BE *ABOUT* SOMETHING?
WE ARE LONG OVERDUE FOR A MEETING.
I MISS YOU GUYS.
YEAH, I MISS STANDING IN A DARK LEAD PIPE LISTENING TO YOU DRONE ON ABOUT HOW YOU *ALMOST* HOOKED UP WITH BLACK CANARY.
THAT REALLY DID HAPPEN!
STOP.
PLEASE TELL ME THIS ISN'T THE REASON WE WERE GATHERED HERE TO--
WHICH ONE OF YOU IS LIGHTING THE FIRES?

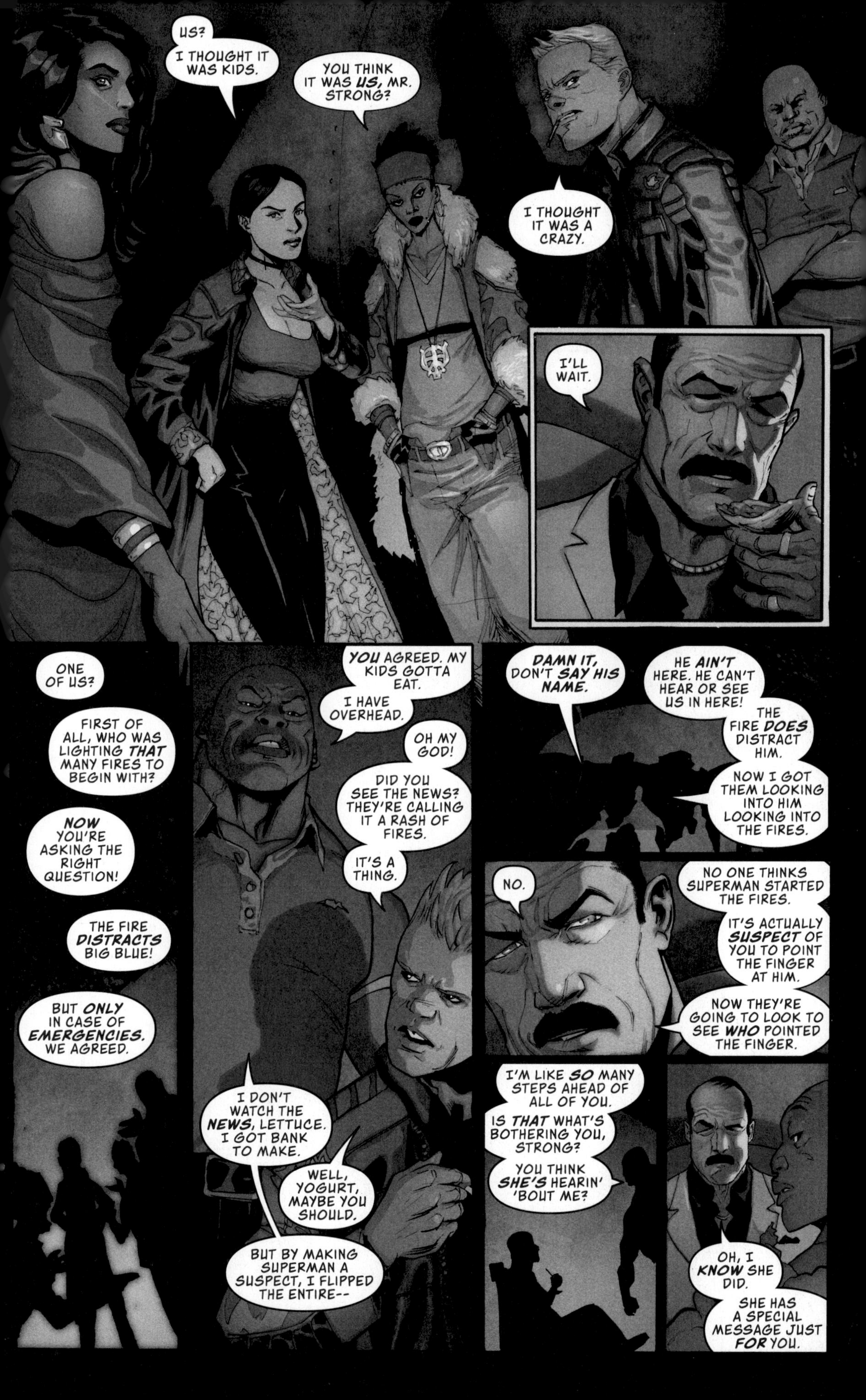
US?
I THOUGHT IT WAS KIDS.
YOU THINK IT WAS US, MR. STRONG?
I THOUGHT IT WAS A CRAZY.
I'LL WAIT.
ONE OF US?
FIRST OF ALL, WHO WAS LIGHTING THAT MANY FIRES TO BEGIN WITH?
NOW YOU'RE ASKING THE RIGHT QUESTION!
THE FIRE DISTRACTS BIG BLUE!
BUT ONLY IN CASE OF EMERGENCIES. WE AGREED.
YOU AGREED. MY KIDS GOTTA EAT.
I HAVE OVERHEAD.
OH MY GOD!
DID YOU SEE THE NEWS? THEY'RE CALLING IT A RASH OF FIRES.
IT'S A THING.
I DON'T WATCH THE NEWS, LETTUCE. I GOT BANK TO MAKE.
WELL, YOGURT, MAYBE YOU SHOULD.
BUT BY MAKING SUPERMAN A SUSPECT, I FLIPPED THE ENTIRE--
DAMN IT, DON'T SAY HIS NAME.
HE AIN'T HERE. HE CAN'T HEAR OR SEE US IN HERE!
THE FIRE DOES DISTRACT HIM.
NOW I GOT THEM LOOKING INTO HIM LOOKING INTO THE FIRES.
NO.
NO ONE THINKS SUPERMAN STARTED THE FIRES.
IT'S ACTUALLY SUSPECT OF YOU TO POINT THE FINGER AT HIM.
NOW THEY'RE GOING TO LOOK TO SEE WHO POINTED THE FINGER.
I'M LIKE SO MANY STEPS AHEAD OF ALL OF YOU.
IS THAT WHAT'S BOTHERING YOU, STRONG?
YOU THINK SHE'S HEARIN' 'BOUT ME?
OH, I KNOW SHE DID.
SHE HAS A SPECIAL MESSAGE JUST FOR YOU.

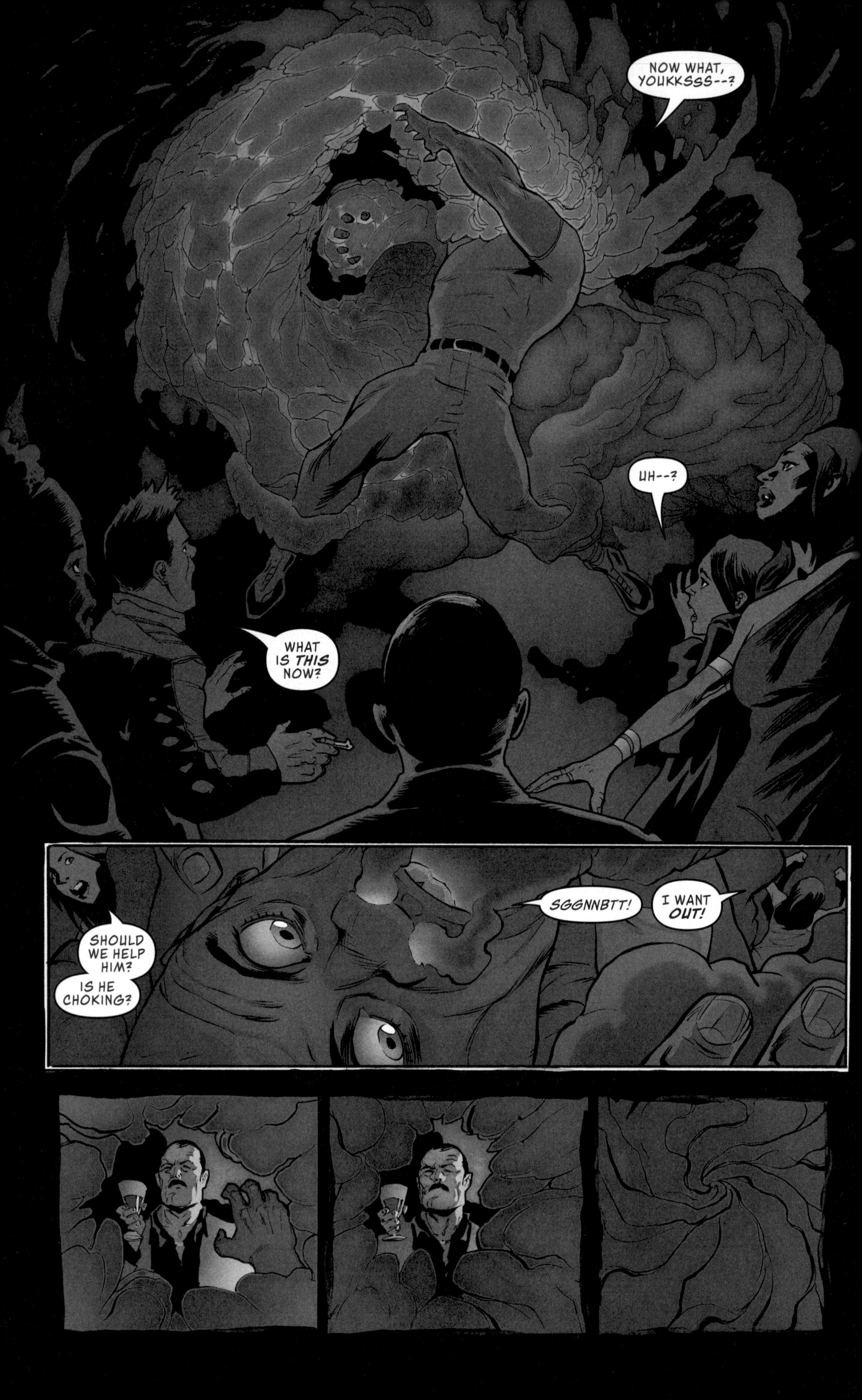
NOW WHAT, YOUKKSSS--?
UH--?
WHAT IS THIS NOW?
SHOULD WE HELP HIM?
IS HE CHOKING?
SGGNNBTT!
I WANT OUT!

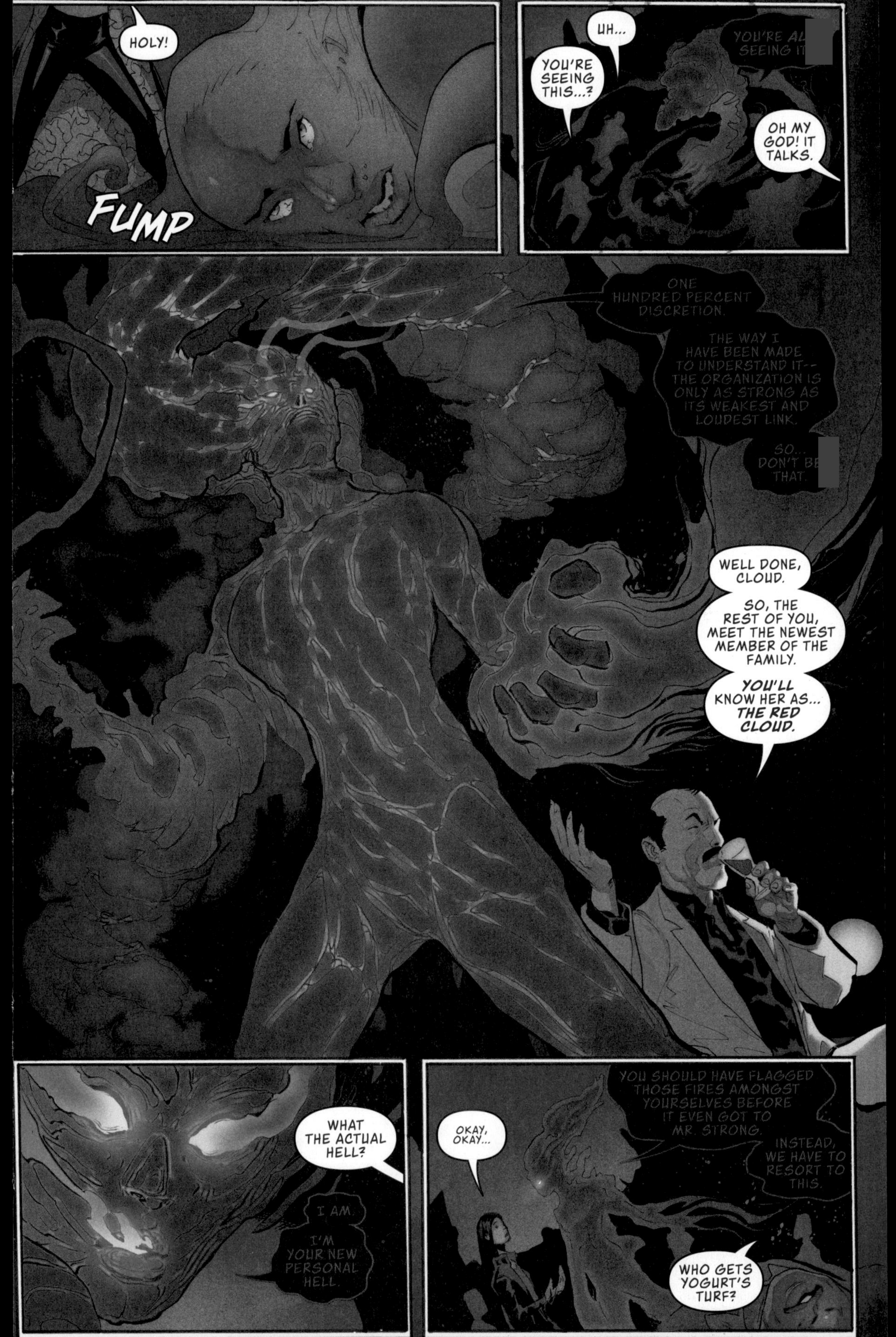
HOLY!
FUMP
UH...
YOU'RE SEEING THIS...?
YOU'RE AL SEEING IT
OH MY GOD! IT TALKS.
ONE HUNDRED PERCENT DISCRETION.
THE WAY I HAVE BEEN MADE TO UNDERSTAND IT-- THE ORGANIZATION IS ONLY AS STRONG AS ITS WEAKEST AND LOUDEST LINK.
SO... DON'T BE THAT.
WELL DONE, CLOUD.
SO, THE REST OF YOU, MEET THE NEWEST MEMBER OF THE FAMILY.
YOU'LL KNOW HER AS... THE RED CLOUD.
WHAT THE ACTUAL HELL?
I AM.
I'M YOUR NEW PERSONAL HELL.
YOU SHOULD HAVE FLAGGED THOSE FIRES AMONGST YOURSELVES BEFORE IT EVEN GOT TO MR. STRONG.
INSTEAD, WE HAVE TO RESORT TO THIS.
OKAY, OKAY...
WHO GETS YOGURT'S TURF?

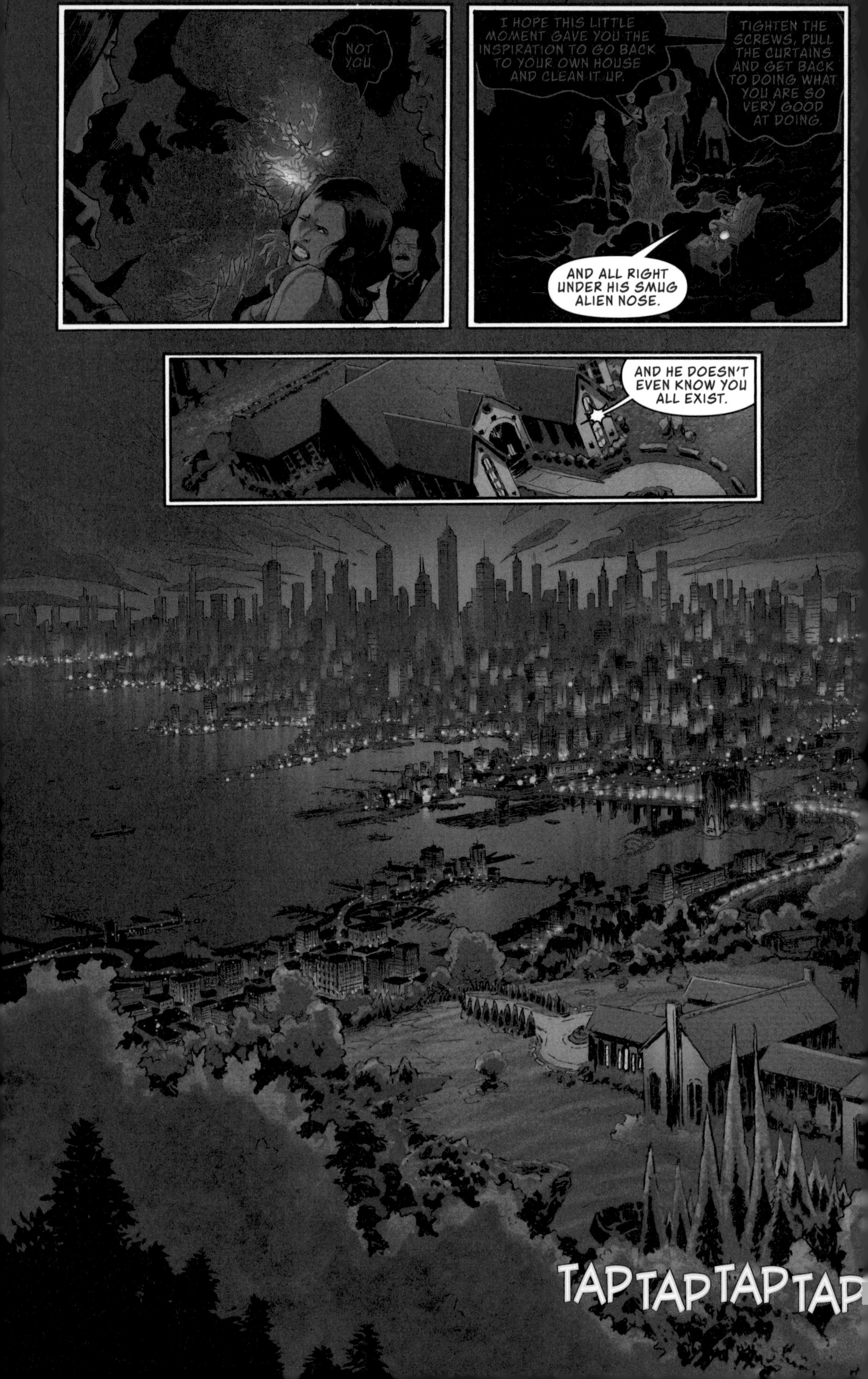
NOT YOU.
I HOPE THIS LITTLE MOMENT GAVE YOU THE INSPIRATION TO GO BACK TO YOUR OWN HOUSE AND CLEAN IT UP.
TIGHTEN THE SCREWS, PULL THE CURTAINS AND GET BACK TO DOING WHAT YOU ARE SO VERY GOOD AT DOING.
AND ALL RIGHT UNDER HIS SMUG ALIEN NOSE.
AND HE DOESN'T EVEN KNOW YOU ALL EXIST.
TAP TAP TAP TAP

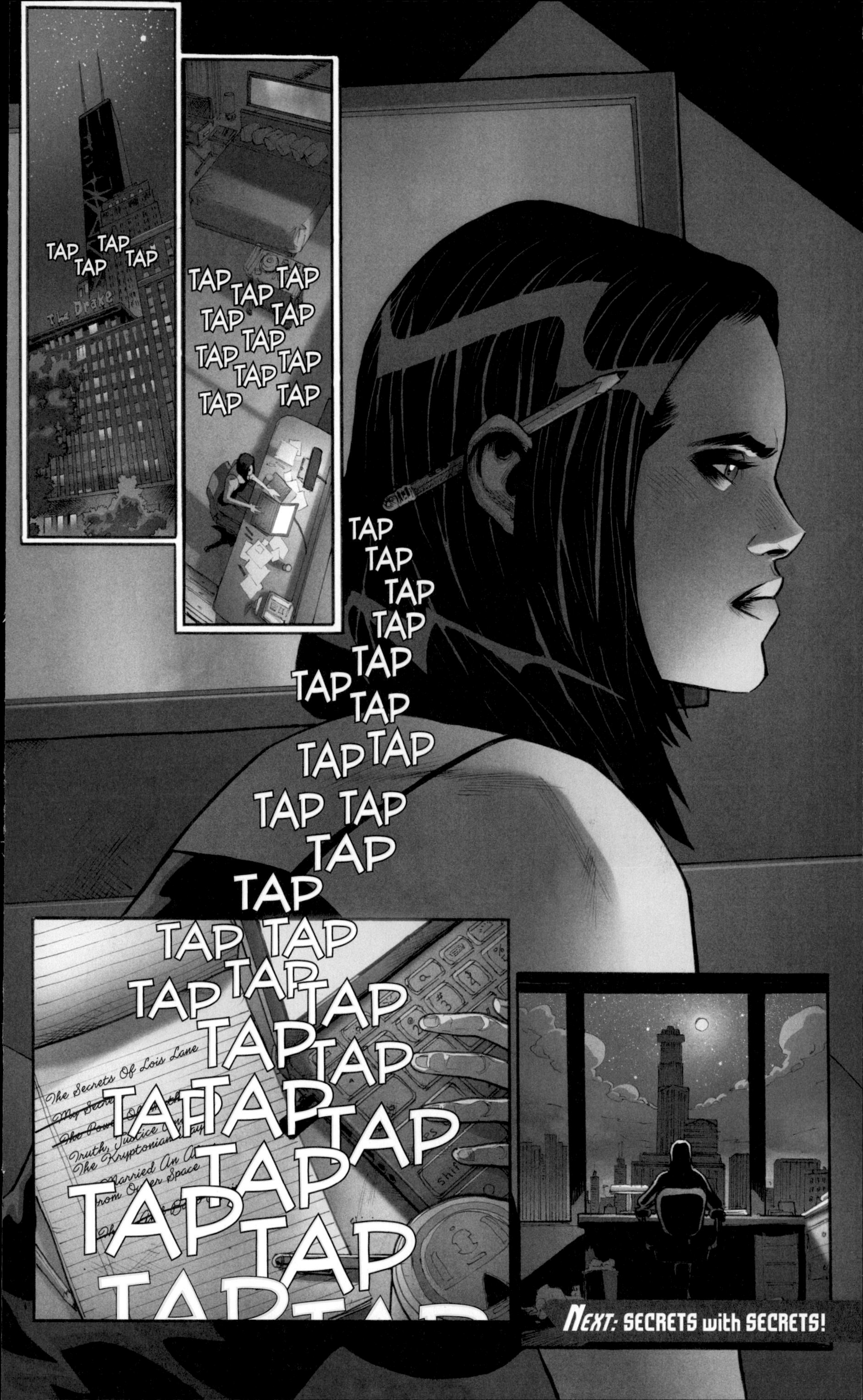
TAP TAP TAP TAP
The Drake
TAP TAP TAP TAP TAP TAP TAP TAP TAP TAP TAP
TAP TAP TAP TAP TAP TAP TAP TAP TAP TAP TAP TAP TAP TAP
The Secrets Of Lois Lane
TAP TAP TAP TAP TAP TAP TAP TAP TAP TAP TAP TAP TAP
NEXT: SECRETS with SECRETS!

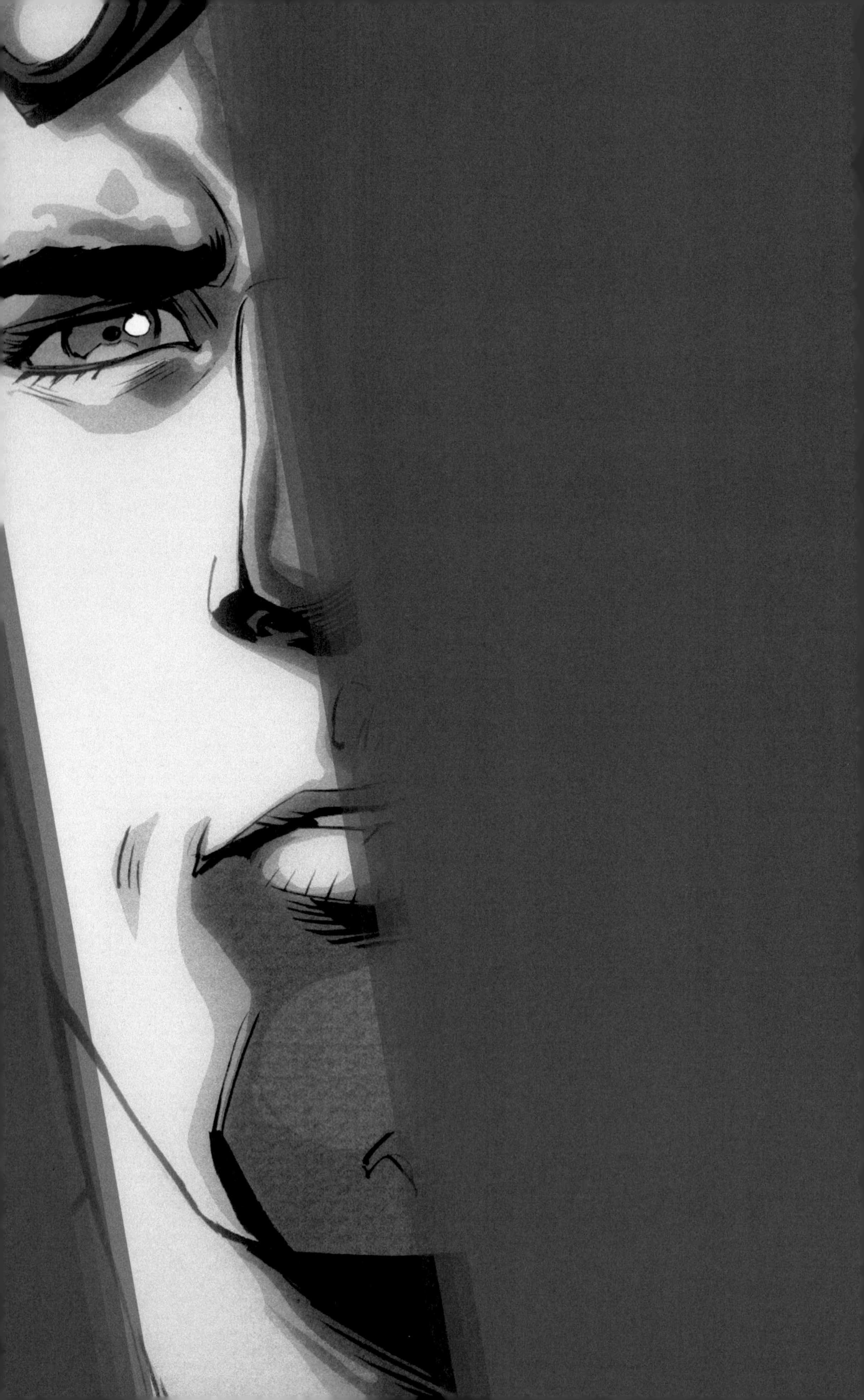

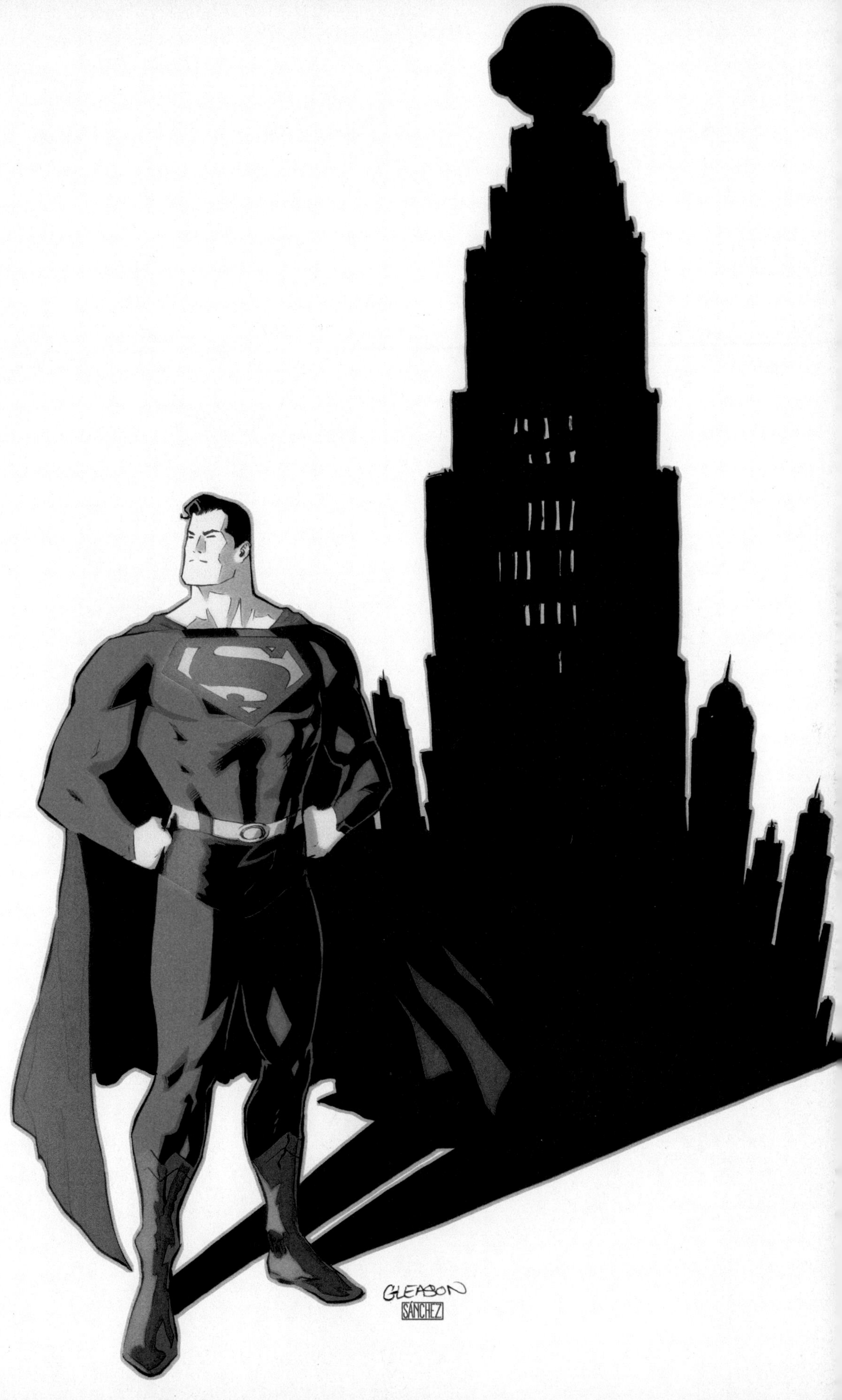
GLEASON
SÁNCHEZ

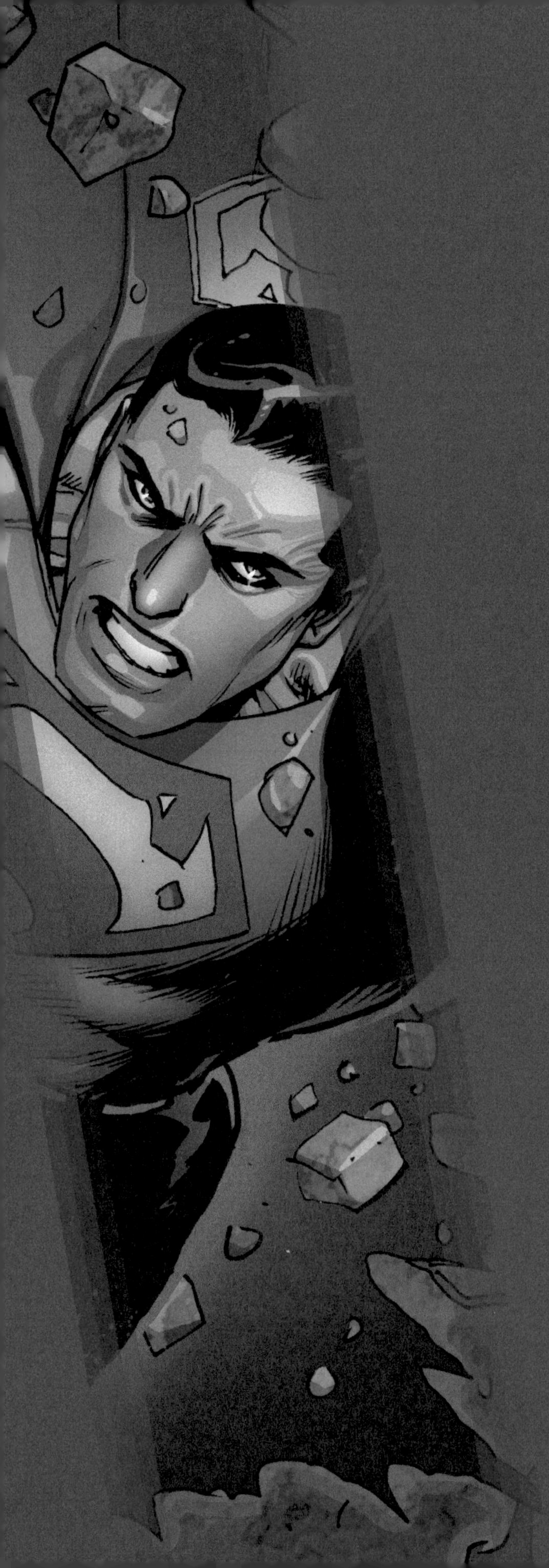

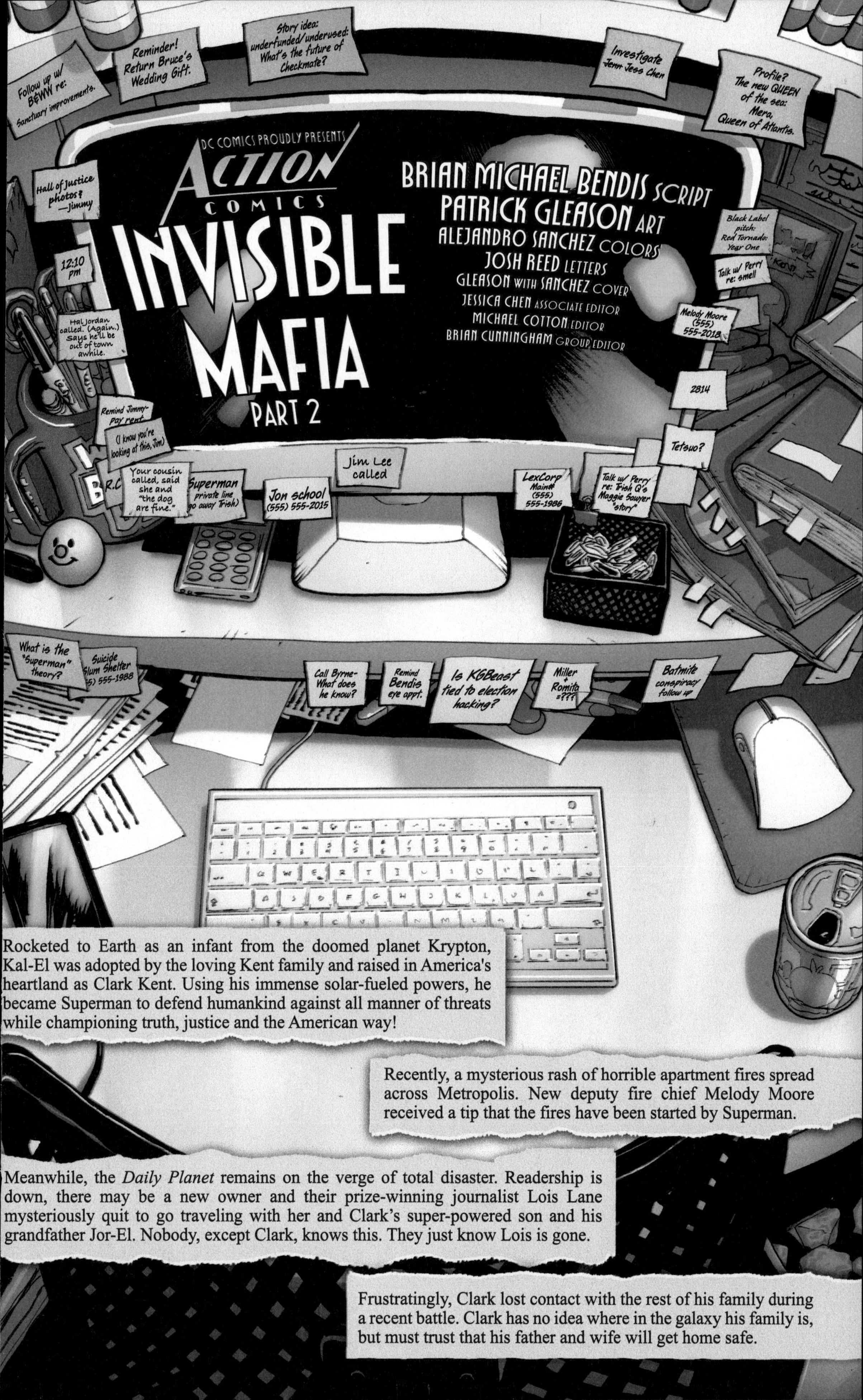

Follow up w/ B&WW re: Sanctuary improvements.
Reminder! Return Bruce's Wedding Gift.
Story idea: underfunded/underused: What's the future of Checkmate?
Investigate ~~Jenn~~ Jess Chen
Profile? The new QUEEN of the sea: Mera, Queen of Atlantis.
DC COMICS PROUDLY PRESENTS
ACTION COMICS
INVISIBLE MAFIA
PART 2
BRIAN MICHAEL BENDIS SCRIPT
PATRICK GLEASON ART
ALEJANDRO SANCHEZ COLORS
JOSH REED LETTERS
GLEASON WITH SANCHEZ COVER
JESSICA CHEN ASSOCIATE EDITOR
MICHAEL COTTON EDITOR
BRIAN CUNNINGHAM GROUP EDITOR
Hall of Justice photos? —Jimmy
12:10 pm
Hal Jordan called. (Again.) Says he'll be out of town awhile.
Remind Jimmy- Pay rent
(I know you're looking at this, Jim)
Your cousin called, said she and "the dog are fine."
Superman private line (go away Trish)
Jon school (555) 555-2015
Jim Lee called
LexCorp Main# (555) 555-1986
Talk w/ Perry re: Trish Q's Maggie Sawyer "story"
Tetsuo?
2814
Melody Moore (555) 555-2018
Talk w/ Perry re: smell
Black Label pitch: Red Tornado: Year One
What is the "Superman" theory?
Suicide Slum Shelter (555) 555-1988
Call Byrne- What does he know?
Remind Bendis eye appt.
Is KGBeast tied to election hacking?
Miller + Romita =???
Batmite conspiracy follow up
Rocketed to Earth as an infant from the doomed planet Krypton, Kal-El was adopted by the loving Kent family and raised in America's heartland as Clark Kent. Using his immense solar-fueled powers, he became Superman to defend humankind against all manner of threats while championing truth, justice and the American way!
Recently, a mysterious rash of horrible apartment fires spread across Metropolis. New deputy fire chief Melody Moore received a tip that the fires have been started by Superman.
Meanwhile, the *Daily Planet* remains on the verge of total disaster. Readership is down, there may be a new owner and their prize-winning journalist Lois Lane mysteriously quit to go traveling with her and Clark's super-powered son and his grandfather Jor-El. Nobody, except Clark, knows this. They just know Lois is gone.
Frustratingly, Clark lost contact with the rest of his family during a recent battle. Clark has no idea where in the galaxy his family is, but must trust that his father and wife will get home safe.

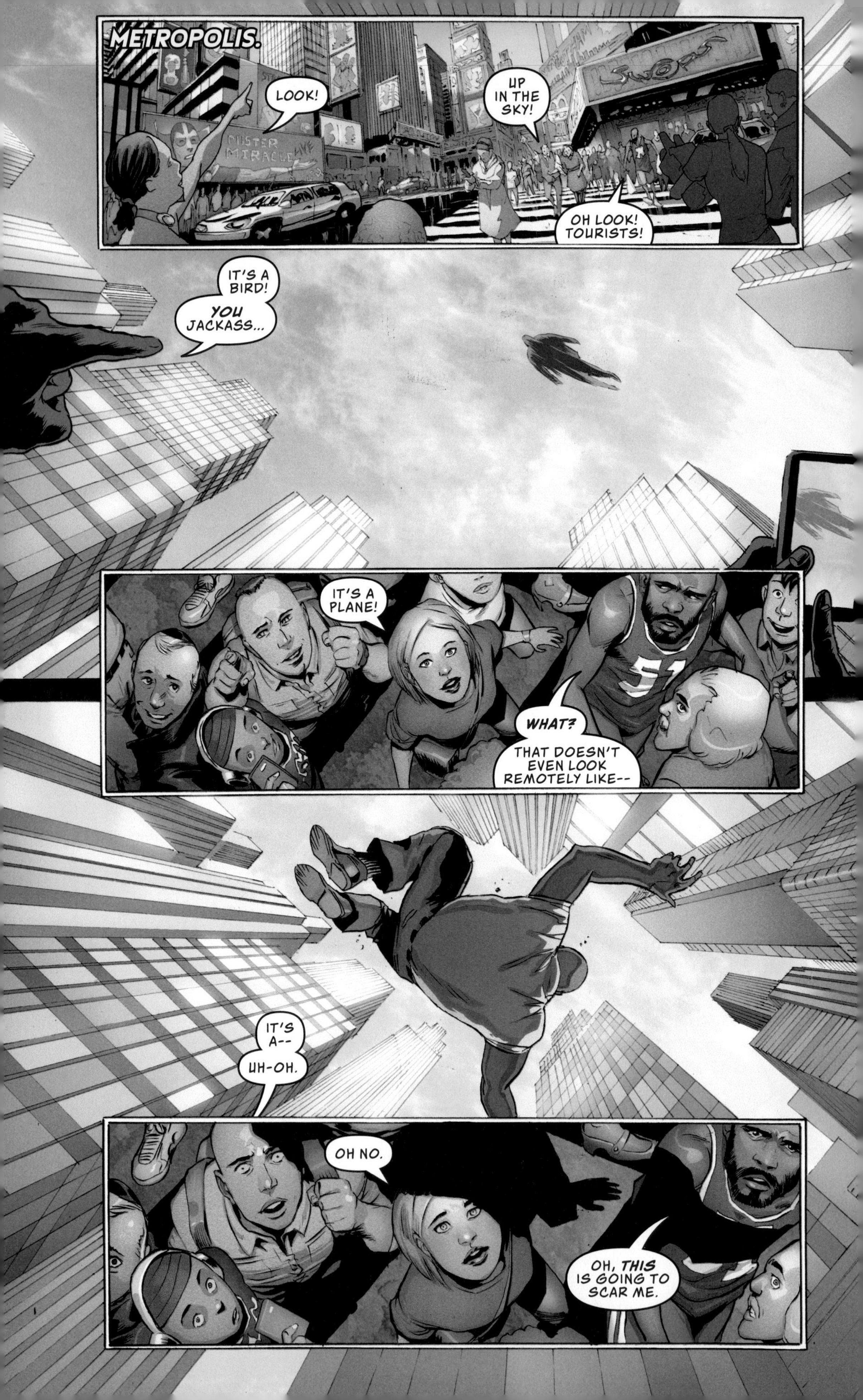
METROPOLIS.
LOOK!
UP IN THE SKY!
OH LOOK! TOURISTS!
IT'S A BIRD!
YOU JACKASS...
IT'S A PLANE!
WHAT?
THAT DOESN'T EVEN LOOK REMOTELY LIKE--
IT'S A--
UH-OH.
OH NO.
OH, THIS IS GOING TO SCAR ME.

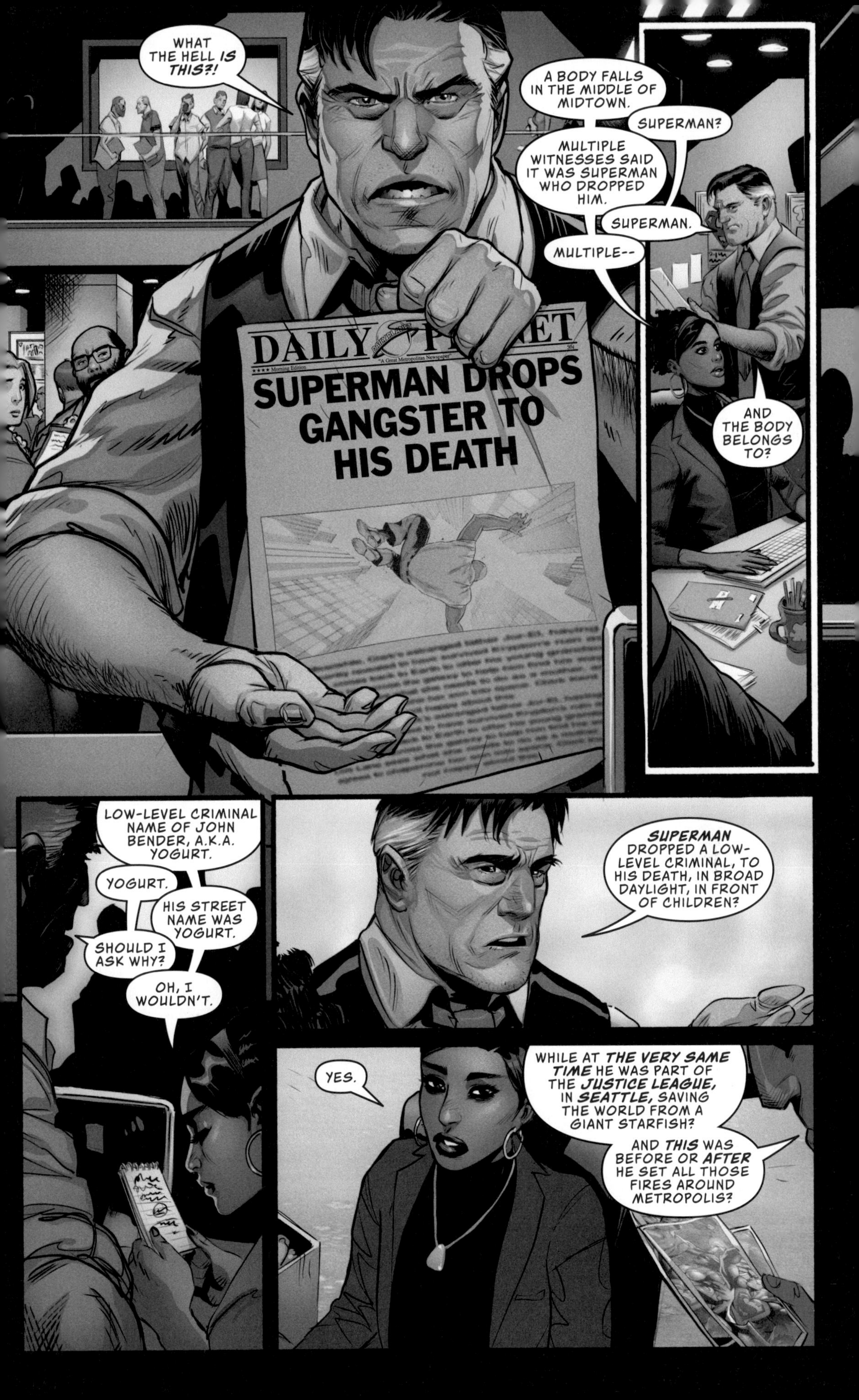
WHAT THE HELL IS THIS?!
DAILY PLANET
"A Great Metropolitan Newspaper"
Morning Edition
SUPERMAN DROPS GANGSTER TO HIS DEATH
A BODY FALLS IN THE MIDDLE OF MIDTOWN.
SUPERMAN?
MULTIPLE WITNESSES SAID IT WAS SUPERMAN WHO DROPPED HIM.
SUPERMAN.
MULTIPLE--
AND THE BODY BELONGS TO?
LOW-LEVEL CRIMINAL NAME OF JOHN BENDER, A.K.A. YOGURT.
YOGURT.
HIS STREET NAME WAS YOGURT.
SHOULD I ASK WHY?
OH, I WOULDN'T.
SUPERMAN DROPPED A LOW-LEVEL CRIMINAL, TO HIS DEATH, IN BROAD DAYLIGHT, IN FRONT OF CHILDREN?
YES.
WHILE AT THE VERY SAME TIME HE WAS PART OF THE JUSTICE LEAGUE, IN SEATTLE, SAVING THE WORLD FROM A GIANT STARFISH?
AND THIS WAS BEFORE OR AFTER HE SET ALL THOSE FIRES AROUND METROPOLIS?

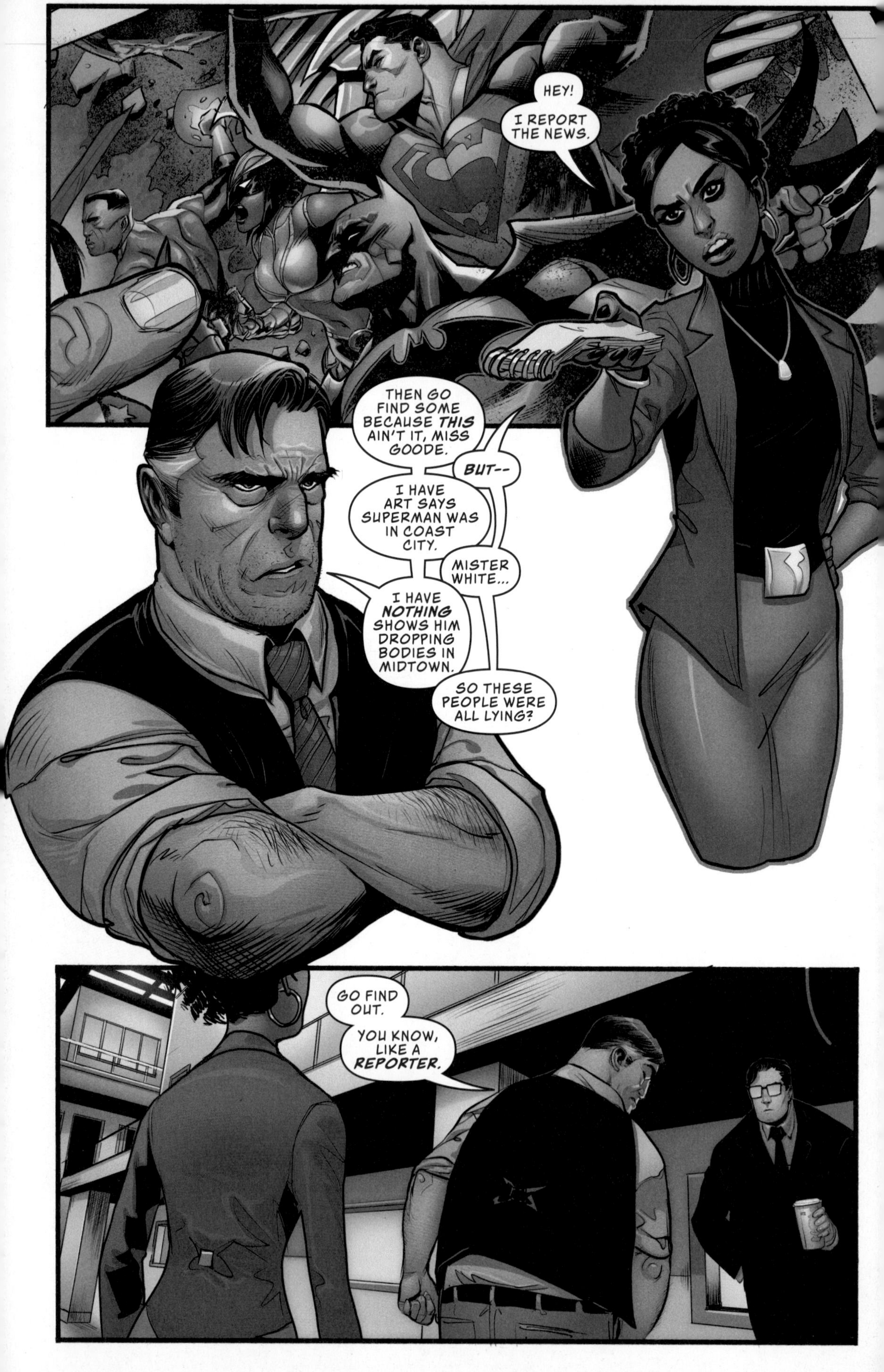
HEY!
I REPORT THE NEWS.
THEN GO FIND SOME BECAUSE *THIS* AIN'T IT, MISS GOODE.
BUT--
I HAVE ART SAYS SUPERMAN WAS IN COAST CITY.
MISTER WHITE...
I HAVE *NOTHING* SHOWS HIM DROPPING BODIES IN MIDTOWN.
SO THESE PEOPLE WERE ALL LYING?
GO FIND OUT.
YOU KNOW, LIKE A *REPORTER.*

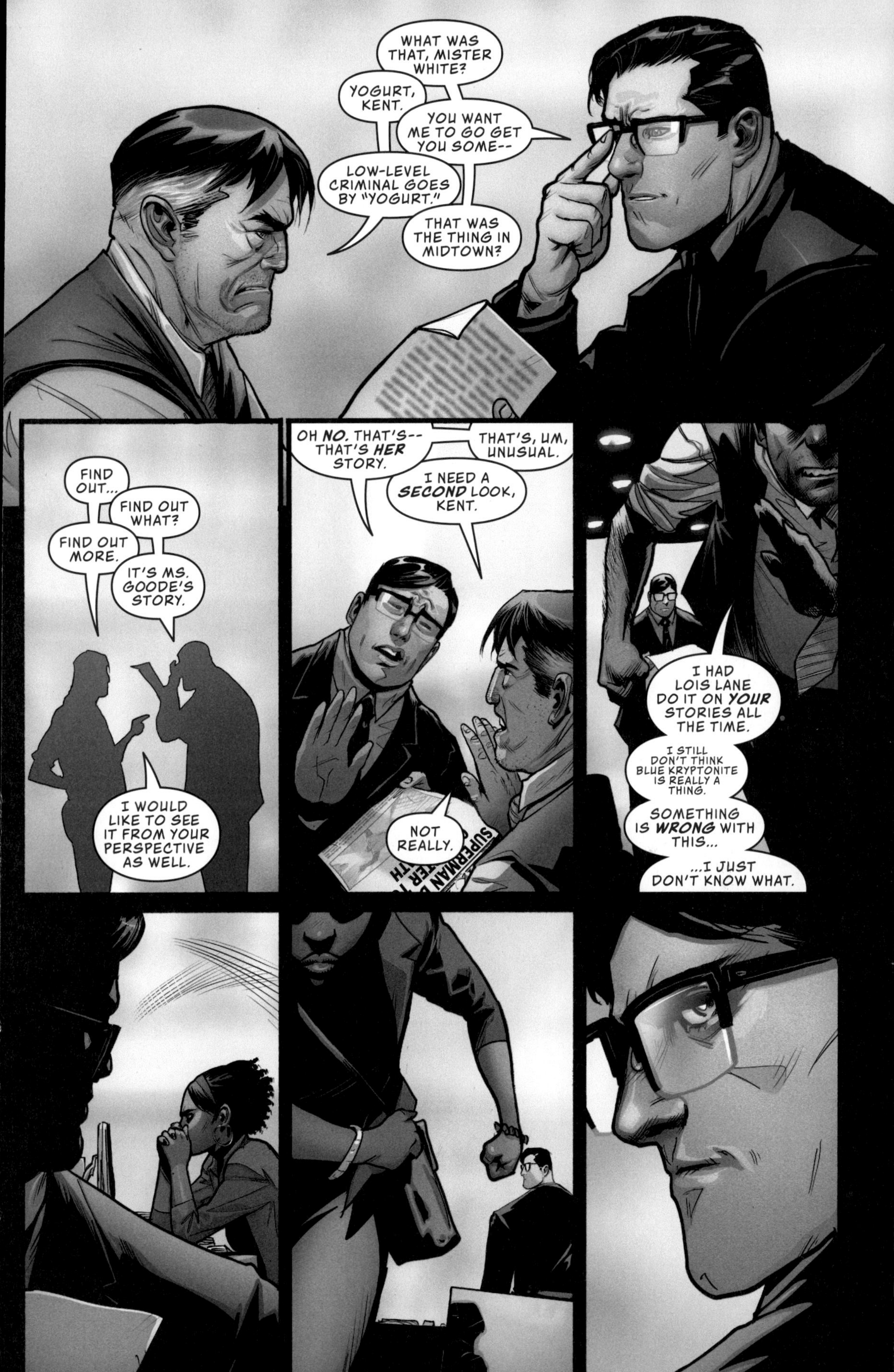
WHAT WAS THAT, MISTER WHITE?
YOGURT, KENT.
YOU WANT ME TO GO GET YOU SOME--
LOW-LEVEL CRIMINAL GOES BY "YOGURT."
THAT WAS THE THING IN MIDTOWN?
FIND OUT...
FIND OUT WHAT?
FIND OUT MORE.
IT'S MS. GOODE'S STORY.
I WOULD LIKE TO SEE IT FROM YOUR PERSPECTIVE AS WELL.
OH NO. THAT'S-- THAT'S HER STORY.
THAT'S, UM, UNUSUAL.
I NEED A SECOND LOOK, KENT.
NOT REALLY.
I HAD LOIS LANE DO IT ON YOUR STORIES ALL THE TIME.
I STILL DON'T THINK BLUE KRYPTONITE IS REALLY A THING.
SOMETHING IS WRONG WITH THIS...
...I JUST DON'T KNOW WHAT.

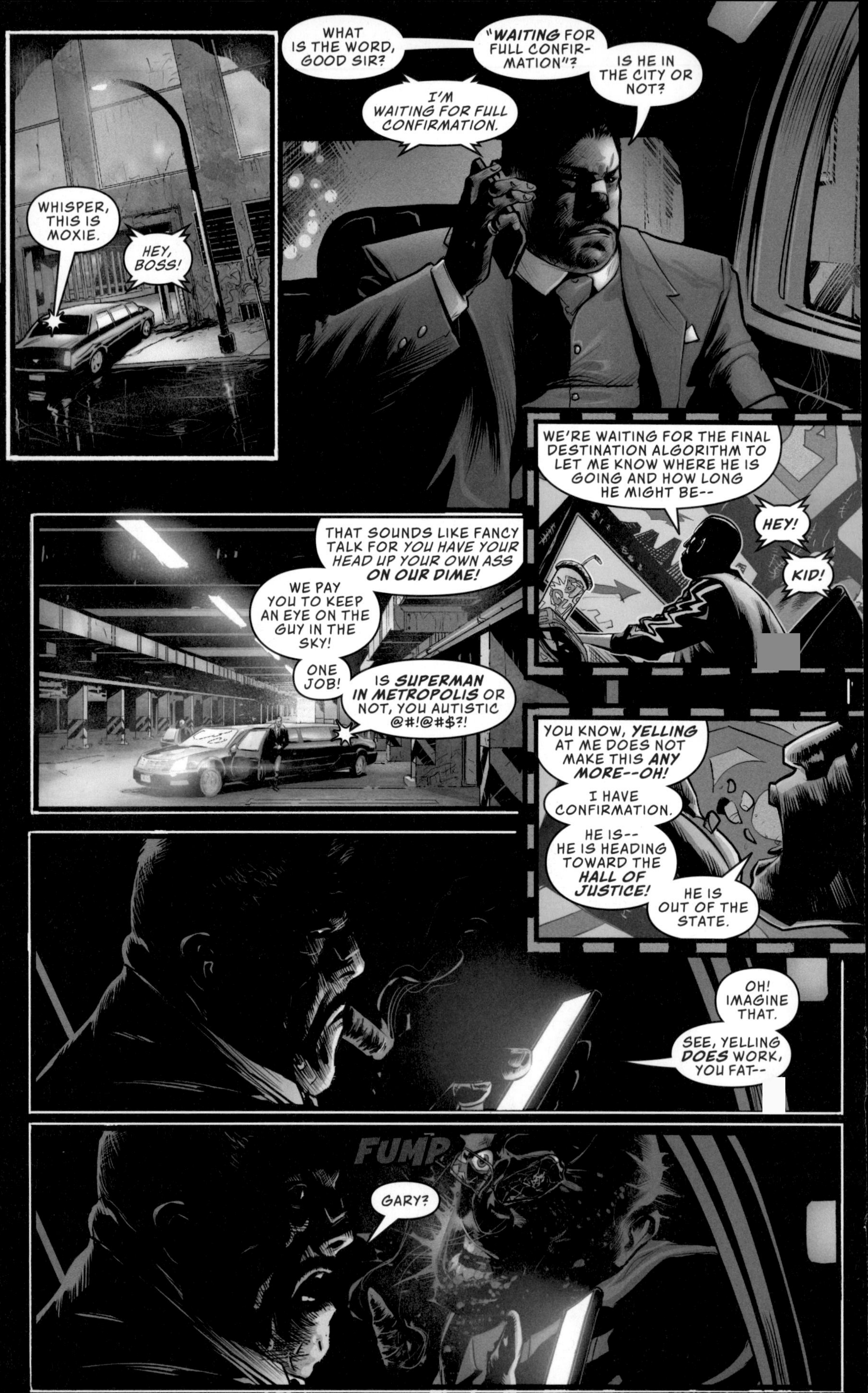
WHISPER, THIS IS MOXIE.
HEY, BOSS!
WHAT IS THE WORD, GOOD SIR?
"WAITING FOR FULL CONFIRMATION"?
IS HE IN THE CITY OR NOT?
I'M WAITING FOR FULL CONFIRMATION.
WE'RE WAITING FOR THE FINAL DESTINATION ALGORITHM TO LET ME KNOW WHERE HE IS GOING AND HOW LONG HE MIGHT BE--
HEY!
KID!
THAT SOUNDS LIKE FANCY TALK FOR YOU HAVE YOUR HEAD UP YOUR OWN ASS ON OUR DIME!
WE PAY YOU TO KEEP AN EYE ON THE GUY IN THE SKY!
ONE JOB!
IS SUPERMAN IN METROPOLIS OR NOT, YOU AUTISTIC @#!@#$?!
YOU KNOW, YELLING AT ME DOES NOT MAKE THIS ANY MORE--OH!
I HAVE CONFIRMATION.
HE IS-- HE IS HEADING TOWARD THE HALL OF JUSTICE!
HE IS OUT OF THE STATE.
OH! IMAGINE THAT.
SEE, YELLING DOES WORK, YOU FAT--
FUMP
GARY?

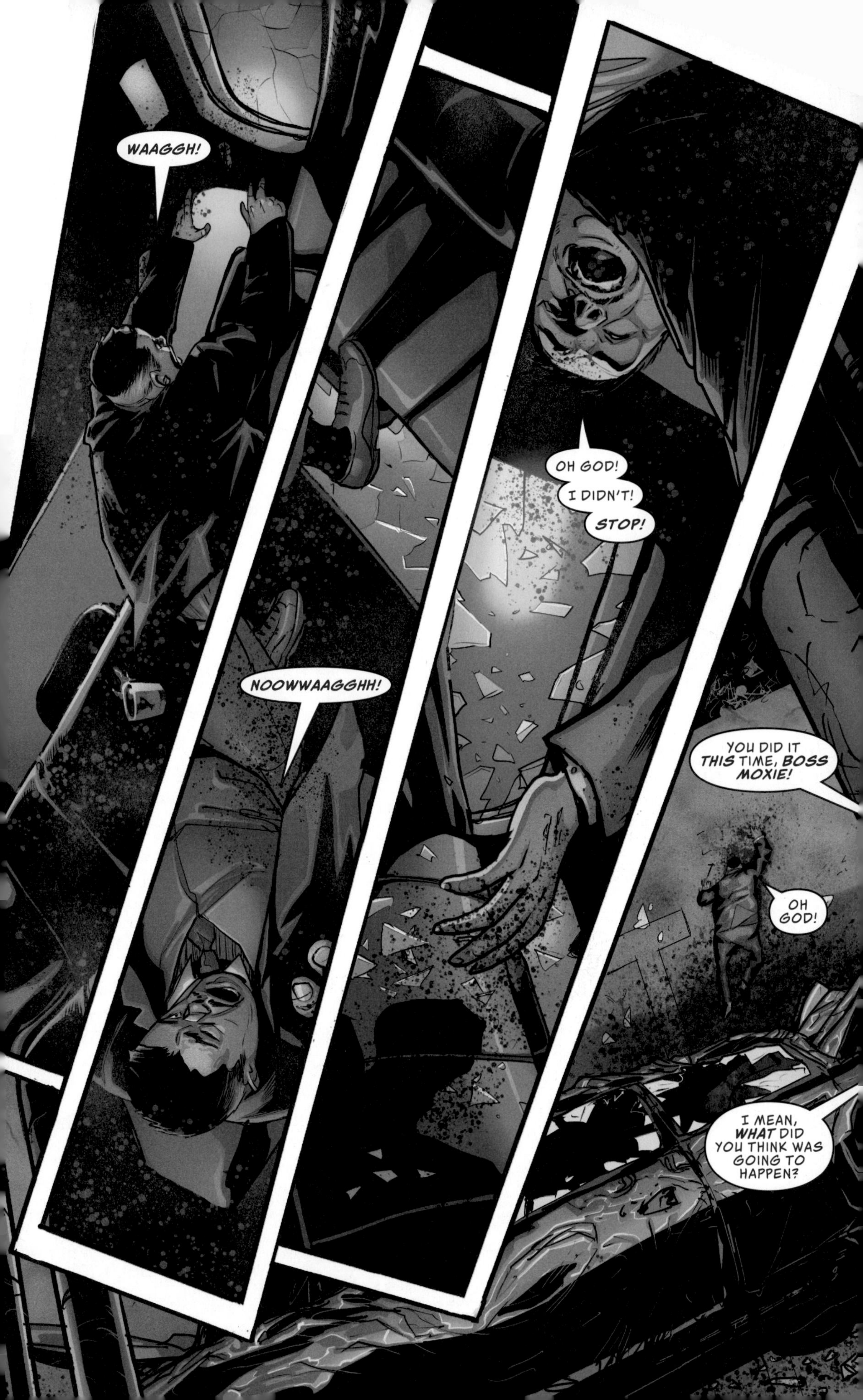
WAAGGH!
NOOWWAAGGHH!
OH GOD!
I DIDN'T!
STOP!
YOU DID IT THIS TIME, BOSS MOXIE!
OH GOD!
I MEAN, WHAT DID YOU THINK WAS GOING TO HAPPEN?

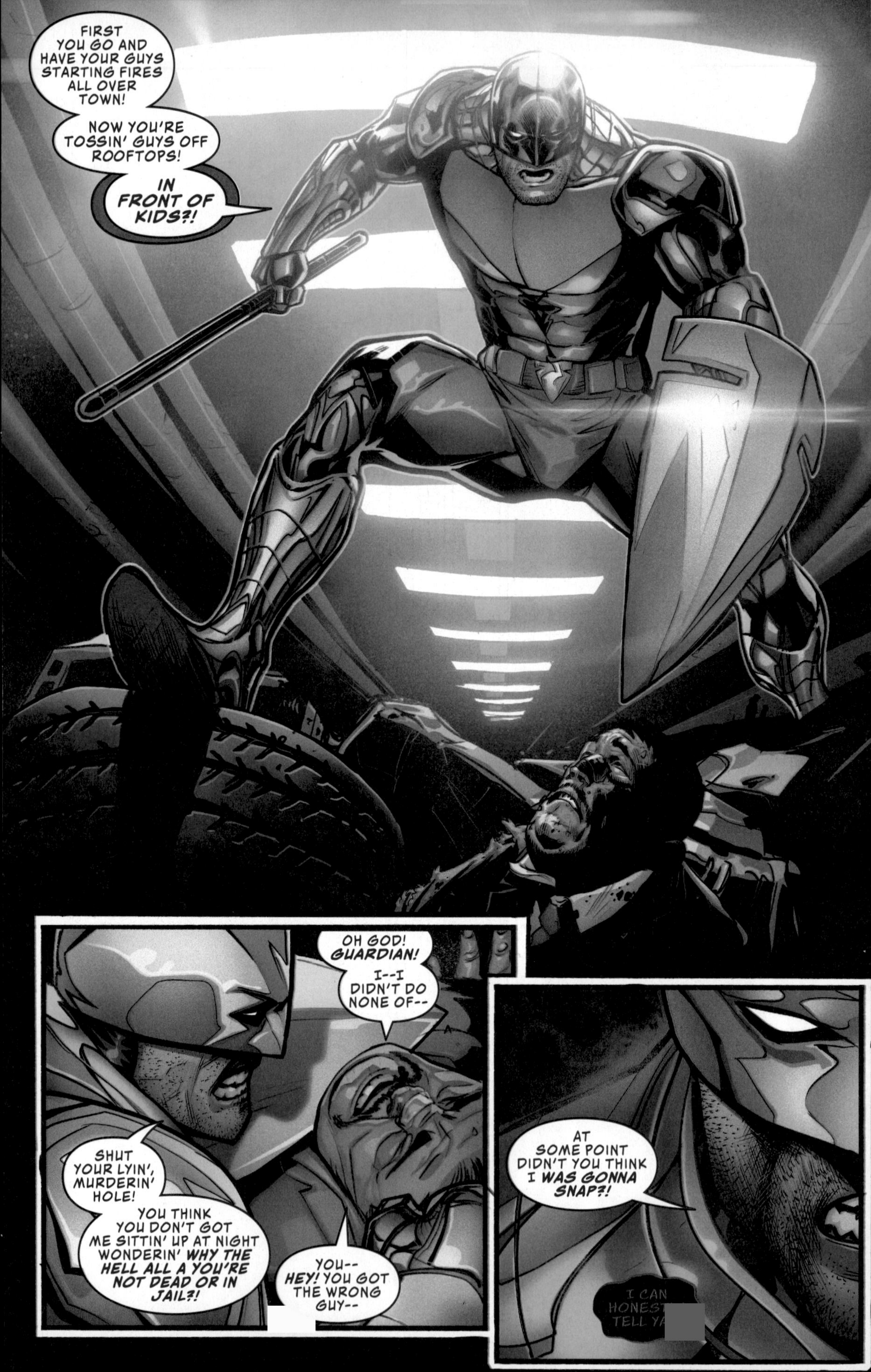
FIRST YOU GO AND HAVE YOUR GUYS STARTING FIRES ALL OVER TOWN!
NOW YOU'RE TOSSIN' GUYS OFF ROOFTOPS!
IN FRONT OF KIDS?!
OH GOD! GUARDIAN!
I--I DIDN'T DO NONE OF--
SHUT YOUR LYIN', MURDERIN' HOLE!
YOU THINK YOU DON'T GOT ME SITTIN' UP AT NIGHT WONDERIN' WHY THE HELL ALL A YOU'RE NOT DEAD OR IN JAIL?!
YOU-- HEY! YOU GOT THE WRONG GUY--
AT SOME POINT DIDN'T YOU THINK I WAS GONNA SNAP?!
I CAN

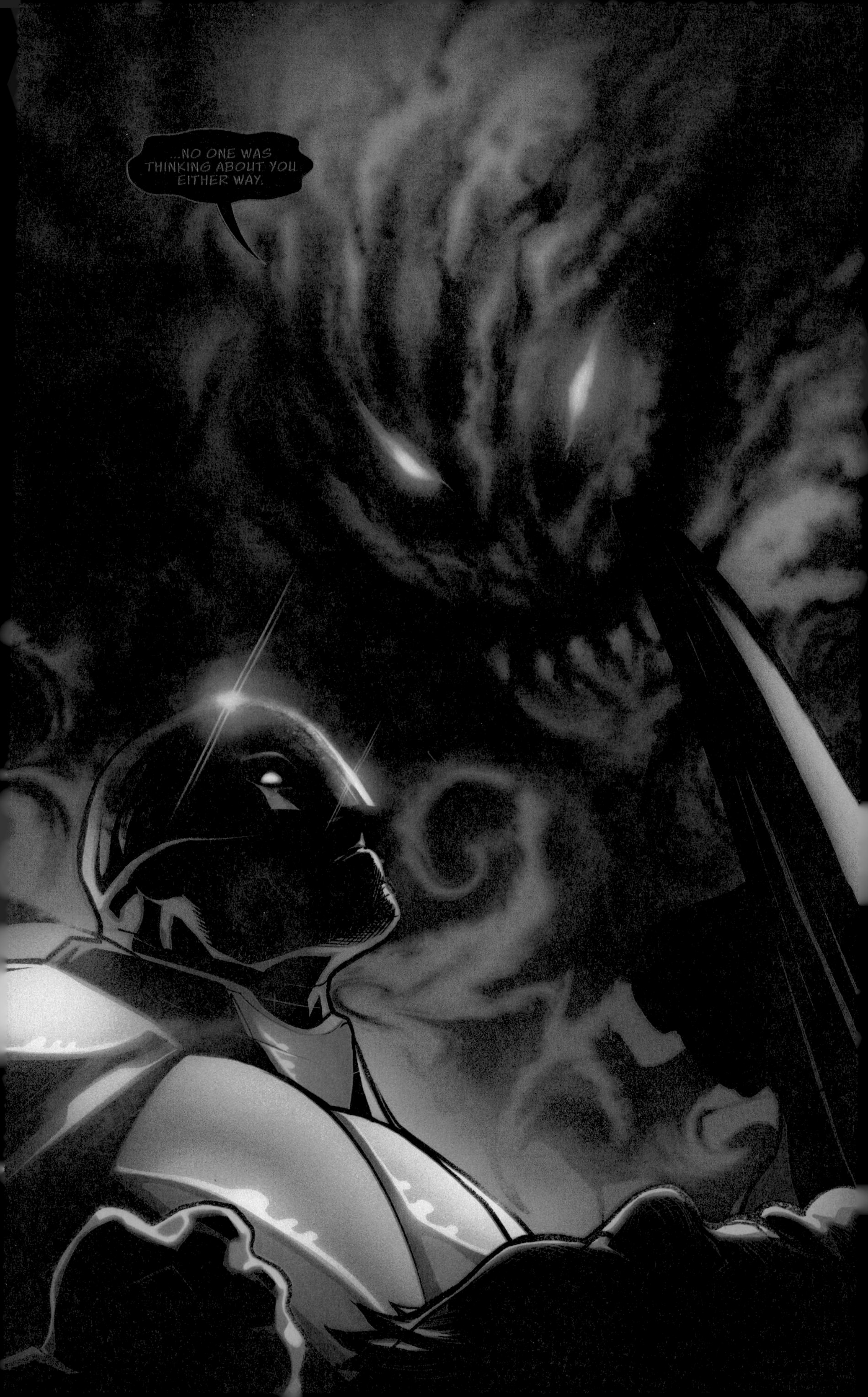
...NO ONE WAS THINKING ABOUT YOU EITHER WAY.

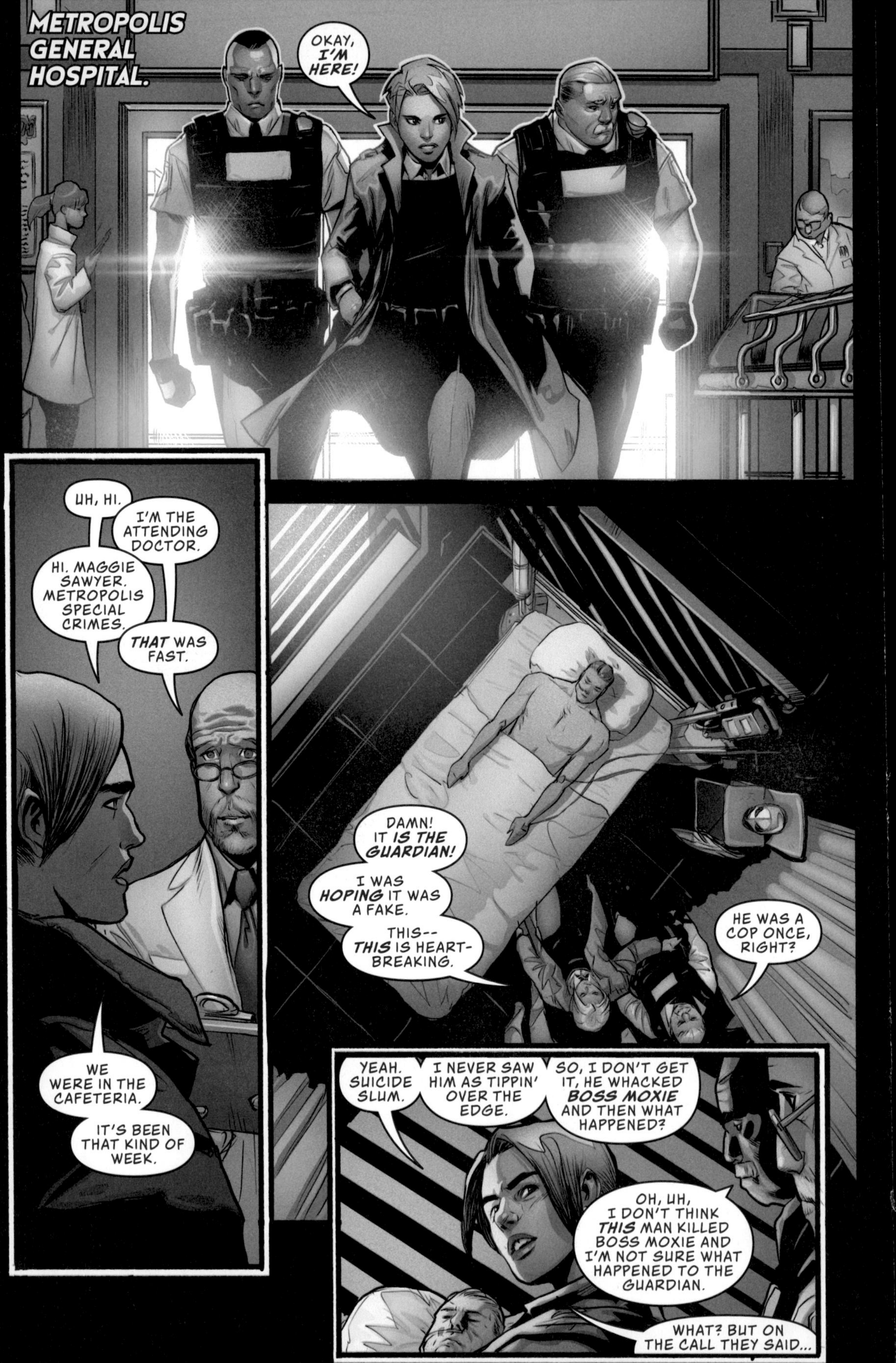
METROPOLIS GENERAL HOSPITAL.
OKAY, I'M HERE!
UH, HI.
I'M THE ATTENDING DOCTOR.
HI. MAGGIE SAWYER. METROPOLIS SPECIAL CRIMES.
THAT WAS FAST.
WE WERE IN THE CAFETERIA.
IT'S BEEN THAT KIND OF WEEK.
DAMN! IT IS THE GUARDIAN!
I WAS HOPING IT WAS A FAKE.
THIS-- THIS IS HEART-BREAKING.
HE WAS A COP ONCE, RIGHT?
YEAH. SUICIDE SLUM.
I NEVER SAW HIM AS TIPPIN' OVER THE EDGE.
SO, I DON'T GET IT, HE WHACKED BOSS MOXIE AND THEN WHAT HAPPENED?
OH, UH, I DON'T THINK THIS MAN KILLED BOSS MOXIE AND I'M NOT SURE WHAT HAPPENED TO THE GUARDIAN.
WHAT? BUT ON THE CALL THEY SAID...

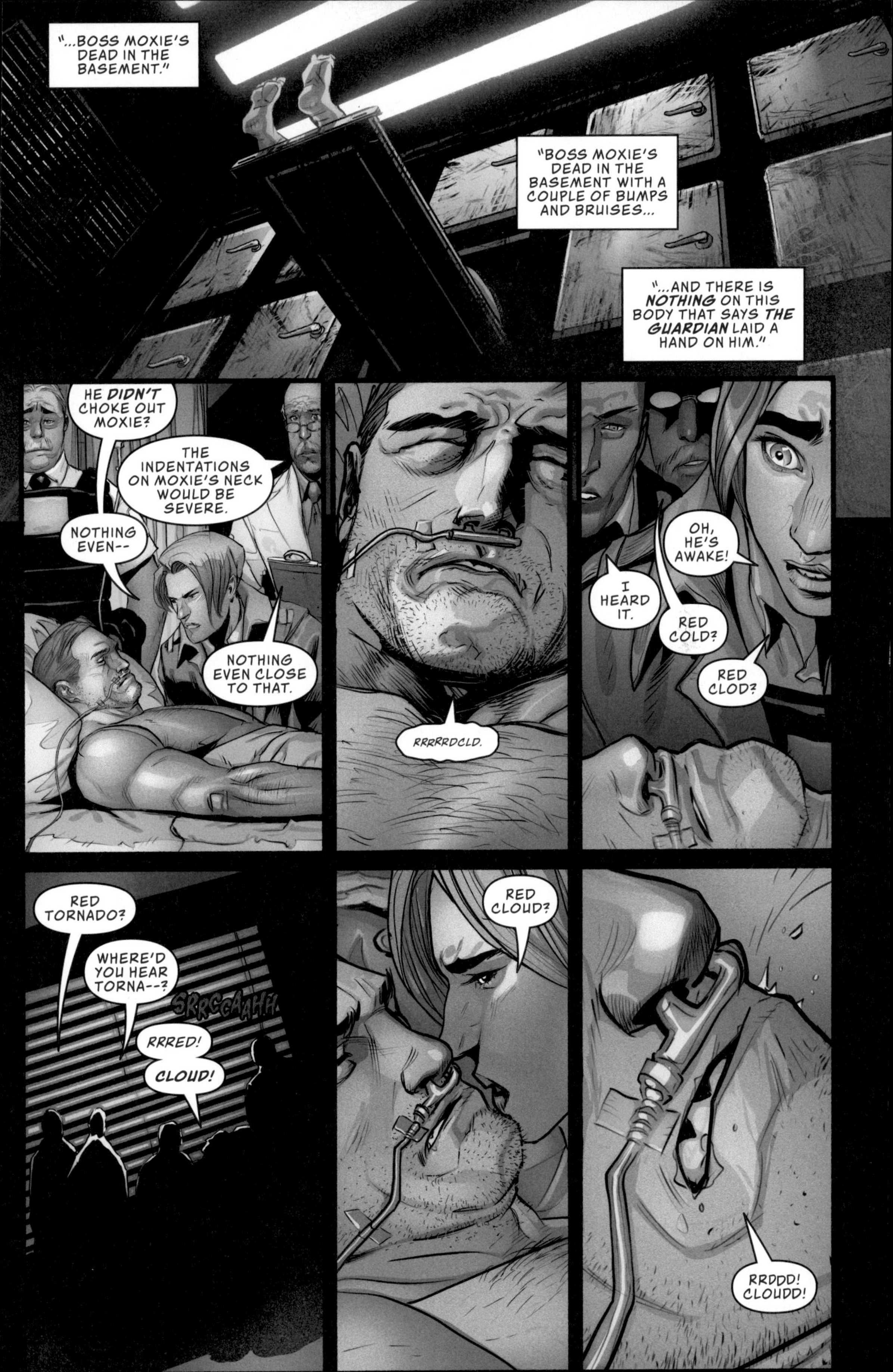
"...BOSS MOXIE'S DEAD IN THE BASEMENT."
"BOSS MOXIE'S DEAD IN THE BASEMENT WITH A COUPLE OF BUMPS AND BRUISES...
"...AND THERE IS NOTHING ON THIS BODY THAT SAYS THE GUARDIAN LAID A HAND ON HIM."
HE DIDN'T CHOKE OUT MOXIE?
THE INDENTATIONS ON MOXIE'S NECK WOULD BE SEVERE.
NOTHING EVEN--
NOTHING EVEN CLOSE TO THAT.
RRRRRDCLD.
OH, HE'S AWAKE!
I HEARD IT.
RED COLD?
RED CLOD?
RED TORNADO?
WHERE'D YOU HEAR TORNA--?
SRRCCAAHH
RRRED!
CLOUD!
RED CLOUD?
RRDDD! CLOUDD!

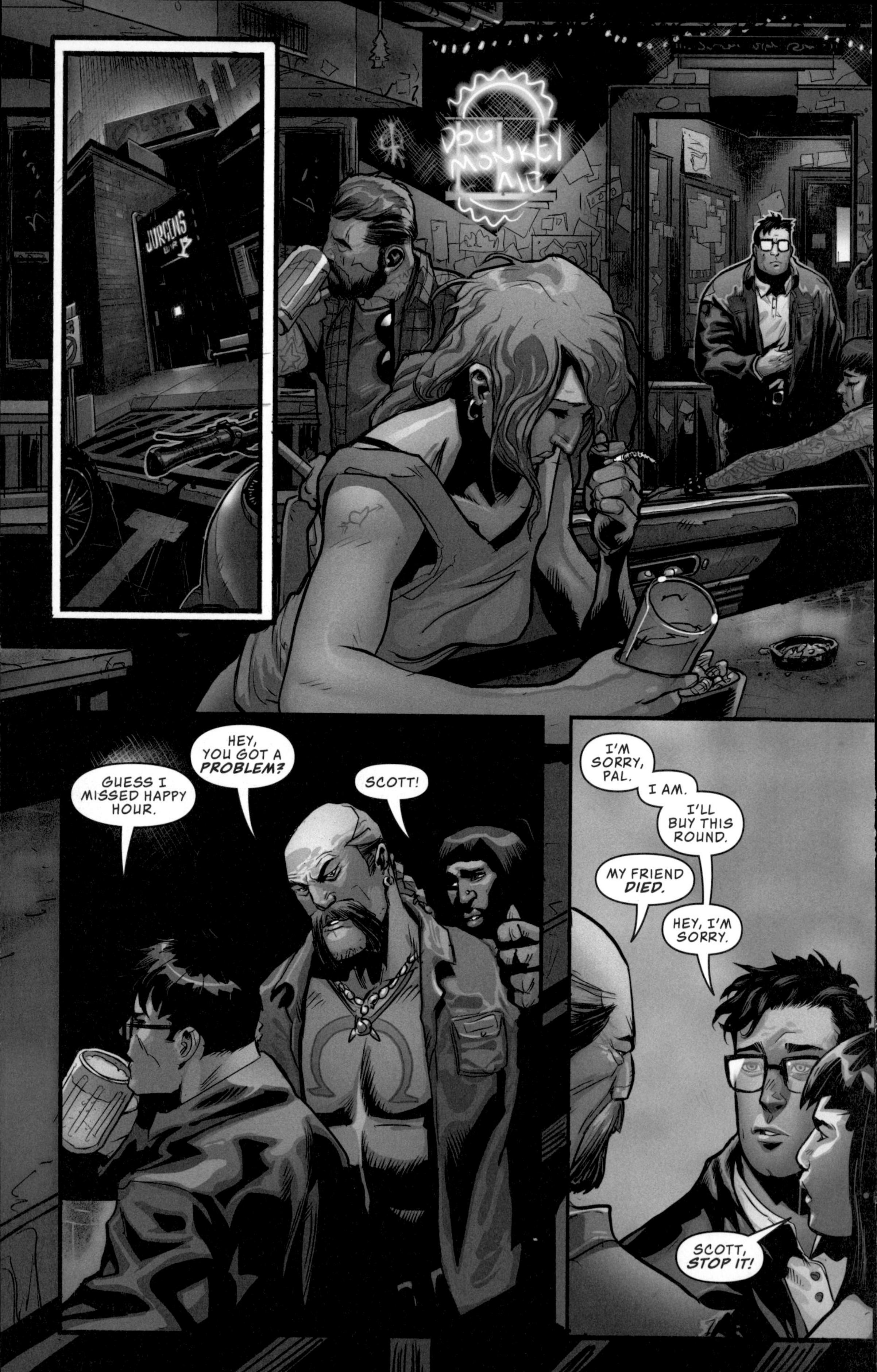
JURGENS BAR
DOG MONKEY ALE
GUESS I MISSED HAPPY HOUR.
HEY, YOU GOT A PROBLEM?
SCOTT!
I'M SORRY, PAL.
I AM.
I'LL BUY THIS ROUND.
MY FRIEND DIED.
HEY, I'M SORRY.
SCOTT, STOP IT!

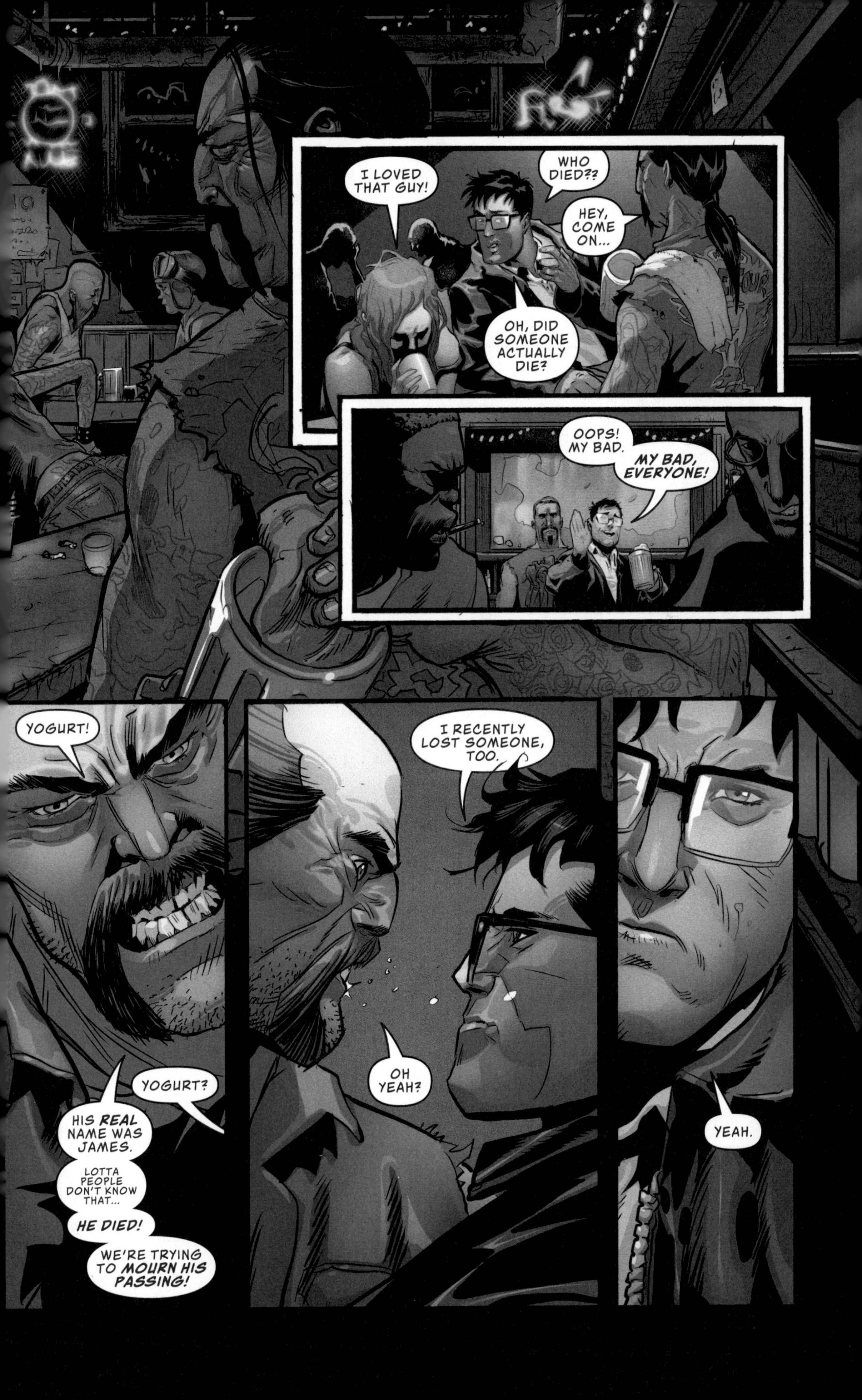
I LOVED THAT GUY!
WHO DIED??
HEY, COME ON...
OH, DID SOMEONE ACTUALLY DIE?
OOPS! MY BAD.
MY BAD, EVERYONE!
YOGURT!
YOGURT?
HIS REAL NAME WAS JAMES.
LOTTA PEOPLE DON'T KNOW THAT...
HE DIED!
WE'RE TRYING TO MOURN HIS PASSING!
I RECENTLY LOST SOMEONE, TOO.
OH YEAH?
YEAH.

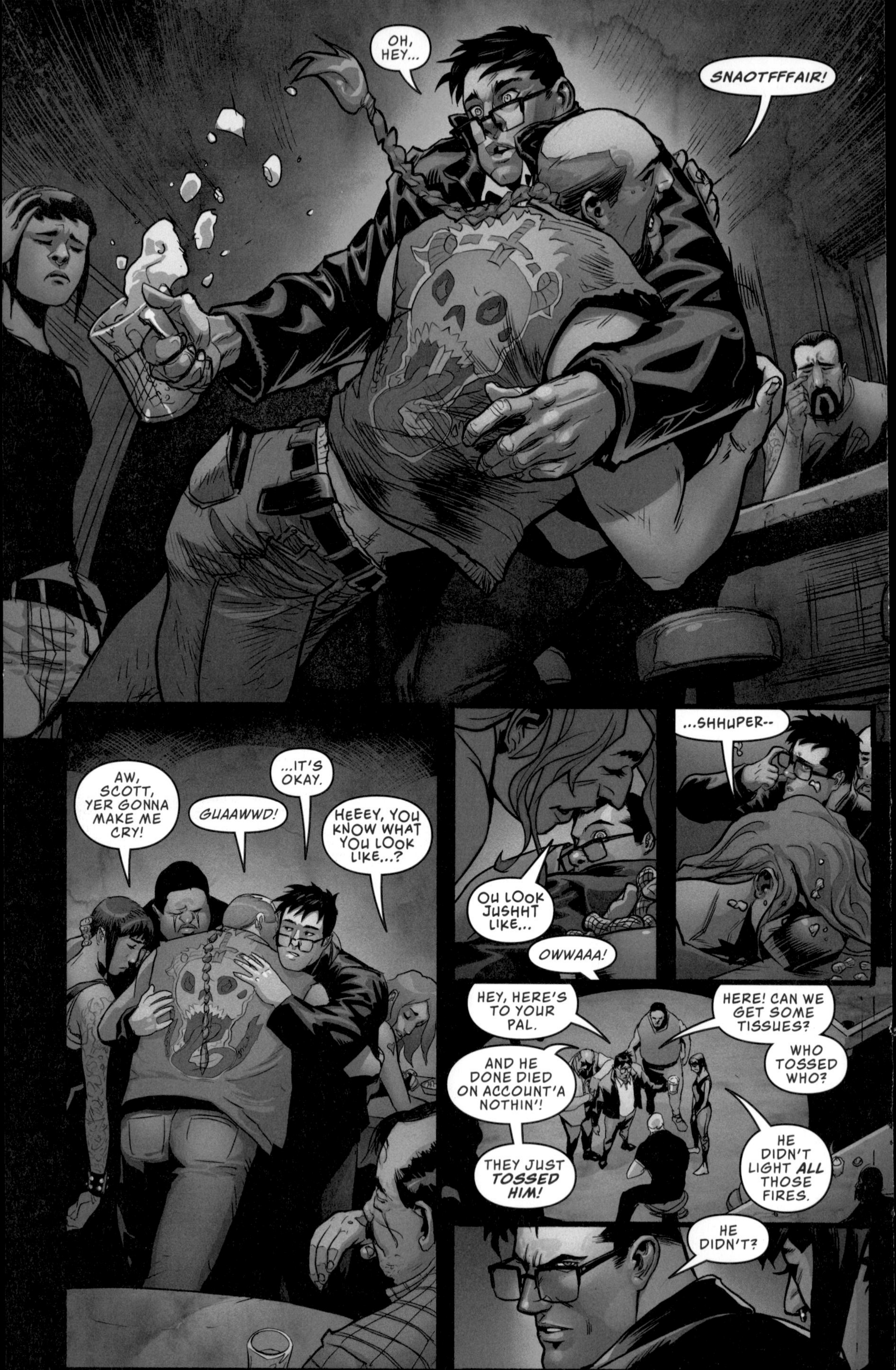
OH, HEY...
SNAOTFFFAIR!
AW, SCOTT, YER GONNA MAKE ME CRY!
GUAAWWD!
...IT'S OKAY.
HEEEY, YOU KNOW WHAT YOU LOOK LIKE...?
OU LOOK JUSHHT LIKE...
OWWAAA!
...SHHUPER--
HEY, HERE'S TO YOUR PAL.
AND HE DONE DIED ON ACCOUNT'A NOTHIN'!
THEY JUST TOSSED HIM!
HERE! CAN WE GET SOME TISSUES?
WHO TOSSED WHO?
HE DIDN'T LIGHT ALL THOSE FIRES.
HE DIDN'T?

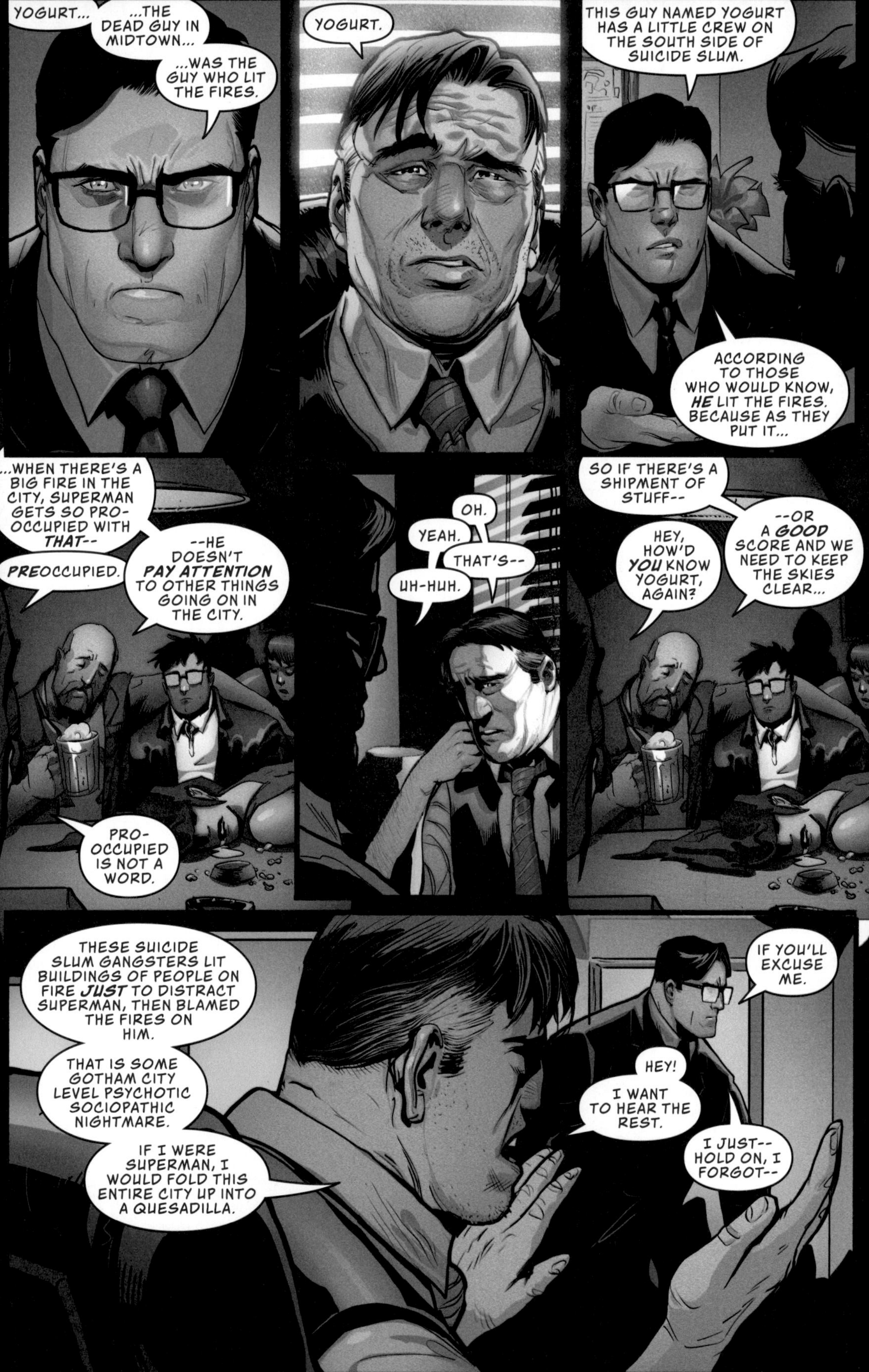
YOGURT...
...THE DEAD GUY IN MIDTOWN...
...WAS THE GUY WHO LIT THE FIRES.
YOGURT.
THIS GUY NAMED YOGURT HAS A LITTLE CREW ON THE SOUTH SIDE OF SUICIDE SLUM.
ACCORDING TO THOSE WHO WOULD KNOW, HE LIT THE FIRES. BECAUSE AS THEY PUT IT...
...WHEN THERE'S A BIG FIRE IN THE CITY, SUPERMAN GETS SO PRO-OCCUPIED WITH THAT--
PREOCCUPIED.
--HE DOESN'T PAY ATTENTION TO OTHER THINGS GOING ON IN THE CITY.
PRO-OCCUPIED IS NOT A WORD.
OH.
YEAH.
THAT'S--
UH-HUH.
SO IF THERE'S A SHIPMENT OF STUFF--
--OR A GOOD SCORE AND WE NEED TO KEEP THE SKIES CLEAR...
HEY, HOW'D YOU KNOW YOGURT, AGAIN?
THESE SUICIDE SLUM GANGSTERS LIT BUILDINGS OF PEOPLE ON FIRE JUST TO DISTRACT SUPERMAN, THEN BLAMED THE FIRES ON HIM.
THAT IS SOME GOTHAM CITY LEVEL PSYCHOTIC SOCIOPATHIC NIGHTMARE.
IF I WERE SUPERMAN, I WOULD FOLD THIS ENTIRE CITY UP INTO A QUESADILLA.
IF YOU'LL EXCUSE ME.
HEY!
I WANT TO HEAR THE REST.
I JUST-- HOLD ON, I FORGOT--

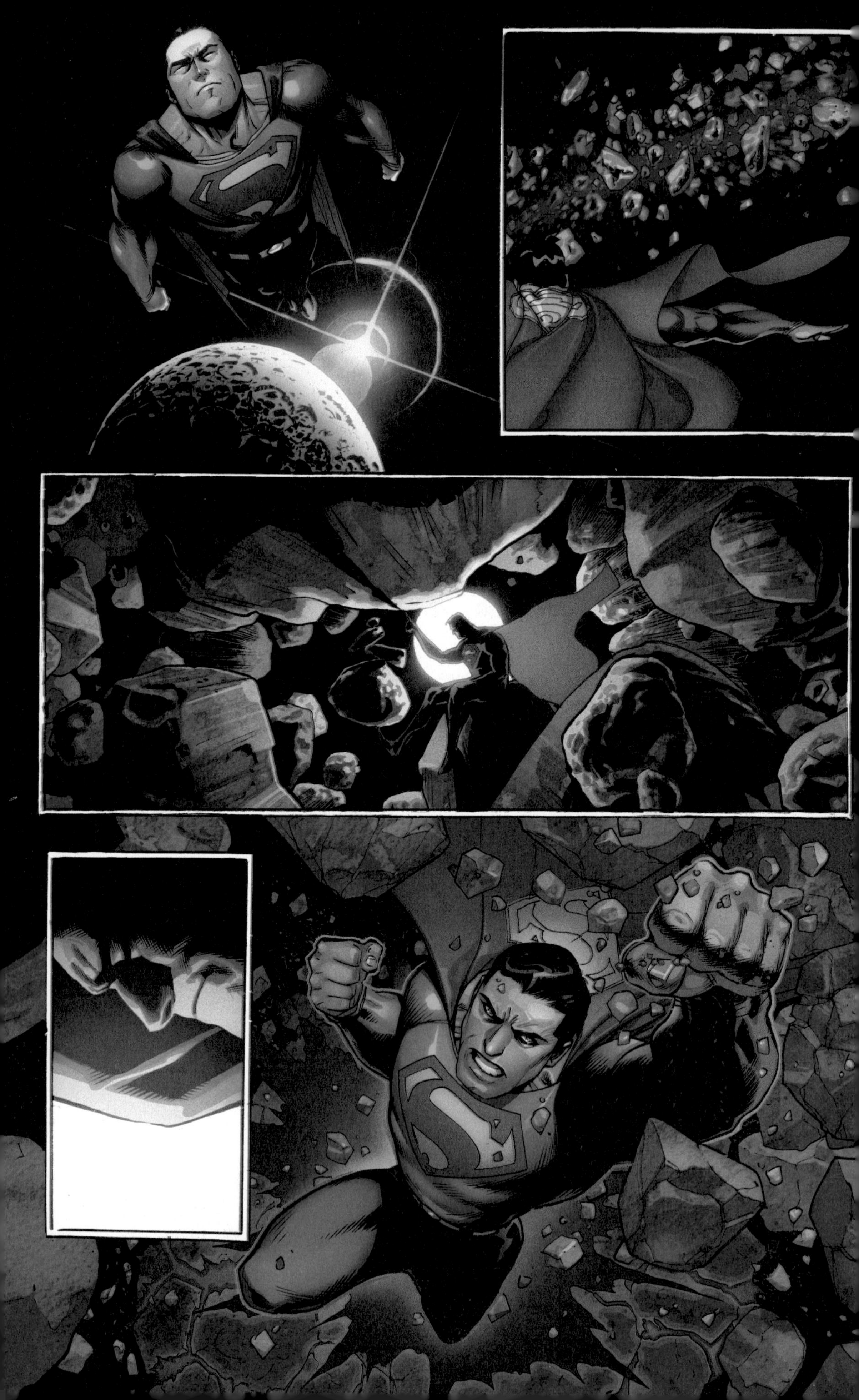

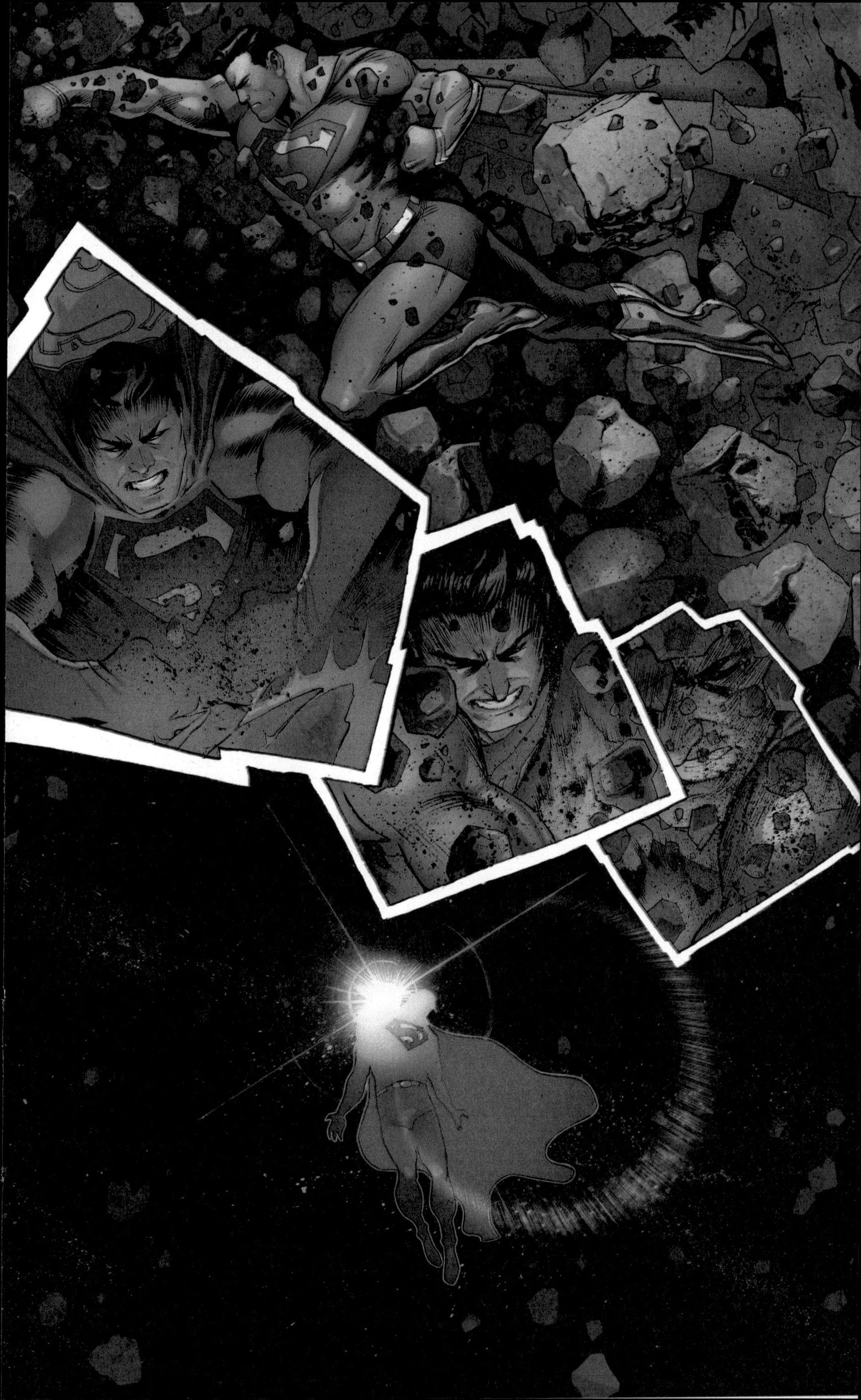

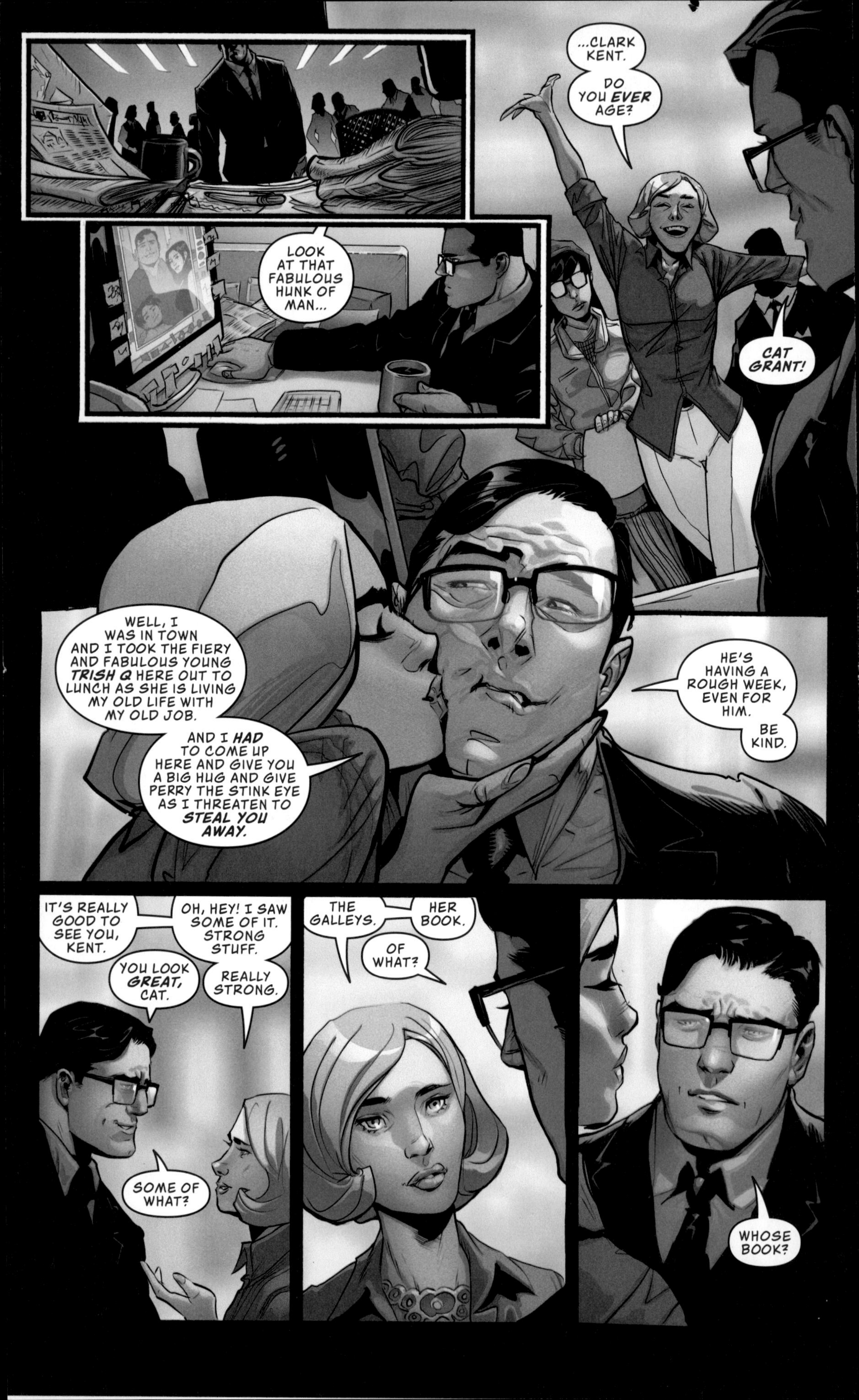
LOOK AT THAT FABULOUS HUNK OF MAN...
...CLARK KENT.
DO YOU EVER AGE?
CAT GRANT!
WELL, I WAS IN TOWN AND I TOOK THE FIERY AND FABULOUS YOUNG TRISH Q HERE OUT TO LUNCH AS SHE IS LIVING MY OLD LIFE WITH MY OLD JOB.
AND I HAD TO COME UP HERE AND GIVE YOU A BIG HUG AND GIVE PERRY THE STINK EYE AS I THREATEN TO STEAL YOU AWAY.
HE'S HAVING A ROUGH WEEK, EVEN FOR HIM.
BE KIND.
IT'S REALLY GOOD TO SEE YOU, KENT.
YOU LOOK GREAT, CAT.
OH, HEY! I SAW SOME OF IT. STRONG STUFF.
REALLY STRONG.
SOME OF WHAT?
THE GALLEYS.
HER BOOK.
OF WHAT?
WHOSE BOOK?

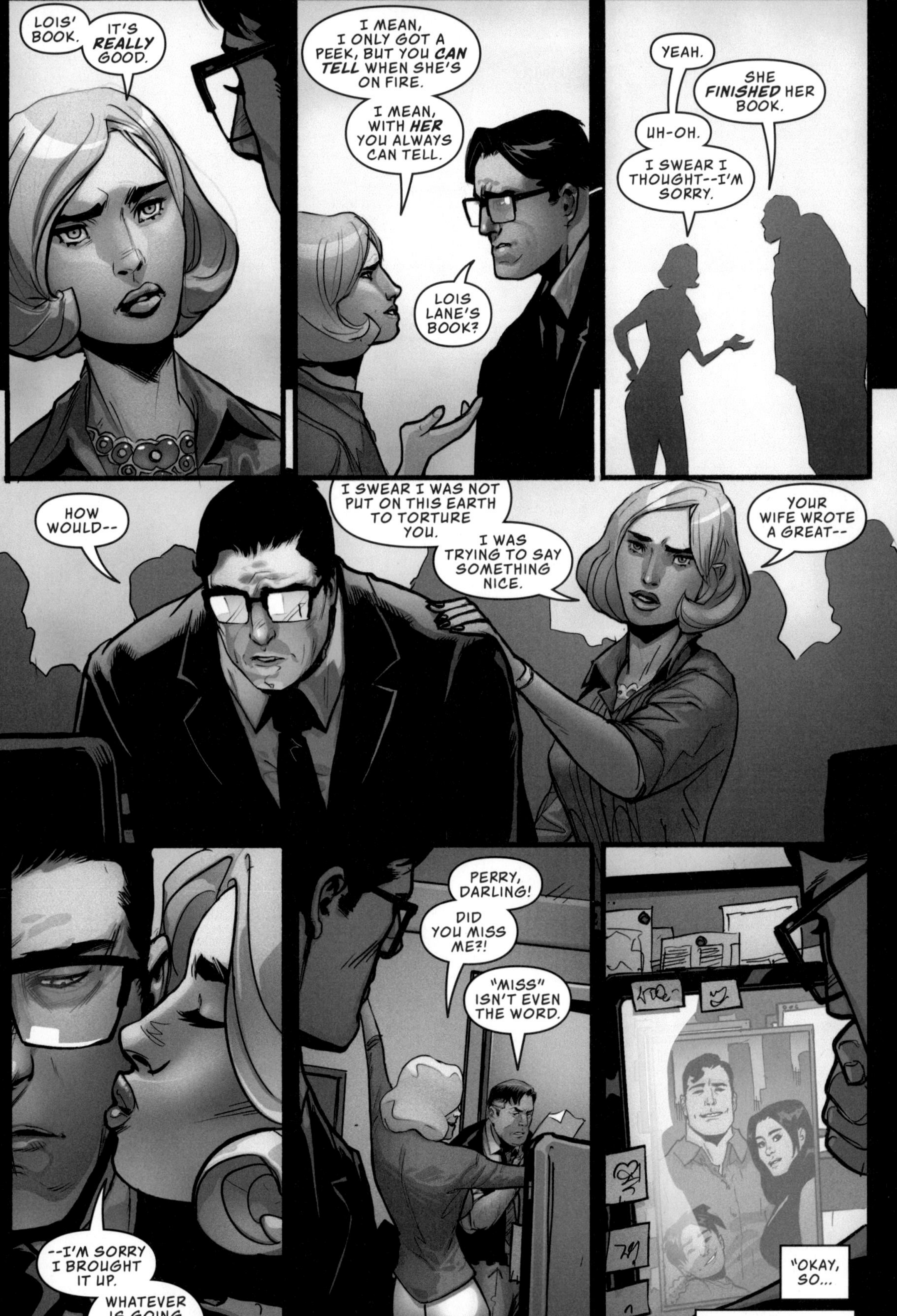
LOIS' BOOK.
IT'S REALLY GOOD.
I MEAN, I ONLY GOT A PEEK, BUT YOU CAN TELL WHEN SHE'S ON FIRE.
I MEAN, WITH HER YOU ALWAYS CAN TELL.
LOIS LANE'S BOOK?
YEAH.
SHE FINISHED HER BOOK.
UH-OH.
I SWEAR I THOUGHT--I'M SORRY.
HOW WOULD--
I SWEAR I WAS NOT PUT ON THIS EARTH TO TORTURE YOU.
I WAS TRYING TO SAY SOMETHING NICE.
YOUR WIFE WROTE A GREAT--
--I'M SORRY I BROUGHT IT UP.
WHATEVER IS GOING ON WITH YOU GUYS--SORRY.
PERRY, DARLING!
DID YOU MISS ME?!
"MISS" ISN'T EVEN THE WORD.
"OKAY, SO...
"...I MAY HAVE UNDERESTIMATED METROPOLIS."

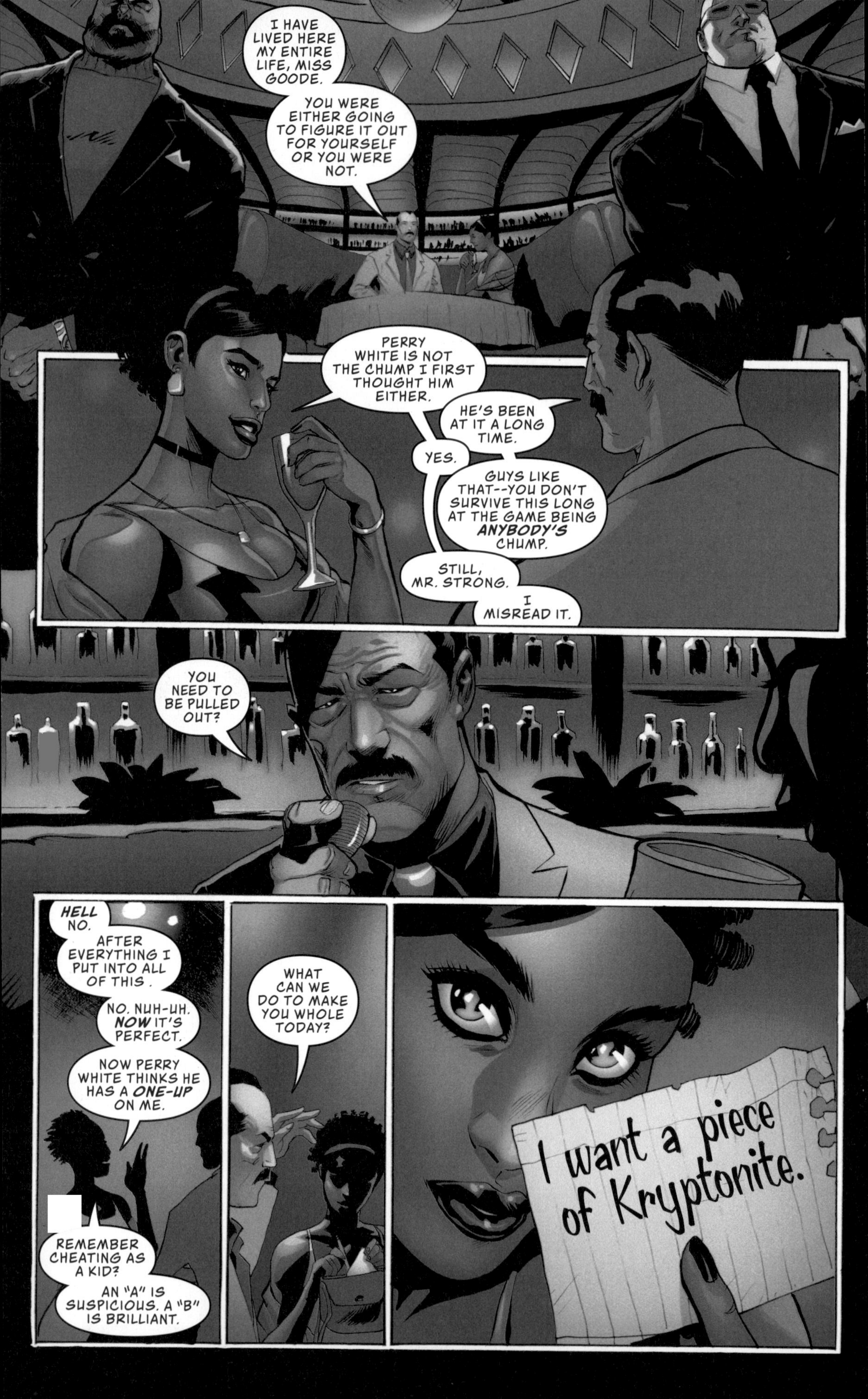
I HAVE LIVED HERE MY ENTIRE LIFE, MISS GOODE.
YOU WERE EITHER GOING TO FIGURE IT OUT FOR YOURSELF OR YOU WERE NOT.
PERRY WHITE IS NOT THE CHUMP I FIRST THOUGHT HIM EITHER.
HE'S BEEN AT IT A LONG TIME.
YES.
GUYS LIKE THAT--YOU DON'T SURVIVE THIS LONG AT THE GAME BEING ANYBODY'S CHUMP.
STILL, MR. STRONG.
I MISREAD IT.
YOU NEED TO BE PULLED OUT?
HELL NO.
AFTER EVERYTHING I PUT INTO ALL OF THIS .
NO. NUH-UH. NOW IT'S PERFECT.
NOW PERRY WHITE THINKS HE HAS A ONE-UP ON ME.
REMEMBER CHEATING AS A KID?
AN "A" IS SUSPICIOUS. A "B" IS BRILLIANT.
WHAT CAN WE DO TO MAKE YOU WHOLE TODAY?
I want a piece of Kryptonite.

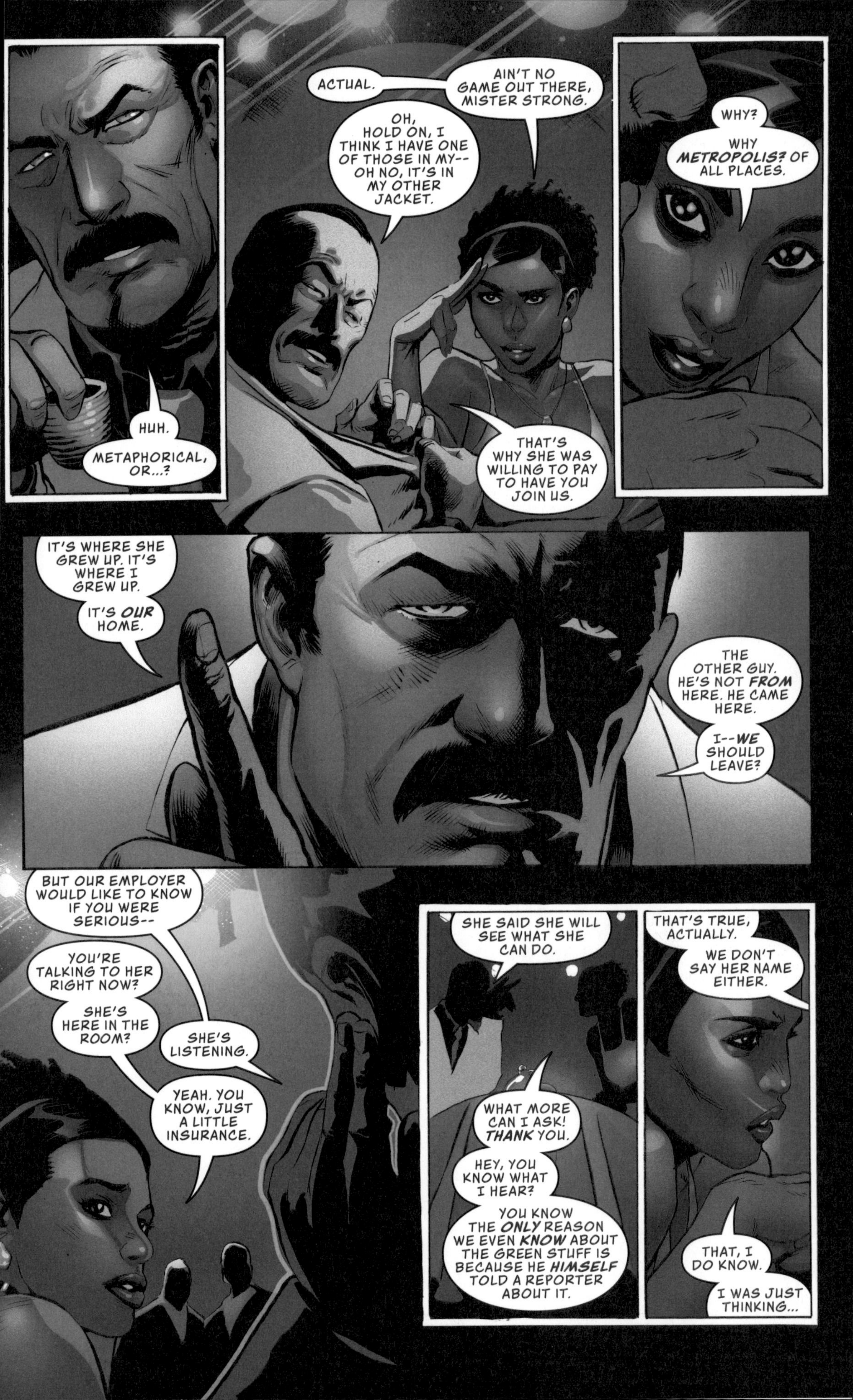
AIN'T NO GAME OUT THERE, MISTER STRONG.
ACTUAL.
OH, HOLD ON, I THINK I HAVE ONE OF THOSE IN MY-- OH NO, IT'S IN MY OTHER JACKET.
HUH.
METAPHORICAL, OR...?
THAT'S WHY SHE WAS WILLING TO PAY TO HAVE YOU JOIN US.
WHY?
WHY *METROPOLIS?* OF ALL PLACES.
IT'S WHERE SHE GREW UP. IT'S WHERE I GREW UP.
IT'S *OUR* HOME.
THE OTHER GUY. HE'S NOT *FROM* HERE. HE CAME HERE.
I--*WE* SHOULD LEAVE?
BUT OUR EMPLOYER WOULD LIKE TO KNOW IF YOU WERE SERIOUS--
YOU'RE TALKING TO HER RIGHT NOW?
SHE'S HERE IN THE ROOM?
SHE'S LISTENING.
YEAH. YOU KNOW, JUST A LITTLE INSURANCE.
SHE SAID SHE WILL SEE WHAT SHE CAN DO.
WHAT MORE CAN I ASK! *THANK* YOU.
HEY, YOU KNOW WHAT I HEAR?
YOU KNOW THE *ONLY* REASON WE EVEN *KNOW* ABOUT THE GREEN STUFF IS BECAUSE HE *HIMSELF* TOLD A REPORTER ABOUT IT.
THAT'S TRUE, ACTUALLY.
WE DON'T SAY HER NAME EITHER.
THAT, I DO KNOW.
I WAS JUST THINKING...

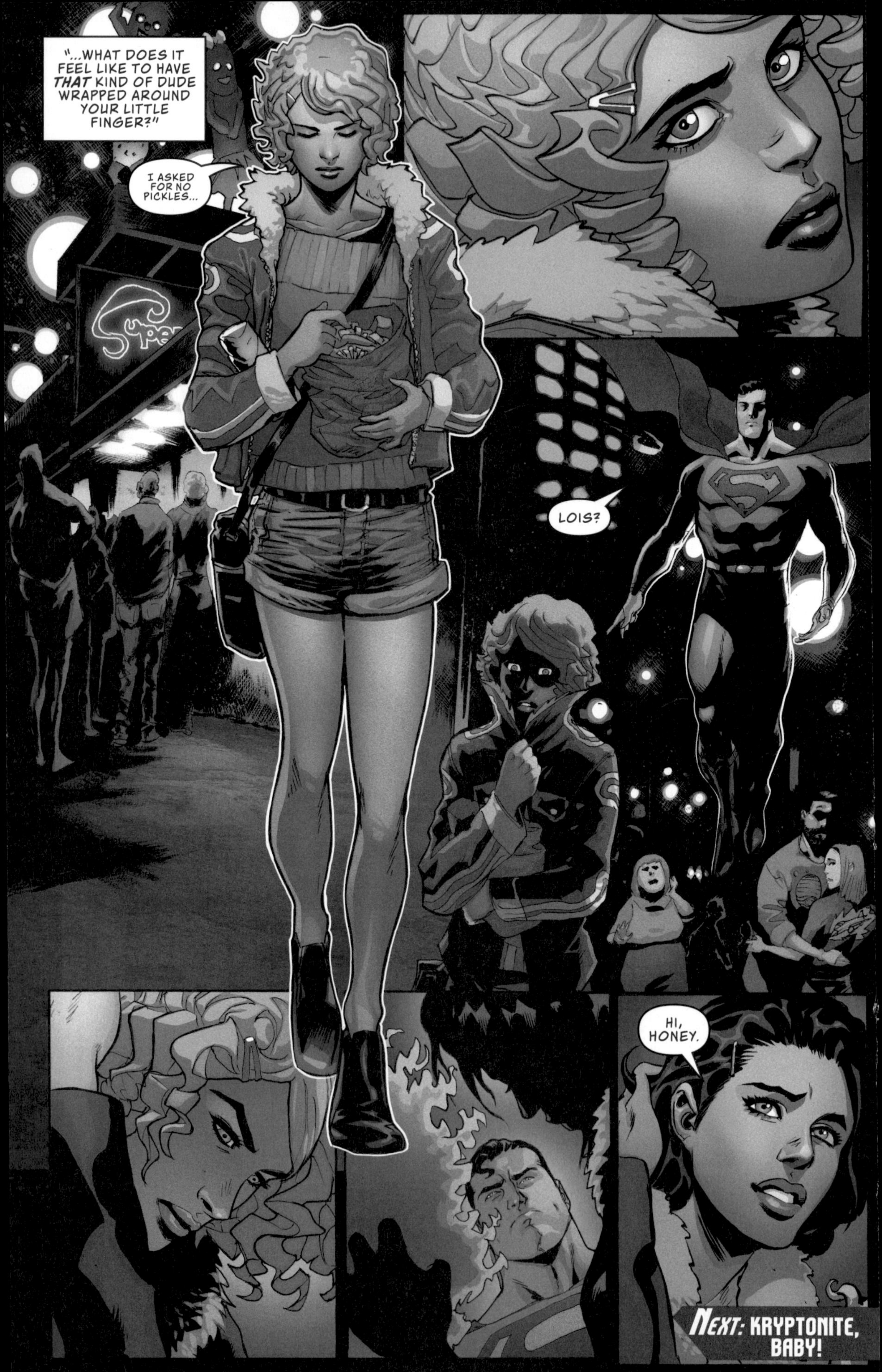
"...WHAT DOES IT FEEL LIKE TO HAVE *THAT* KIND OF DUDE WRAPPED AROUND YOUR LITTLE FINGER?"
I ASKED FOR NO PICKLES...
LOIS?
HI, HONEY.
NEXT: KRYPTONITE, BABY!

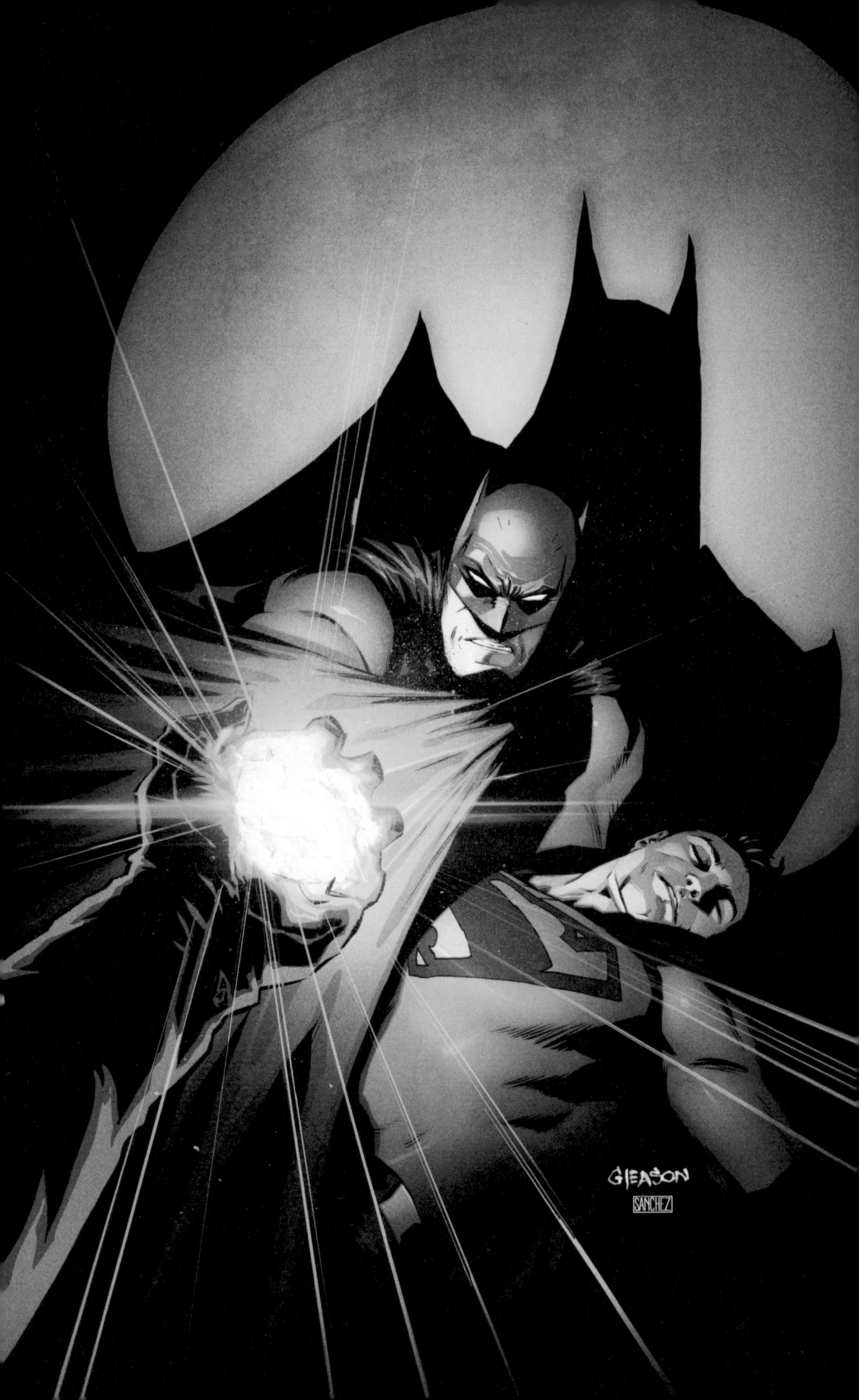
GLEASON
SÁNCHEZ

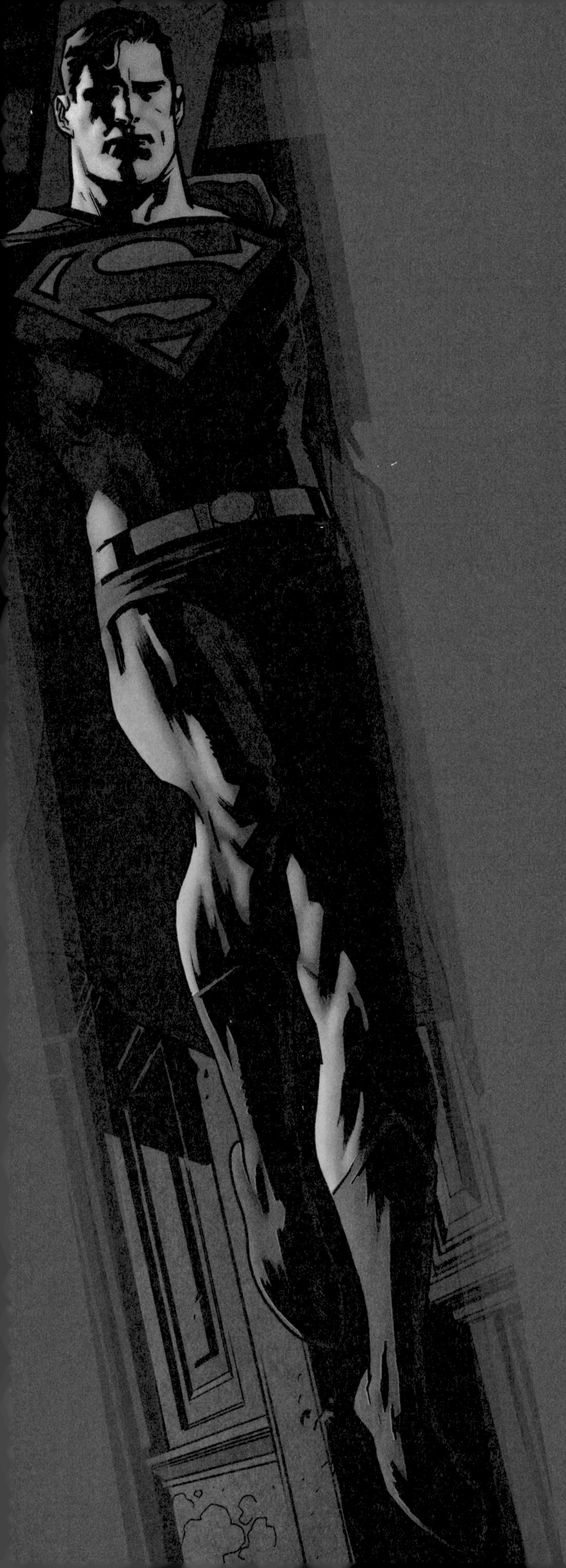

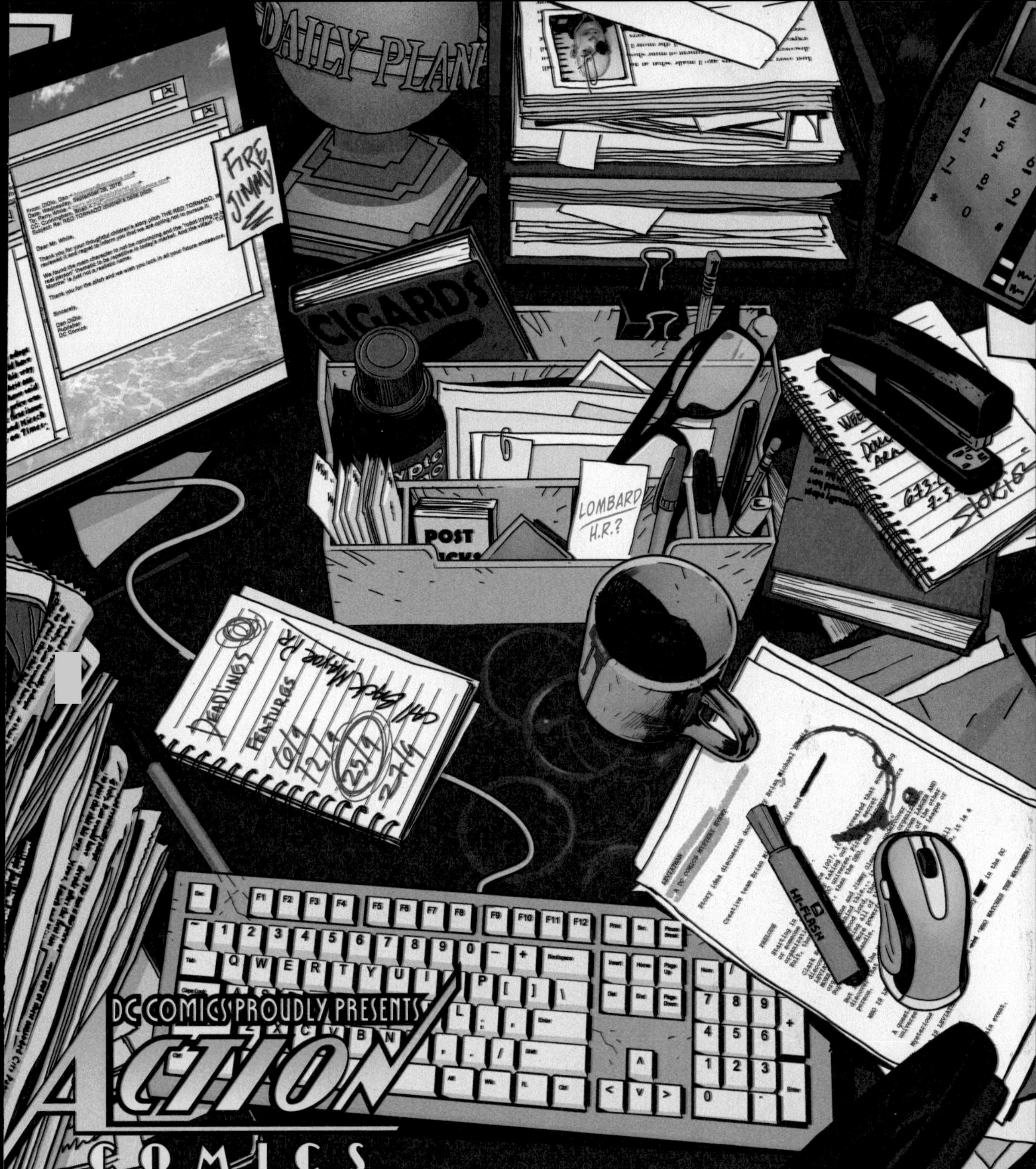

FIRE JIMMY
LOMBARD
H.R.?
DEADLINES
FEATURES

DC COMICS PROUDLY PRESENTS

ACTION COMICS

INVISIBLE MAFIA

PART 3

BRIAN MICHAEL BENDIS SCRIPT • YANICK PAQUETTE ART

NATHAN FAIRBAIRN COLORS • JOSH REED LETTERS

PATRICK GLEASON & BRAD ANDERSON COVER

JESSICA CHEN ASSOCIATE EDITOR • MICHAEL COTTON EDITOR • BRIAN CUNNINGHAM GROUP EDITOR

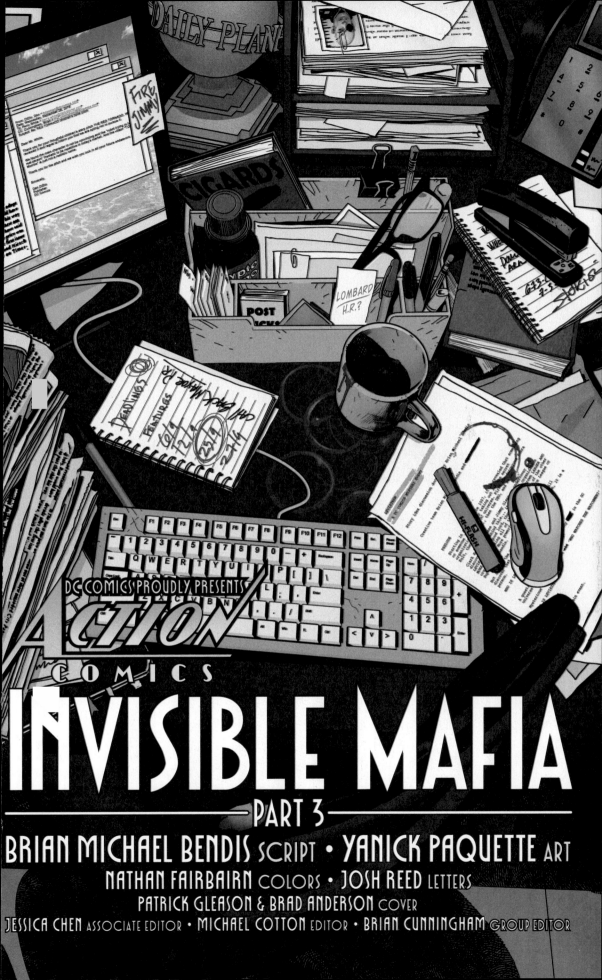

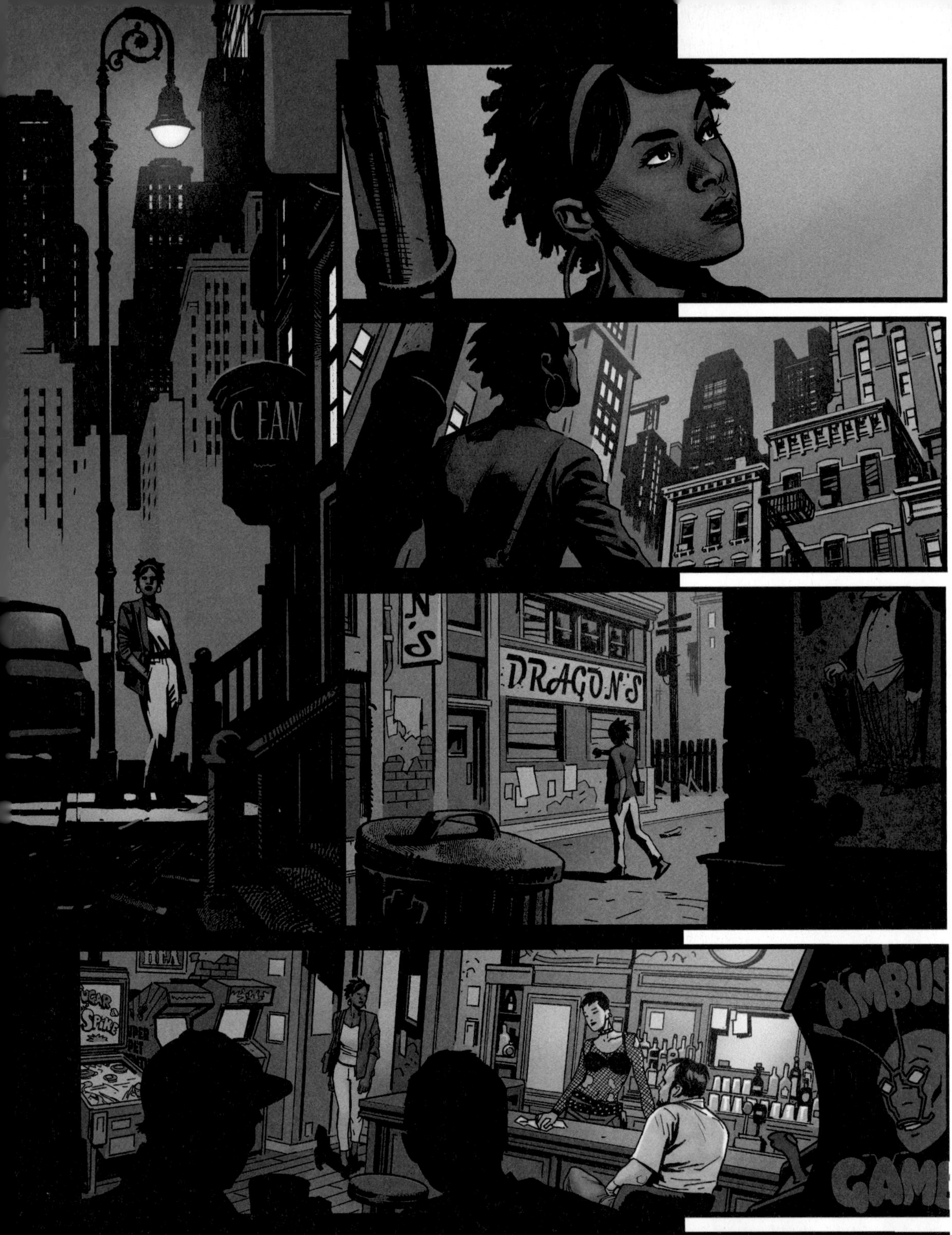
C EAN
DRAGON'S
AMBUS
GAME
I'M--
IN THE BACK.
CANDY?

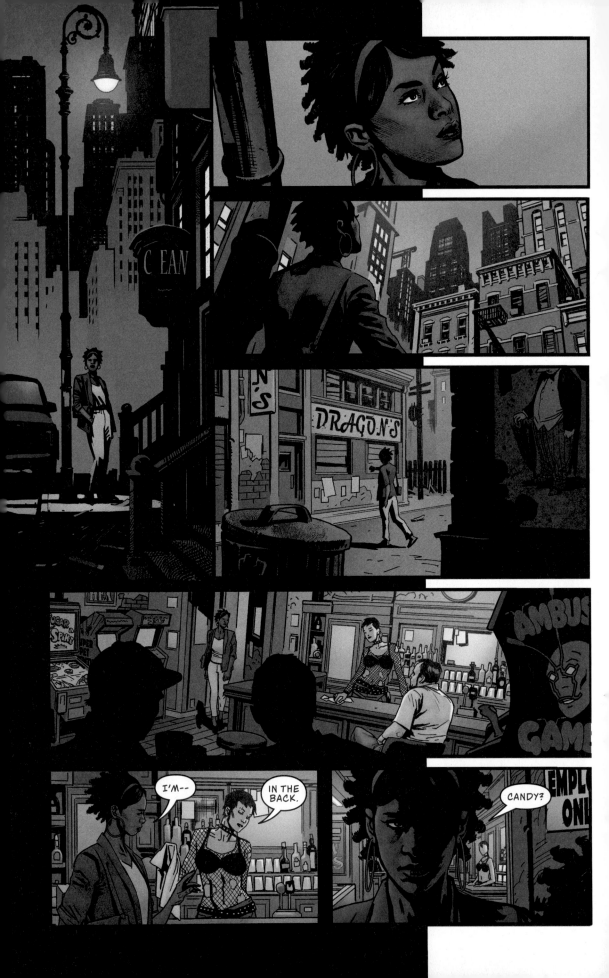

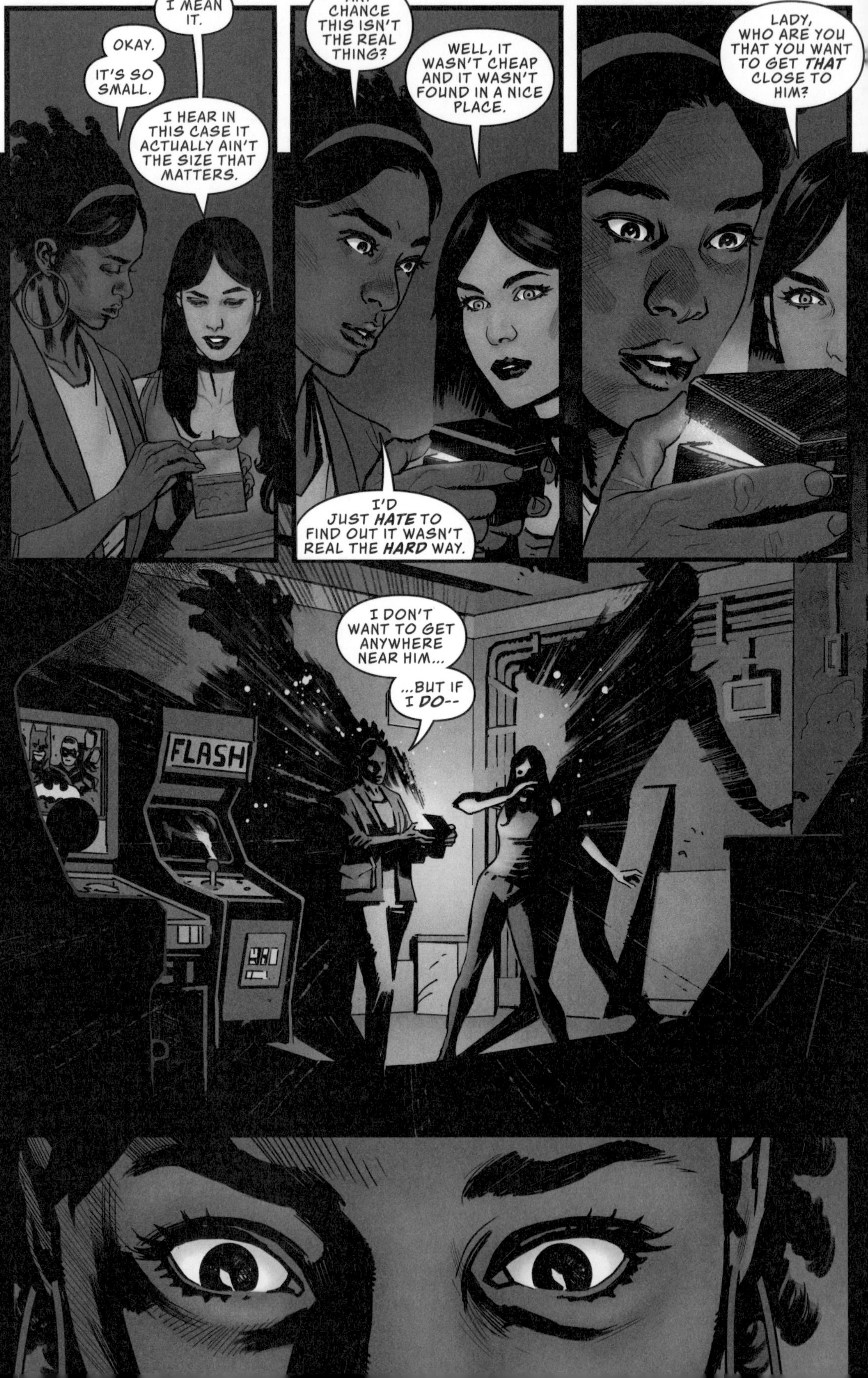

I MEAN IT.
OKAY.
IT'S SO SMALL.
I HEAR IN THIS CASE IT ACTUALLY AIN'T THE SIZE THAT MATTERS.
ANY CHANCE THIS ISN'T THE REAL THING?
WELL, IT WASN'T CHEAP AND IT WASN'T FOUND IN A NICE PLACE.
I'D JUST HATE TO FIND OUT IT WASN'T REAL THE HARD WAY.
LADY, WHO ARE YOU THAT YOU WANT TO GET THAT CLOSE TO HIM?
I DON'T WANT TO GET ANYWHERE NEAR HIM...
...BUT IF I DO--
FLASH

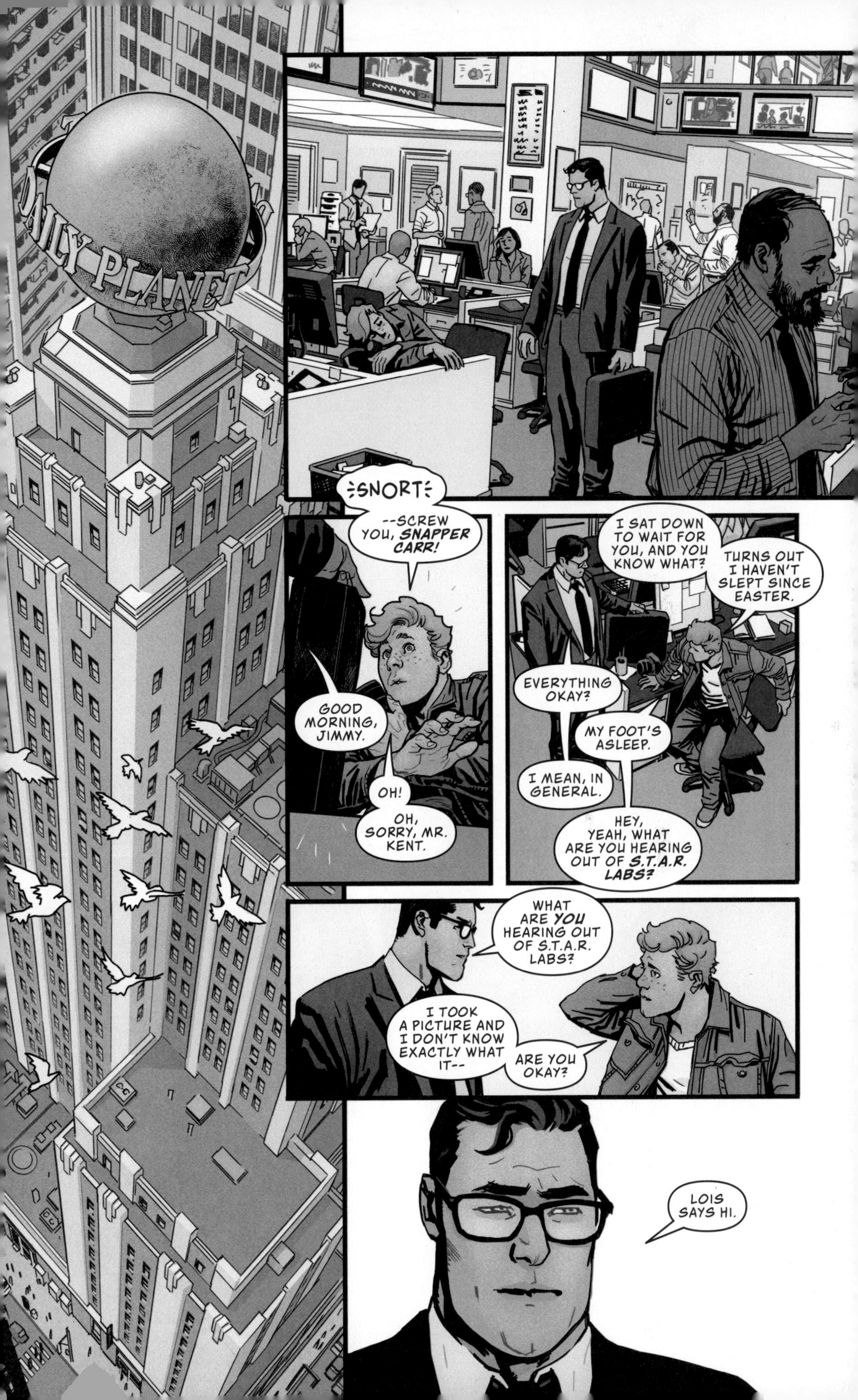
DAILY PLANET
SNORT
--SCREW YOU, SNAPPER CARR!
GOOD MORNING, JIMMY.
OH!
OH, SORRY, MR. KENT.
I SAT DOWN TO WAIT FOR YOU, AND YOU KNOW WHAT?
TURNS OUT I HAVEN'T SLEPT SINCE EASTER.
EVERYTHING OKAY?
MY FOOT'S ASLEEP.
I MEAN, IN GENERAL.
HEY, YEAH, WHAT ARE YOU HEARING OUT OF S.T.A.R. LABS?
WHAT ARE YOU HEARING OUT OF S.T.A.R. LABS?
I TOOK A PICTURE AND I DON'T KNOW EXACTLY WHAT IT--
ARE YOU OKAY?
LOIS SAYS HI.

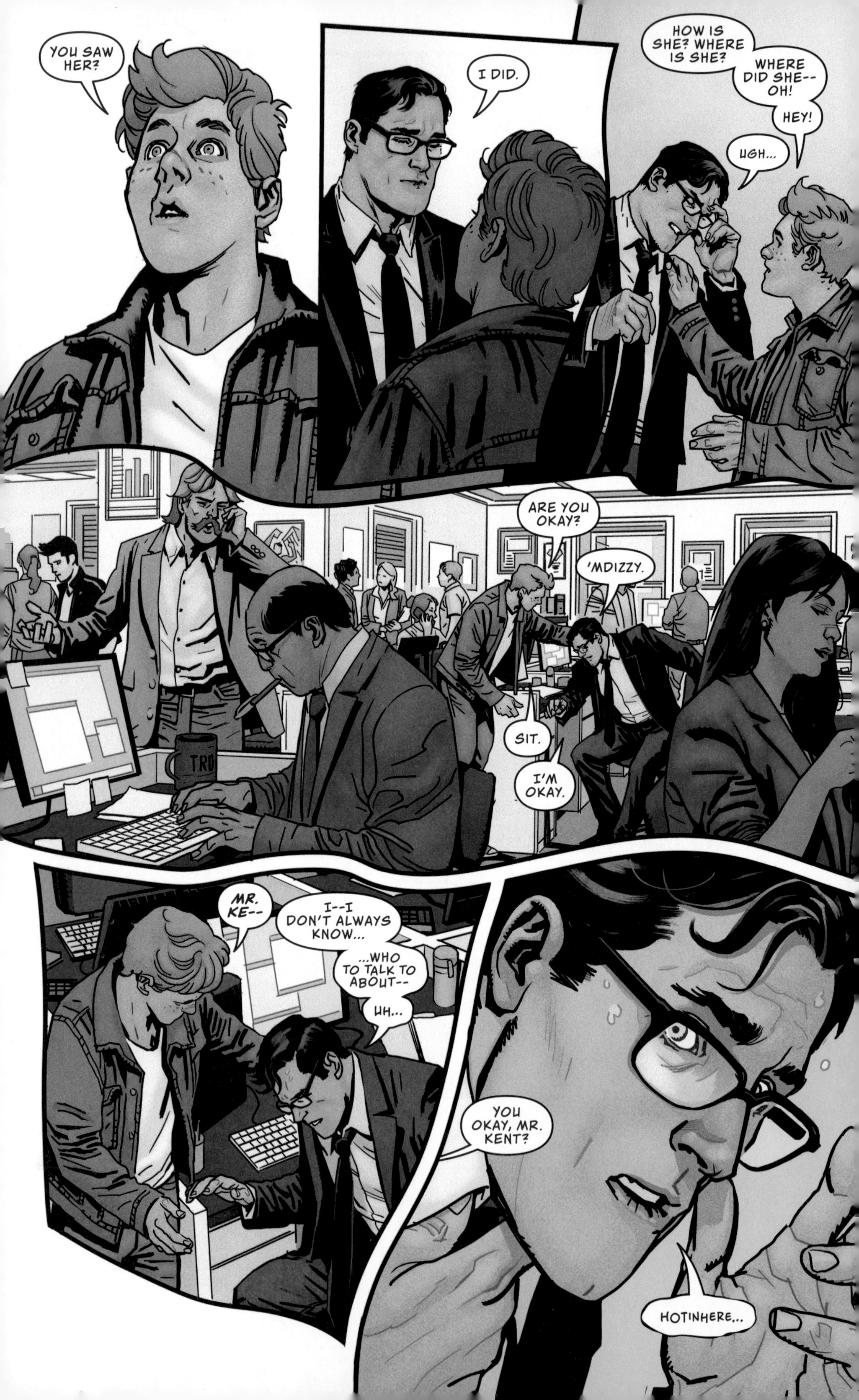
YOU SAW HER?
I DID.
HOW IS SHE? WHERE IS SHE?
WHERE DID SHE-- OH!
HEY!
UGH...
ARE YOU OKAY?
'MDIZZY.
SIT.
I'M OKAY.
MR. KE--
I--I DON'T ALWAYS KNOW...
...WHO TO TALK TO ABOUT--
UH...
YOU OKAY, MR. KENT?
HOTINHERE...

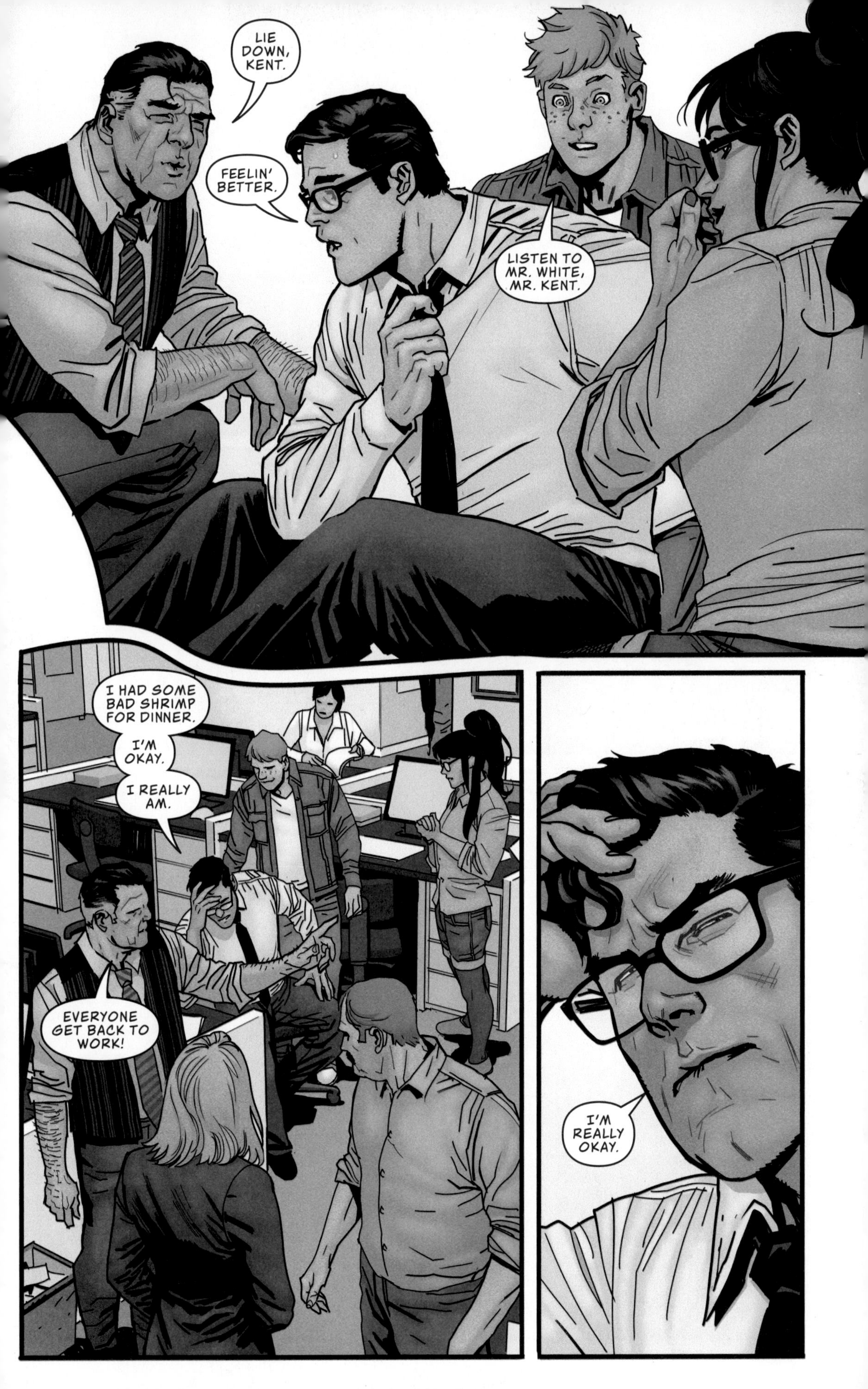
LIE DOWN, KENT.
FEELIN' BETTER.
LISTEN TO MR. WHITE, MR. KENT.
I HAD SOME BAD SHRIMP FOR DINNER.
I'M OKAY.
I REALLY AM.
EVERYONE GET BACK TO WORK!
I'M REALLY OKAY.

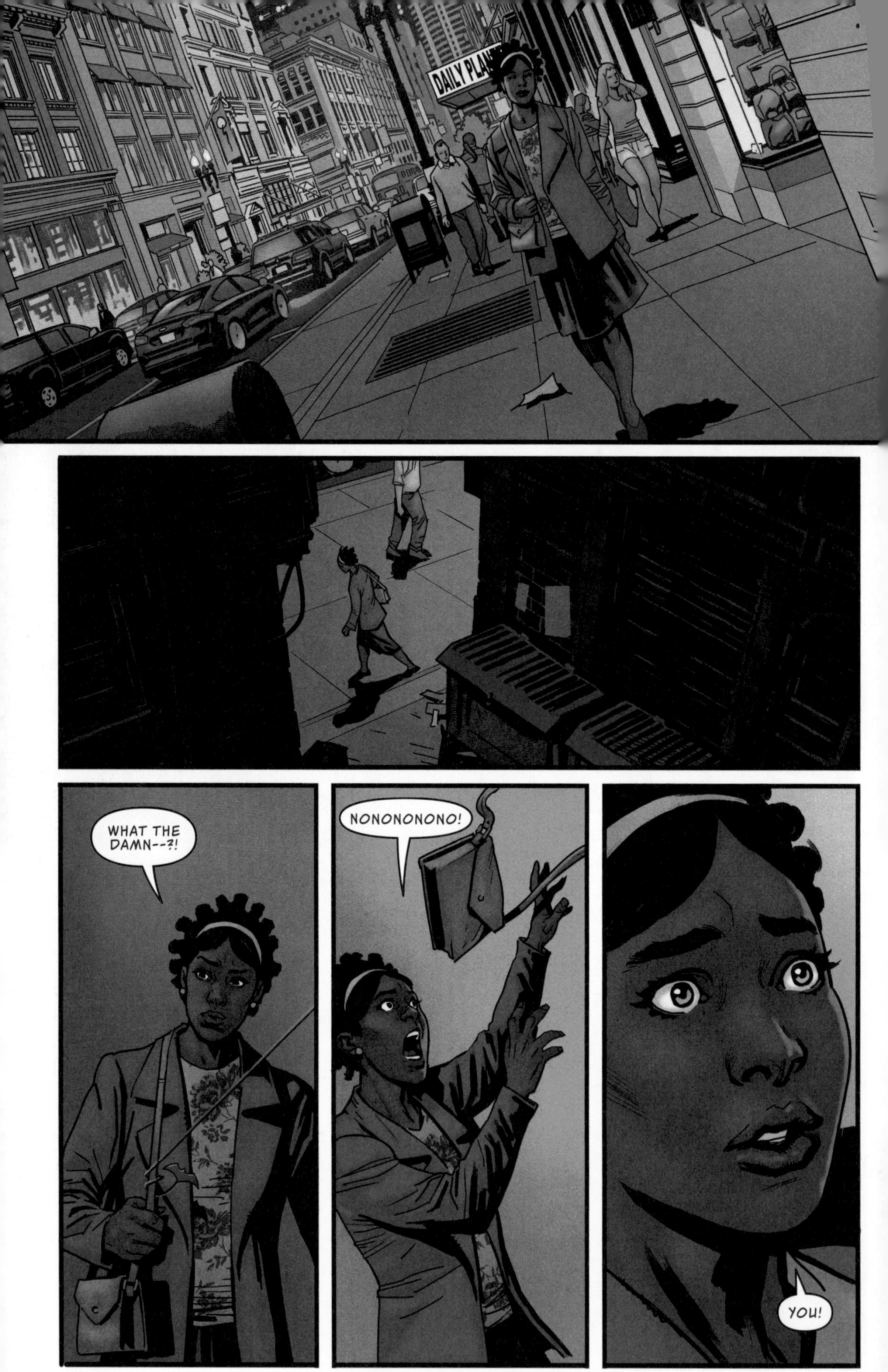
DAILY PLA
WHAT THE DAMN--?!
NONONONONO!
YOU!

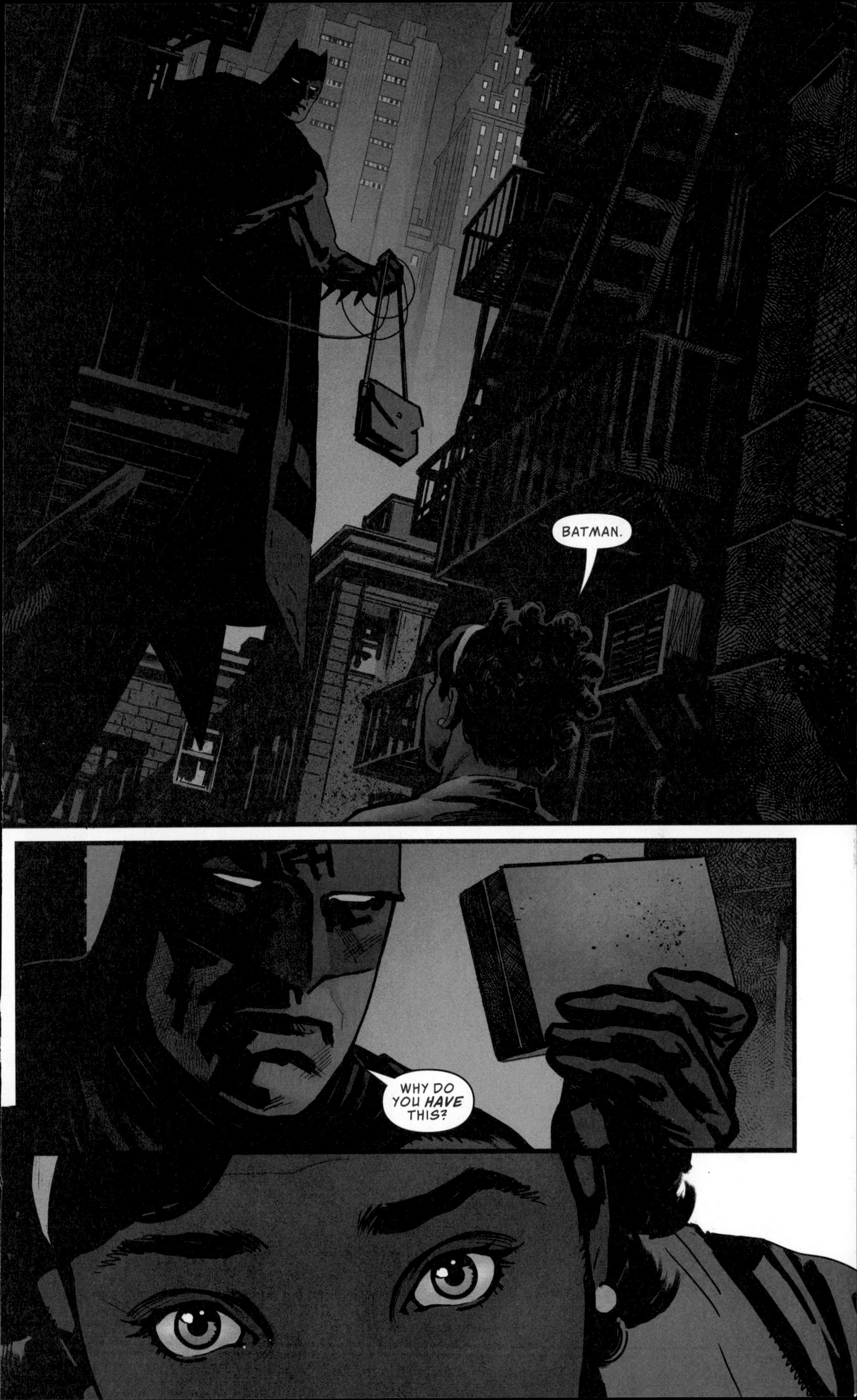
BATMAN.
WHY DO YOU HAVE THIS?

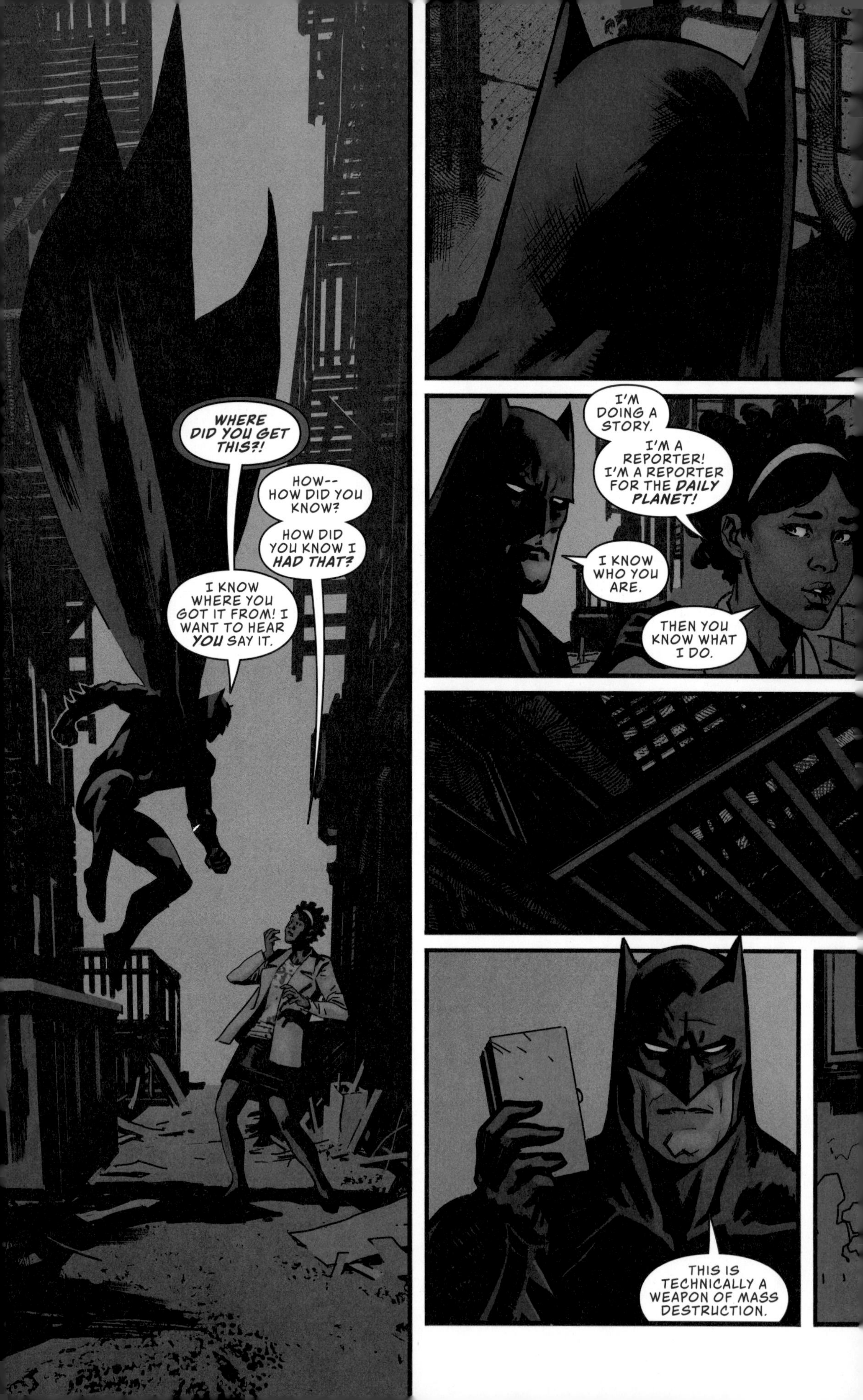

WHERE DID YOU GET THIS?!
HOW-- HOW DID YOU KNOW?
HOW DID YOU KNOW I HAD THAT?
I KNOW WHERE YOU GOT IT FROM! I WANT TO HEAR YOU SAY IT.
I'M DOING A STORY.
I'M A REPORTER! I'M A REPORTER FOR THE DAILY PLANET!
I KNOW WHO YOU ARE.
THEN YOU KNOW WHAT I DO.
THIS IS TECHNICALLY A WEAPON OF MASS DESTRUCTION.

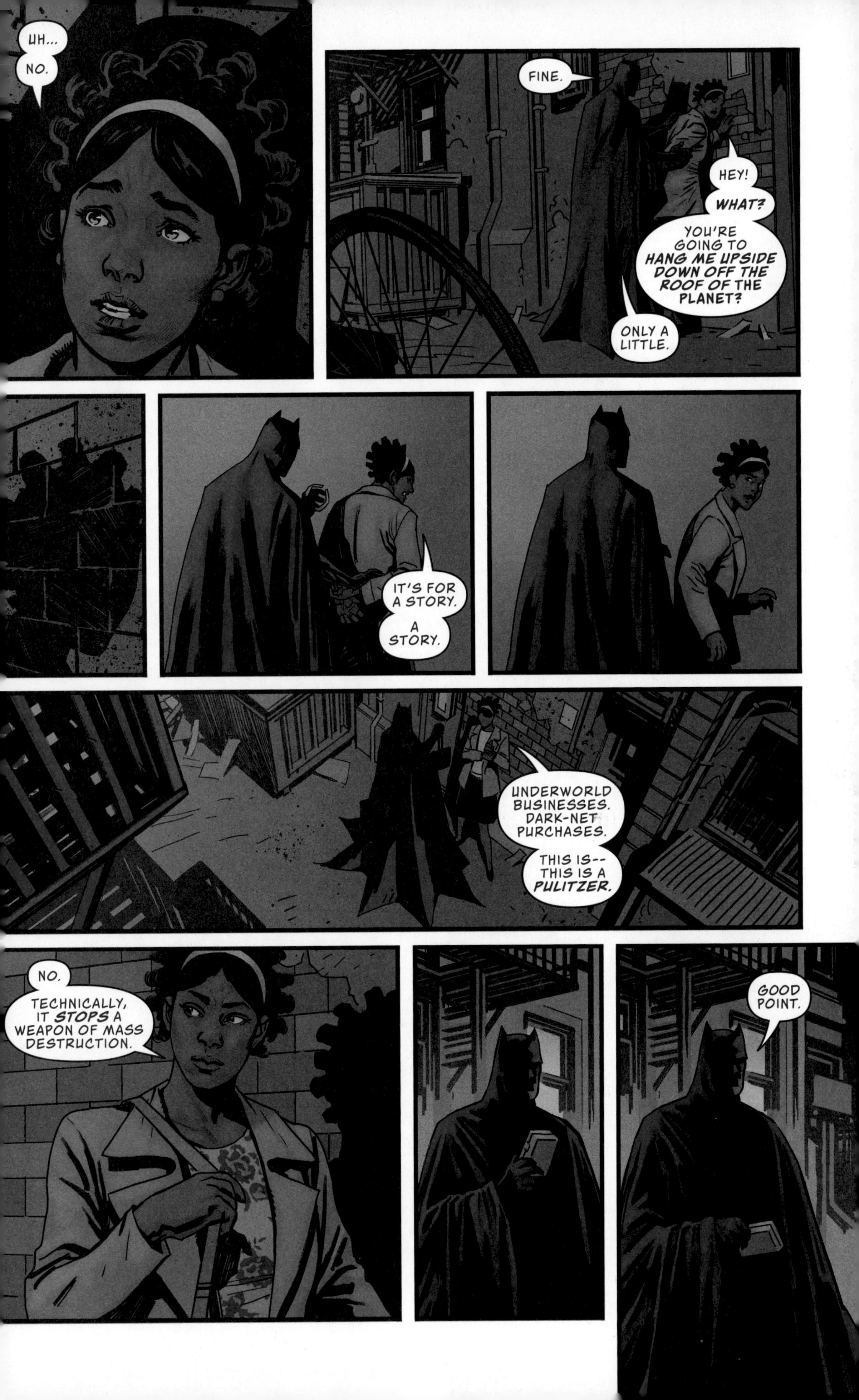
UH...
NO.
FINE.
HEY!
WHAT?
YOU'RE GOING TO HANG ME UPSIDE DOWN OFF THE ROOF OF THE PLANET?
ONLY A LITTLE.
IT'S FOR A STORY.
A STORY.
UNDERWORLD BUSINESSES. DARK-NET PURCHASES.
THIS IS-- THIS IS A PULITZER.
NO.
TECHNICALLY, IT STOPS A WEAPON OF MASS DESTRUCTION.
GOOD POINT.

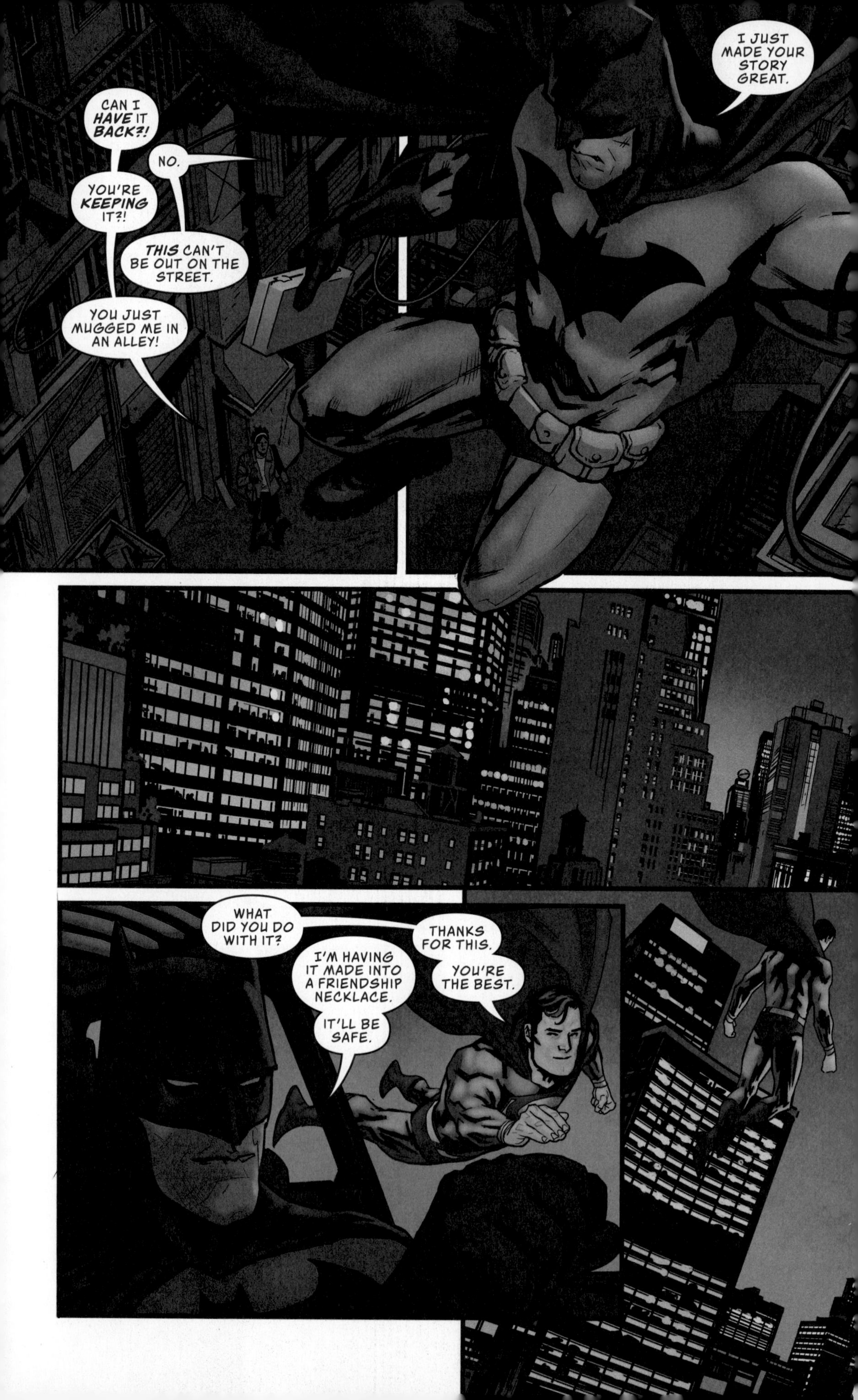
CAN I HAVE IT BACK?!
NO.
YOU'RE KEEPING IT?!
THIS CAN'T BE OUT ON THE STREET.
YOU JUST MUGGED ME IN AN ALLEY!
I JUST MADE YOUR STORY GREAT.
WHAT DID YOU DO WITH IT?
I'M HAVING IT MADE INTO A FRIENDSHIP NECKLACE.
IT'LL BE SAFE.
THANKS FOR THIS.
YOU'RE THE BEST.

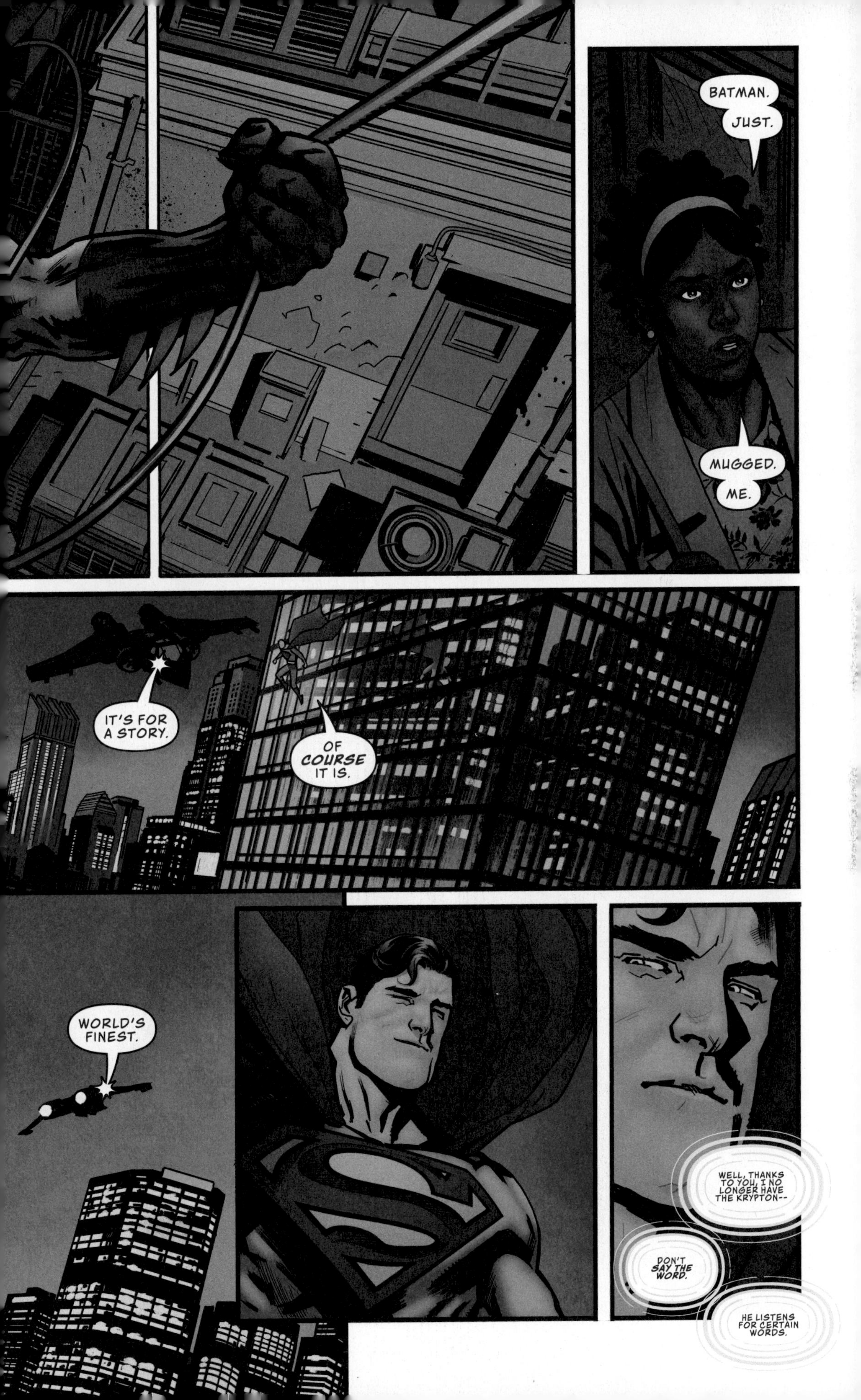
BATMAN.
JUST.
MUGGED.
ME.
IT'S FOR A STORY.
OF COURSE IT IS.
WORLD'S FINEST.
WELL, THANKS TO YOU, I NO LONGER HAVE THE KRYPTON--
DON'T SAY THE WORD.
HE LISTENS FOR CERTAIN WORDS.

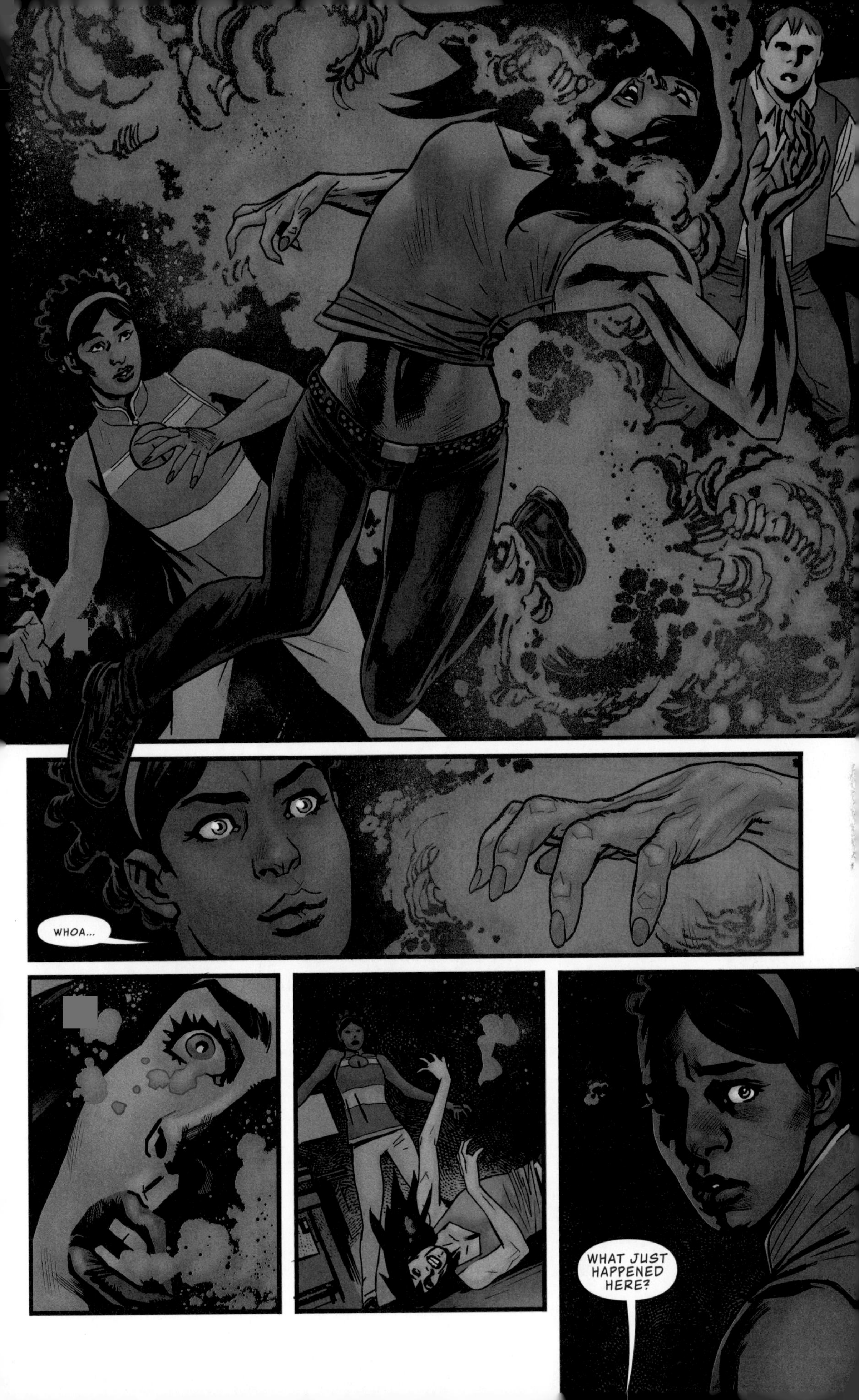
WHOA...
WHAT JUST HAPPENED HERE?

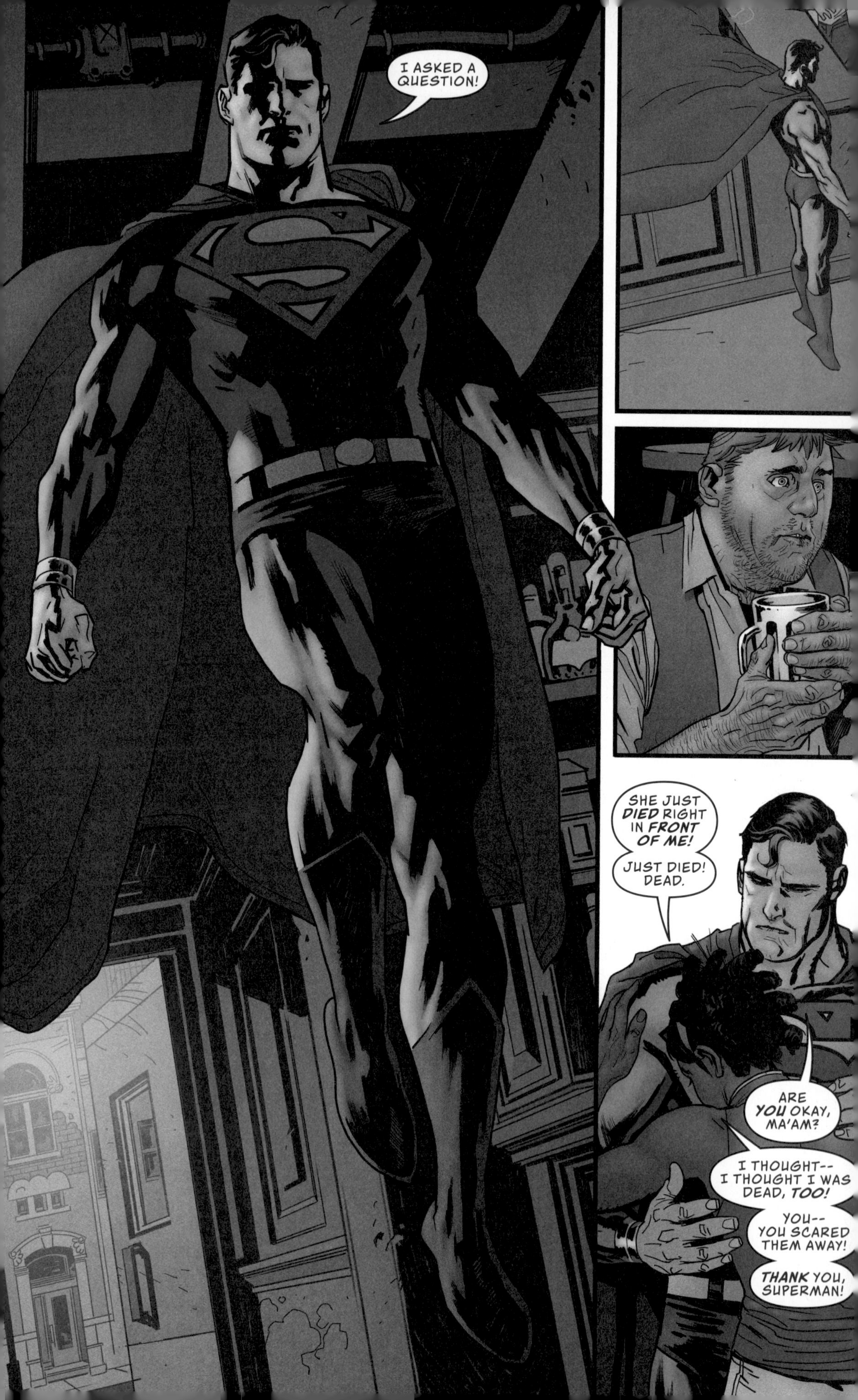
I ASKED A QUESTION!
SHE JUST DIED RIGHT IN FRONT OF ME!
JUST DIED! DEAD.
ARE YOU OKAY, MA'AM?
I THOUGHT-- I THOUGHT I WAS DEAD, TOO!
YOU-- YOU SCARED THEM AWAY!
THANK YOU, SUPERMAN!

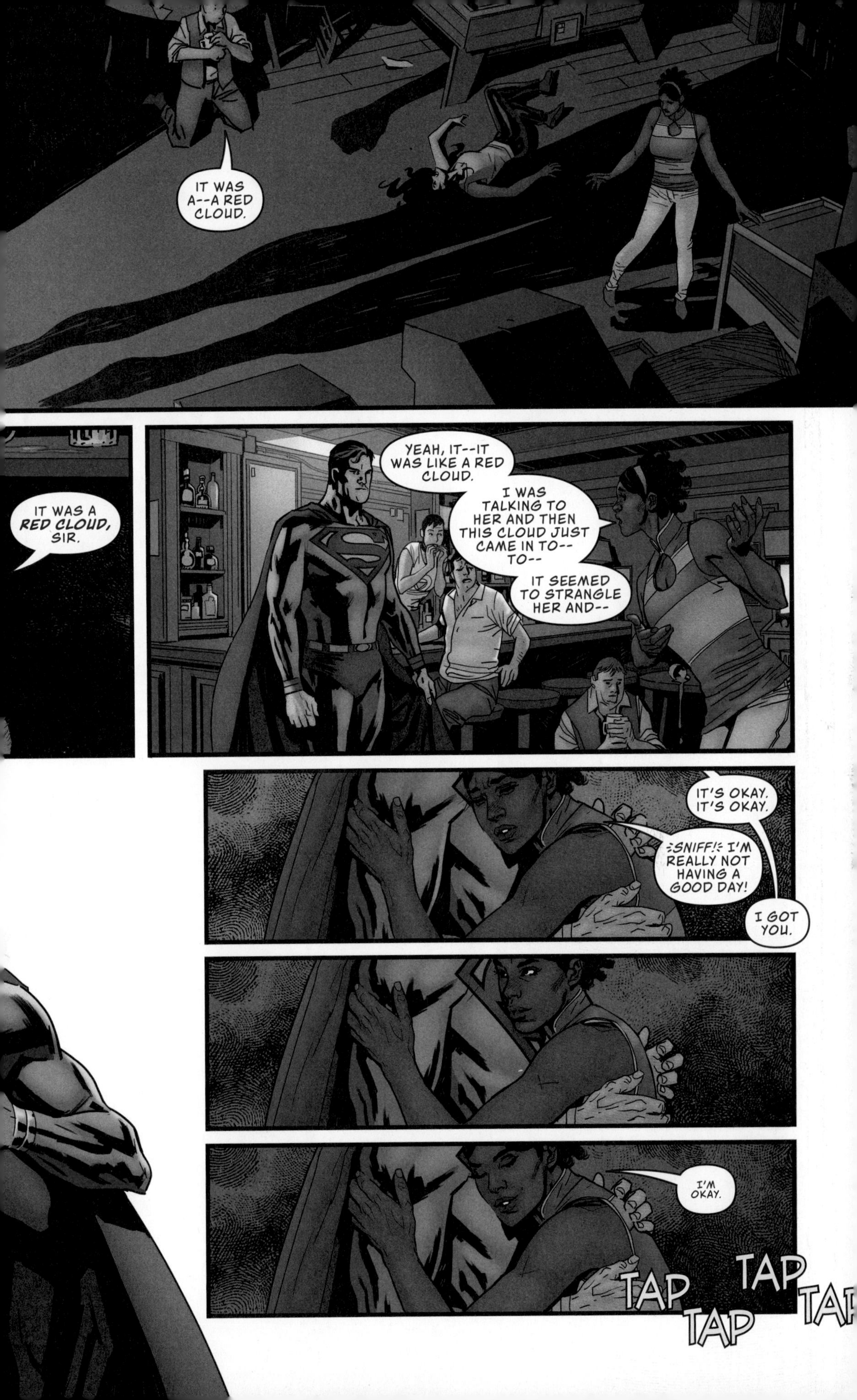
IT WAS A--A RED CLOUD.
IT WAS A RED CLOUD, SIR.
YEAH, IT--IT WAS LIKE A RED CLOUD.
I WAS TALKING TO HER AND THEN THIS CLOUD JUST CAME IN TO-- TO--
IT SEEMED TO STRANGLE HER AND--
IT'S OKAY. IT'S OKAY.
SNIFF! I'M REALLY NOT HAVING A GOOD DAY!
I GOT YOU.
I'M OKAY.
TAP TAP TAP TAP

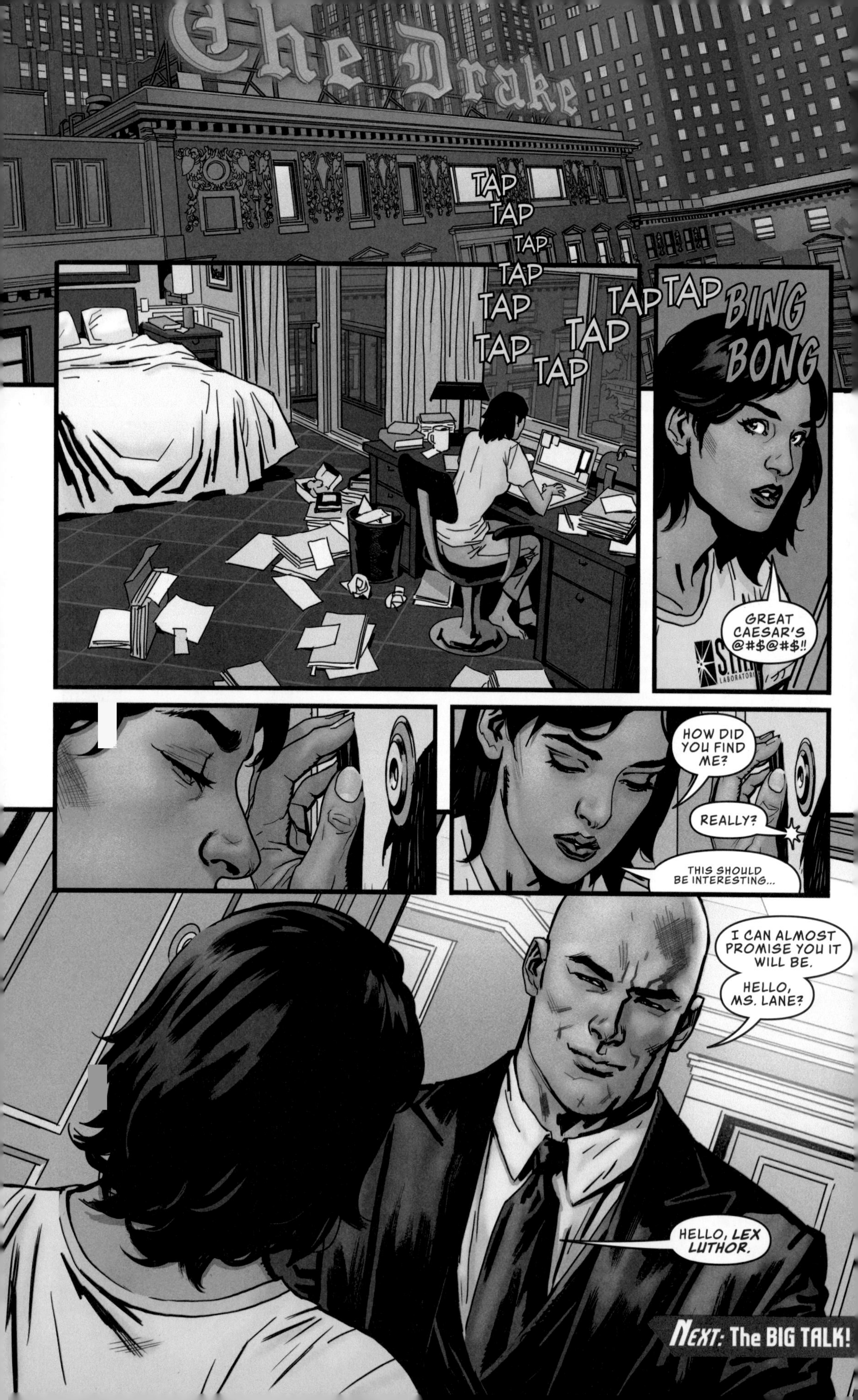
The Drake
TAP TAP TAP TAP TAP TAP TAP TAP TAP TAP
BING BONG
GREAT CAESAR'S @#$@#$!!
HOW DID YOU FIND ME?
REALLY?
THIS SHOULD BE INTERESTING...
I CAN ALMOST PROMISE YOU IT WILL BE.
HELLO, MS. LANE?
HELLO, *LEX LUTHOR.*
NEXT: The BIG TALK!

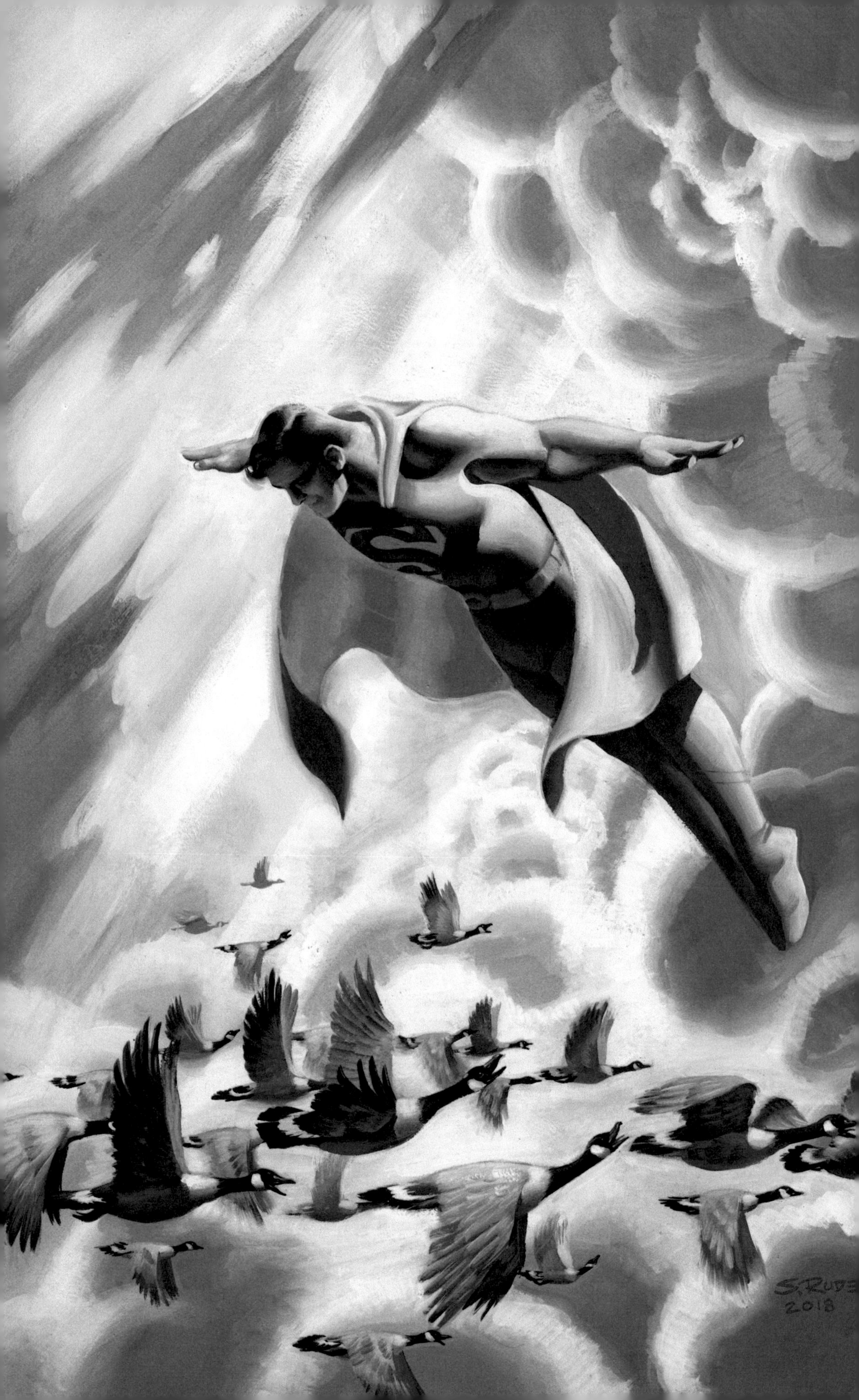
S. RUDE
2018

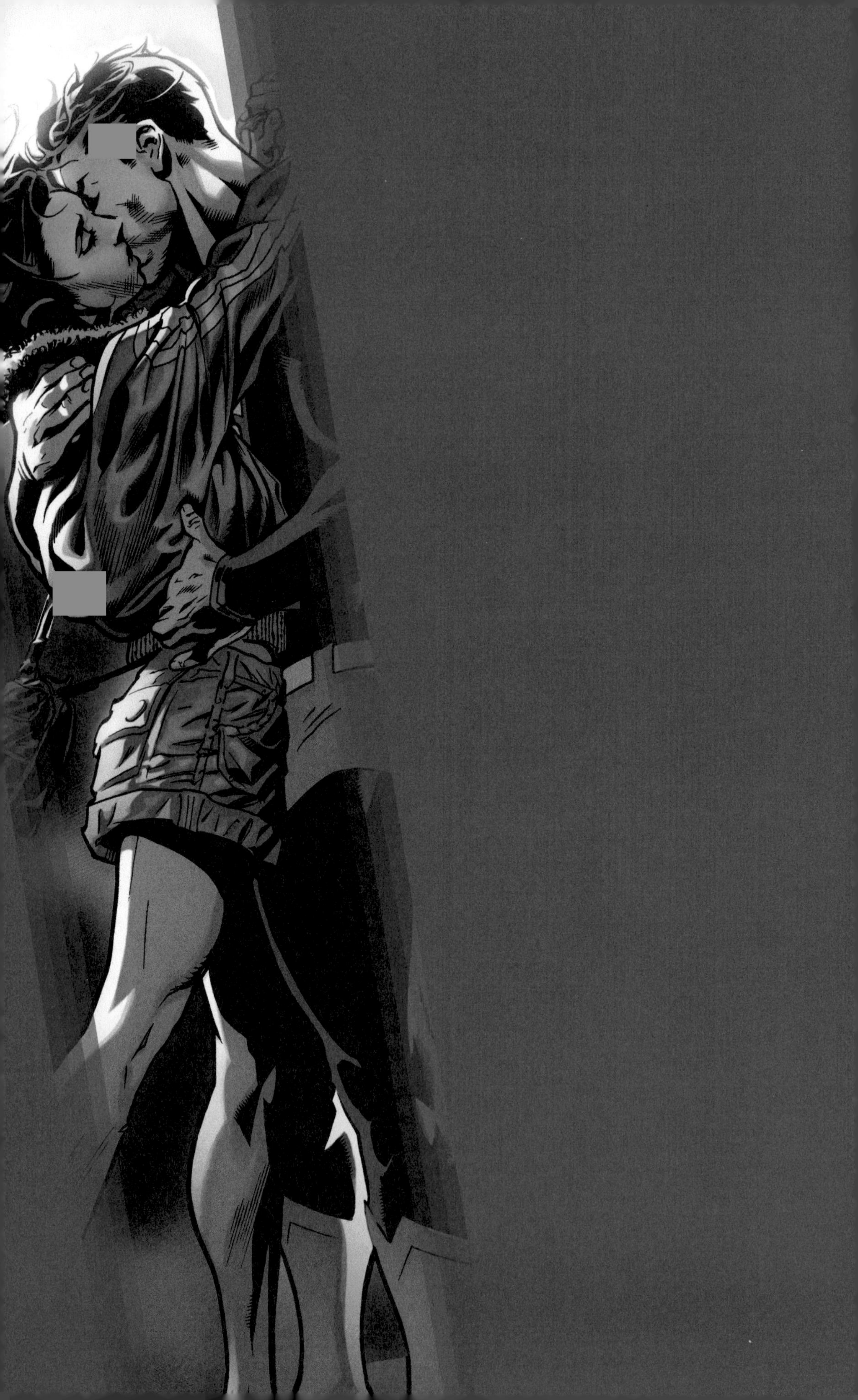

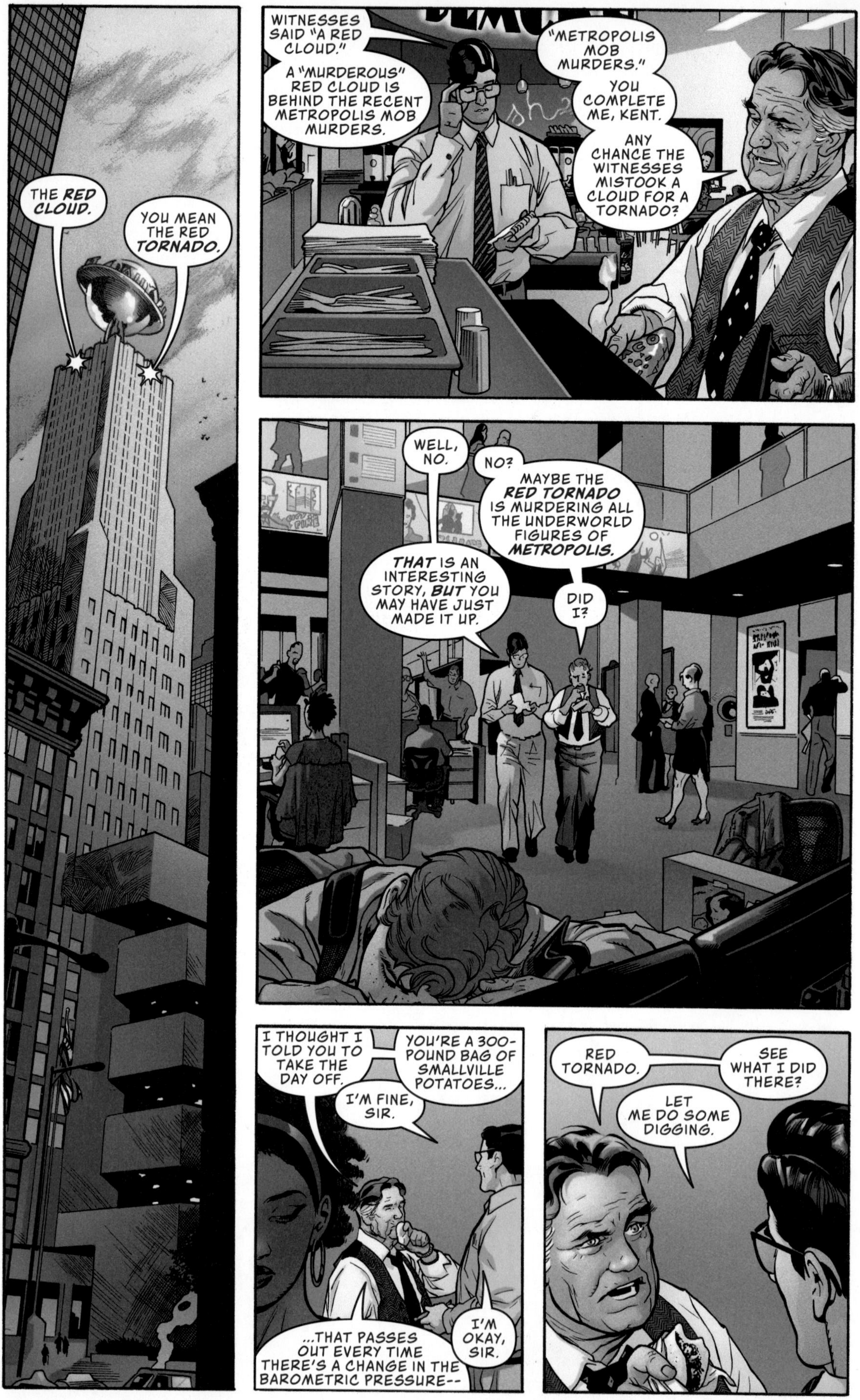
THE RED CLOUD.
YOU MEAN THE RED TORNADO.
WITNESSES SAID "A RED CLOUD."
A "MURDEROUS" RED CLOUD IS BEHIND THE RECENT METROPOLIS MOB MURDERS.
"METROPOLIS MOB MURDERS."
YOU COMPLETE ME, KENT.
ANY CHANCE THE WITNESSES MISTOOK A CLOUD FOR A TORNADO?
WELL, NO.
NO?
MAYBE THE RED TORNADO IS MURDERING ALL THE UNDERWORLD FIGURES OF METROPOLIS.
THAT IS AN INTERESTING STORY, BUT YOU MAY HAVE JUST MADE IT UP.
DID I?
I THOUGHT I TOLD YOU TO TAKE THE DAY OFF.
I'M FINE, SIR.
YOU'RE A 300-POUND BAG OF SMALLVILLE POTATOES...
...THAT PASSES OUT EVERY TIME THERE'S A CHANGE IN THE BAROMETRIC PRESSURE--
I'M OKAY, SIR.
RED TORNADO.
SEE WHAT I DID THERE?
LET ME DO SOME DIGGING.

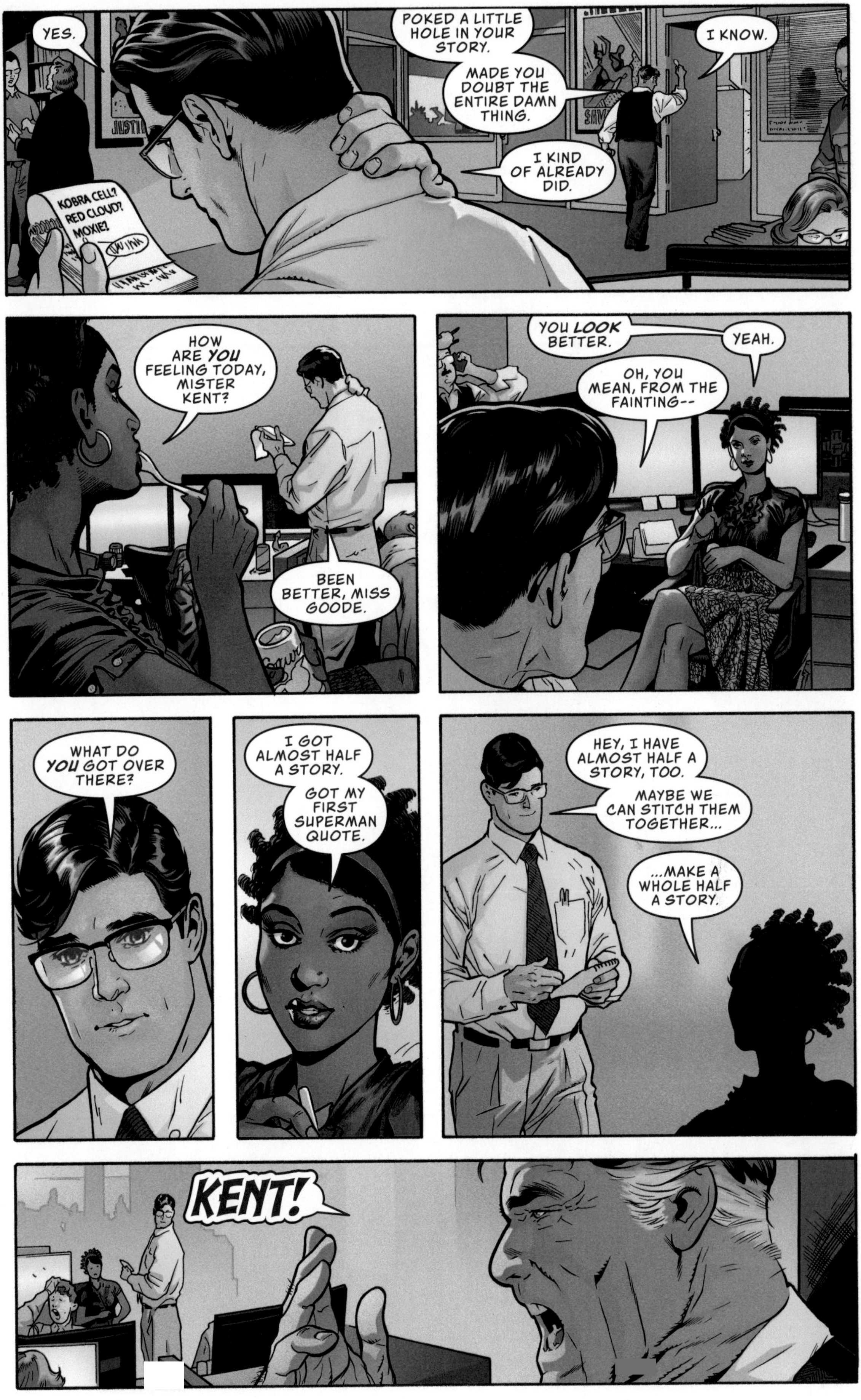
YES.
POKED A LITTLE HOLE IN YOUR STORY.
MADE YOU DOUBT THE ENTIRE DAMN THING.
I KNOW.
I KIND OF ALREADY DID.
KOBRA CELL? RED CLOUD? MOXIE?
HOW ARE YOU FEELING TODAY, MISTER KENT?
BEEN BETTER, MISS GOODE.
YOU LOOK BETTER.
YEAH.
OH, YOU MEAN, FROM THE FAINTING--
WHAT DO YOU GOT OVER THERE?
I GOT ALMOST HALF A STORY.
GOT MY FIRST SUPERMAN QUOTE.
HEY, I HAVE ALMOST HALF A STORY, TOO.
MAYBE WE CAN STITCH THEM TOGETHER...
...MAKE A WHOLE HALF A STORY.
KENT!

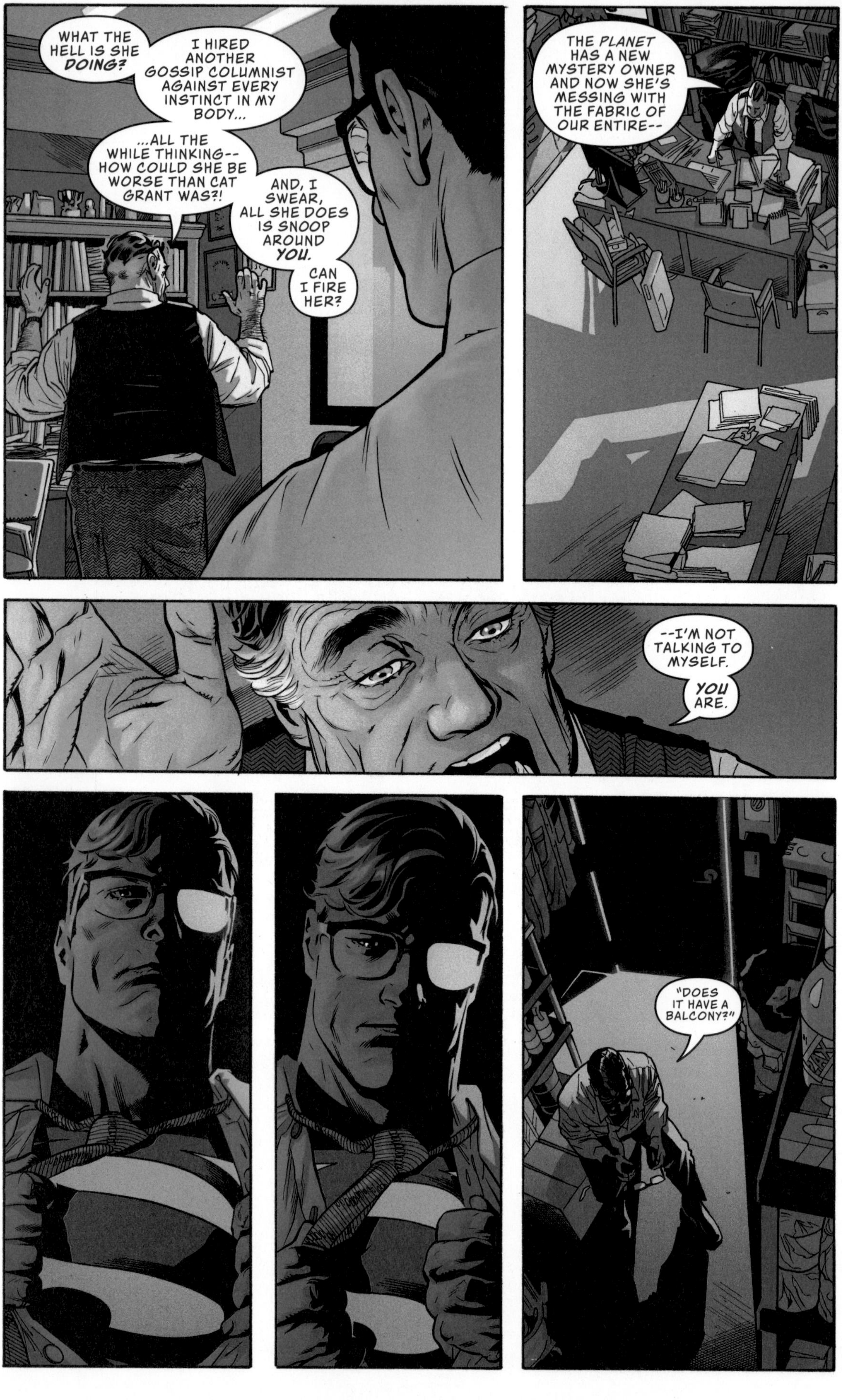
WHAT THE HELL IS SHE DOING?
I HIRED ANOTHER GOSSIP COLUMNIST AGAINST EVERY INSTINCT IN MY BODY...
...ALL THE WHILE THINKING-- HOW COULD SHE BE WORSE THAN CAT GRANT WAS?!
AND, I SWEAR, ALL SHE DOES IS SNOOP AROUND YOU.
CAN I FIRE HER?
THE PLANET HAS A NEW MYSTERY OWNER AND NOW SHE'S MESSING WITH THE FABRIC OF OUR ENTIRE--
--I'M NOT TALKING TO MYSELF.
YOU ARE.
"DOES IT HAVE A BALCONY?"

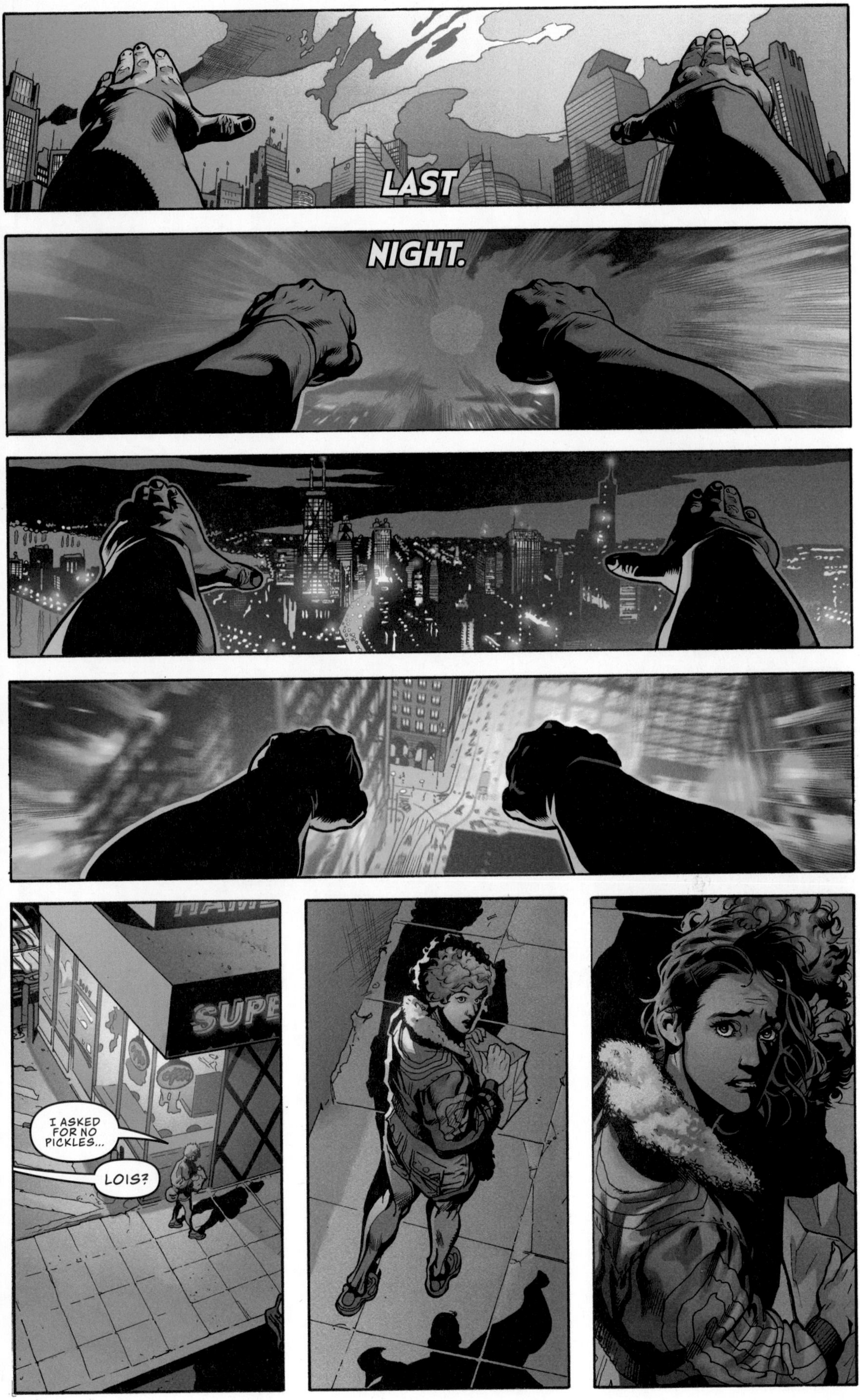
LAST
NIGHT.
HAME
SUPE
I ASKED FOR NO PICKLES...
LOIS?

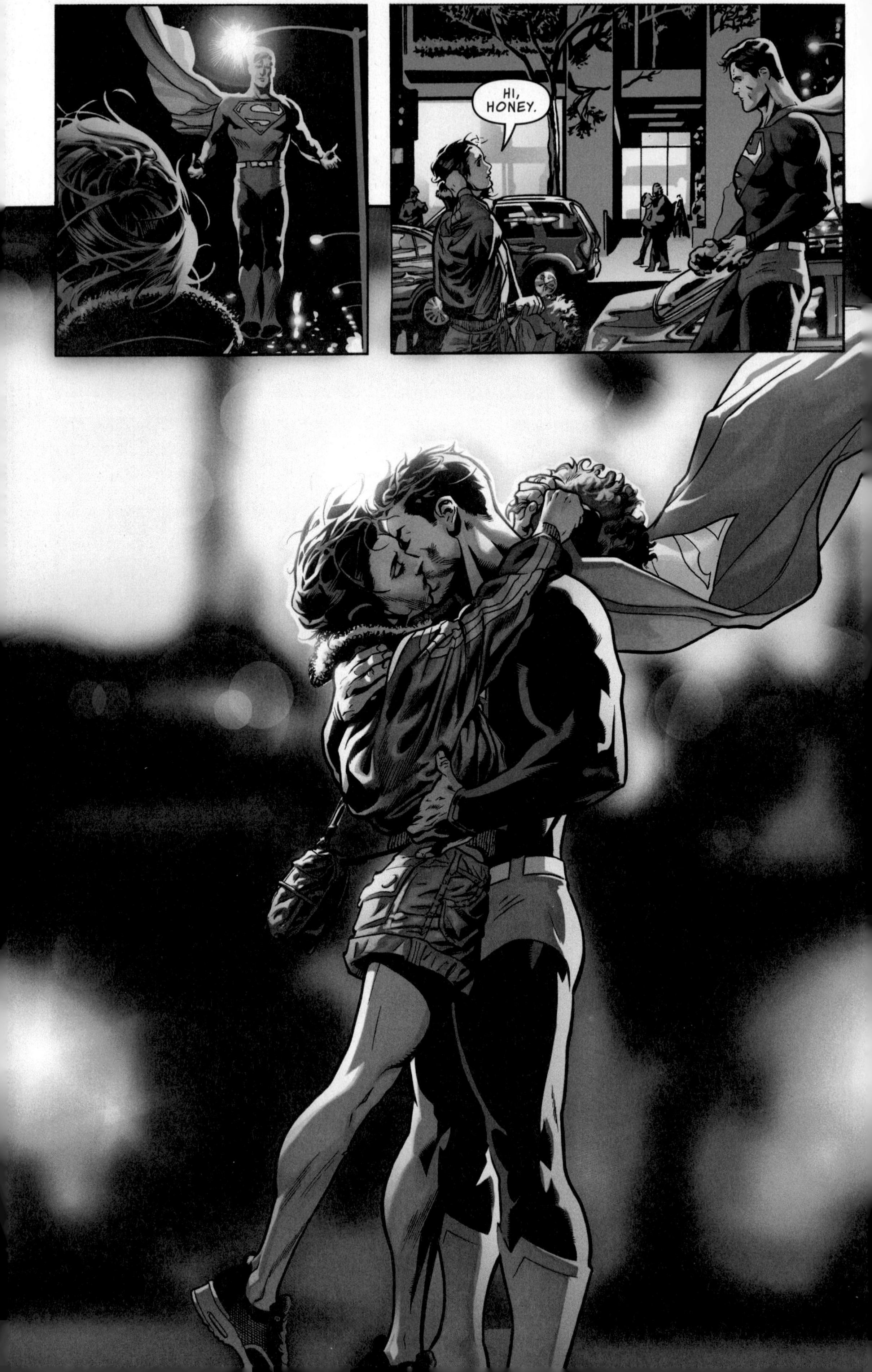
HI, HONEY.

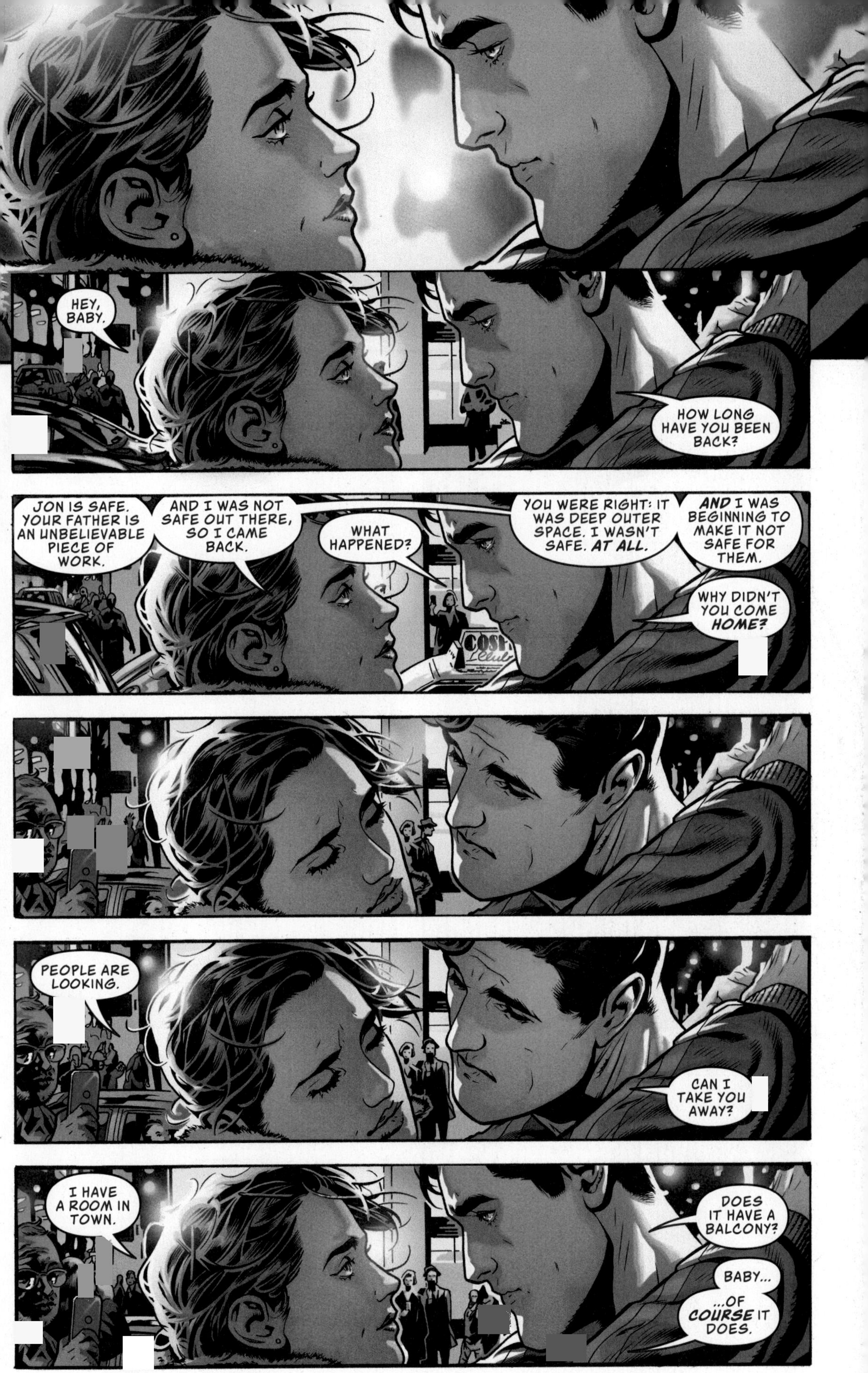
HEY, BABY.
HOW LONG HAVE YOU BEEN BACK?
JON IS SAFE. YOUR FATHER IS AN UNBELIEVABLE PIECE OF WORK.
AND I WAS NOT SAFE OUT THERE, SO I CAME BACK.
WHAT HAPPENED?
YOU WERE RIGHT: IT WAS DEEP OUTER SPACE. I WASN'T SAFE. AT ALL.
AND I WAS BEGINNING TO MAKE IT NOT SAFE FOR THEM.
WHY DIDN'T YOU COME HOME?
PEOPLE ARE LOOKING.
CAN I TAKE YOU AWAY?
I HAVE A ROOM IN TOWN.
DOES IT HAVE A BALCONY?
BABY...
...OF COURSE IT DOES.

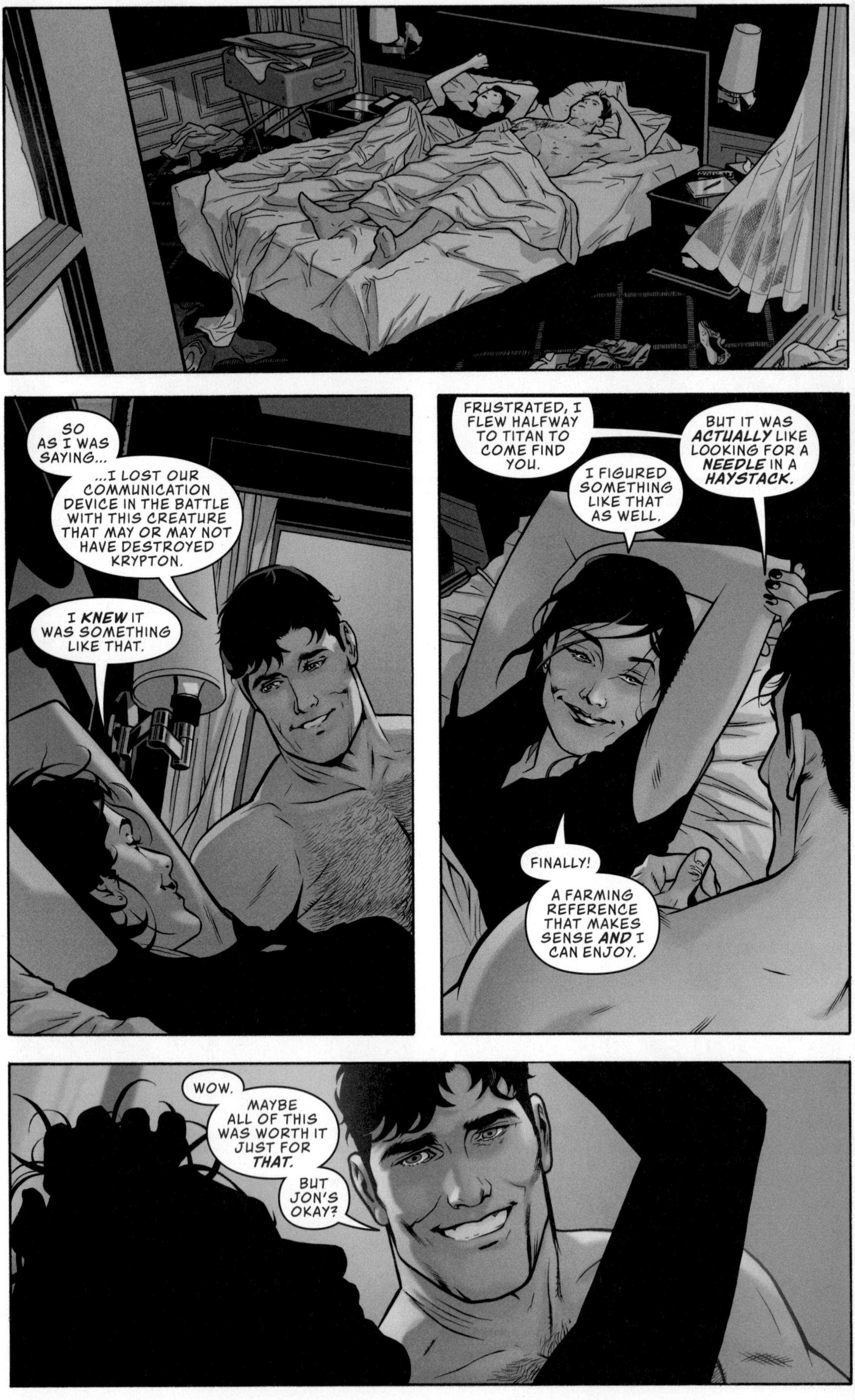
SO AS I WAS SAYING...
...I LOST OUR COMMUNICATION DEVICE IN THE BATTLE WITH THIS CREATURE THAT MAY OR MAY NOT HAVE DESTROYED KRYPTON.
I KNEW IT WAS SOMETHING LIKE THAT.
FRUSTRATED, I FLEW HALFWAY TO TITAN TO COME FIND YOU.
BUT IT WAS ACTUALLY LIKE LOOKING FOR A NEEDLE IN A HAYSTACK.
I FIGURED SOMETHING LIKE THAT AS WELL.
FINALLY!
A FARMING REFERENCE THAT MAKES SENSE AND I CAN ENJOY.
WOW.
MAYBE ALL OF THIS WAS WORTH IT JUST FOR THAT.
BUT JON'S OKAY?

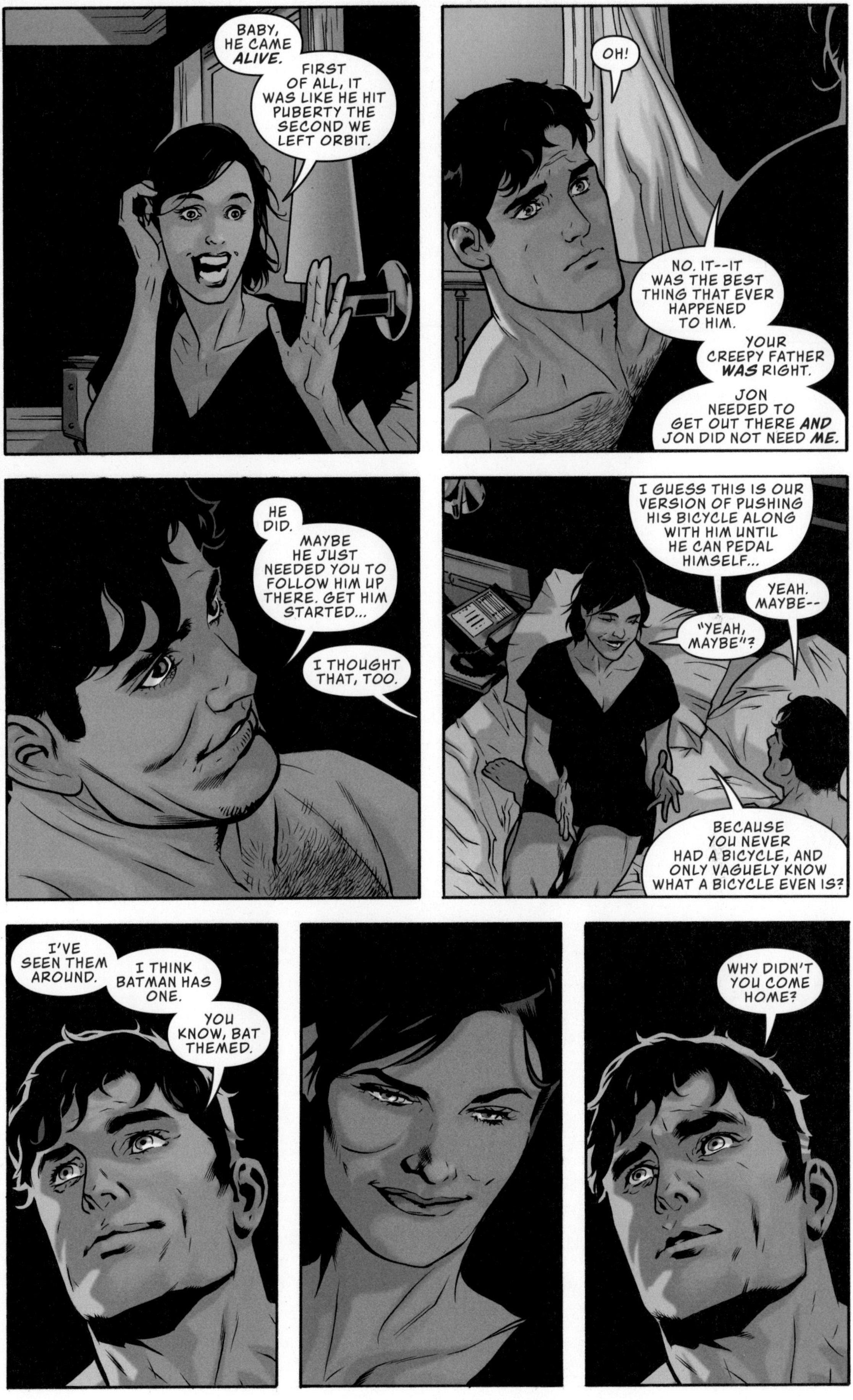
BABY, HE CAME ALIVE.
FIRST OF ALL, IT WAS LIKE HE HIT PUBERTY THE SECOND WE LEFT ORBIT.
OH!
NO. IT--IT WAS THE BEST THING THAT EVER HAPPENED TO HIM.
YOUR CREEPY FATHER WAS RIGHT.
JON NEEDED TO GET OUT THERE AND JON DID NOT NEED ME.
HE DID.
MAYBE HE JUST NEEDED YOU TO FOLLOW HIM UP THERE. GET HIM STARTED...
I THOUGHT THAT, TOO.
I GUESS THIS IS OUR VERSION OF PUSHING HIS BICYCLE ALONG WITH HIM UNTIL HE CAN PEDAL HIMSELF...
YEAH. MAYBE--
"YEAH, MAYBE"?
BECAUSE YOU NEVER HAD A BICYCLE, AND ONLY VAGUELY KNOW WHAT A BICYCLE EVEN IS?
I'VE SEEN THEM AROUND.
I THINK BATMAN HAS ONE.
YOU KNOW, BAT THEMED.
WHY DIDN'T YOU COME HOME?

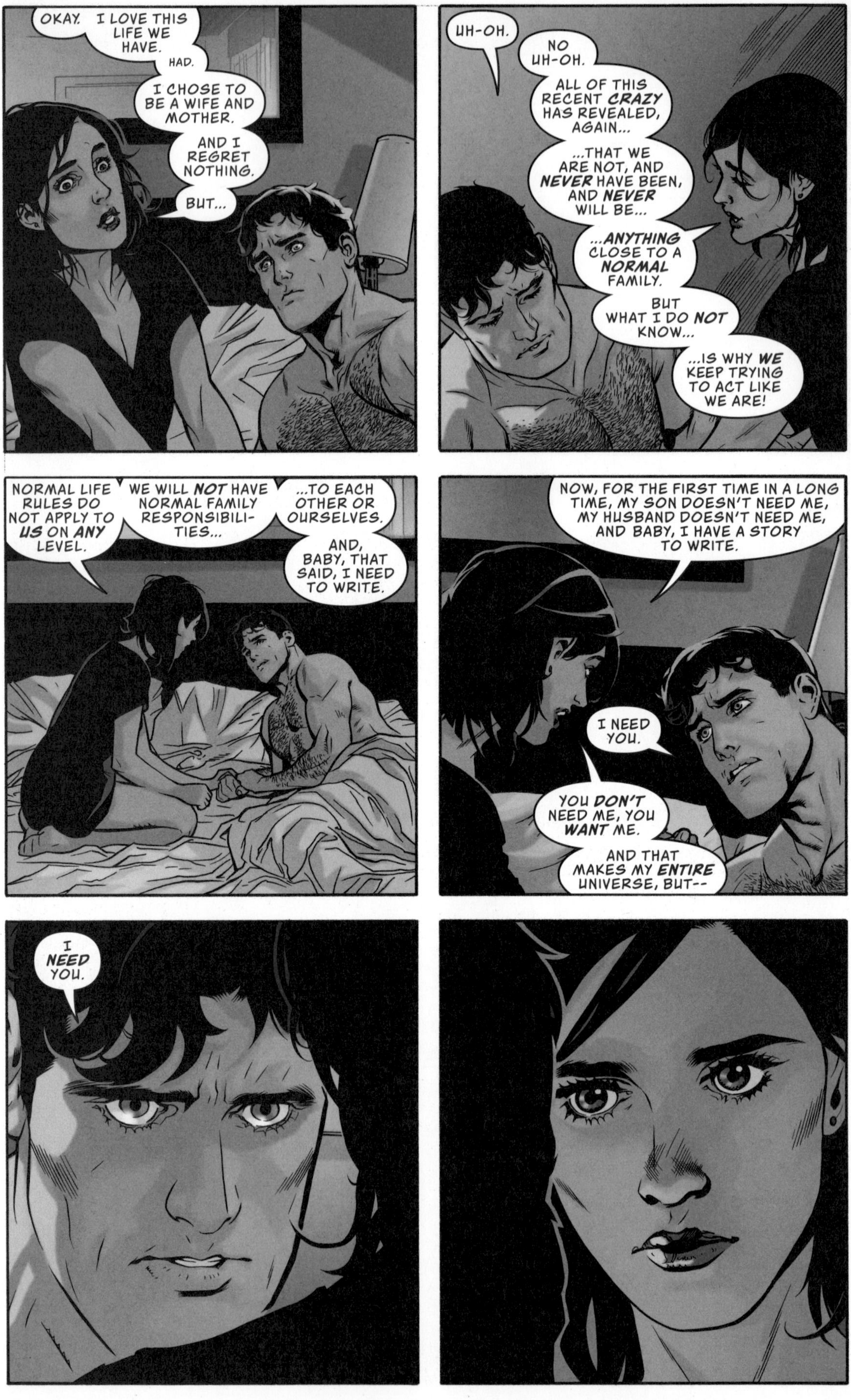
OKAY. I LOVE THIS LIFE WE HAVE.
HAD.
I CHOSE TO BE A WIFE AND MOTHER.
AND I REGRET NOTHING.
BUT...
UH-OH.
NO UH-OH.
ALL OF THIS RECENT CRAZY HAS REVEALED, AGAIN...
...THAT WE ARE NOT, AND NEVER HAVE BEEN, AND NEVER WILL BE...
...ANYTHING CLOSE TO A NORMAL FAMILY.
BUT WHAT I DO NOT KNOW...
...IS WHY WE KEEP TRYING TO ACT LIKE WE ARE!
NORMAL LIFE RULES DO NOT APPLY TO US ON ANY LEVEL.
WE WILL NOT HAVE NORMAL FAMILY RESPONSIBILI-TIES...
...TO EACH OTHER OR OURSELVES.
AND, BABY, THAT SAID, I NEED TO WRITE.
NOW, FOR THE FIRST TIME IN A LONG TIME, MY SON DOESN'T NEED ME, MY HUSBAND DOESN'T NEED ME, AND BABY, I HAVE A STORY TO WRITE.
I NEED YOU.
YOU DON'T NEED ME, YOU WANT ME.
AND THAT MAKES MY ENTIRE UNIVERSE, BUT--
I NEED YOU.

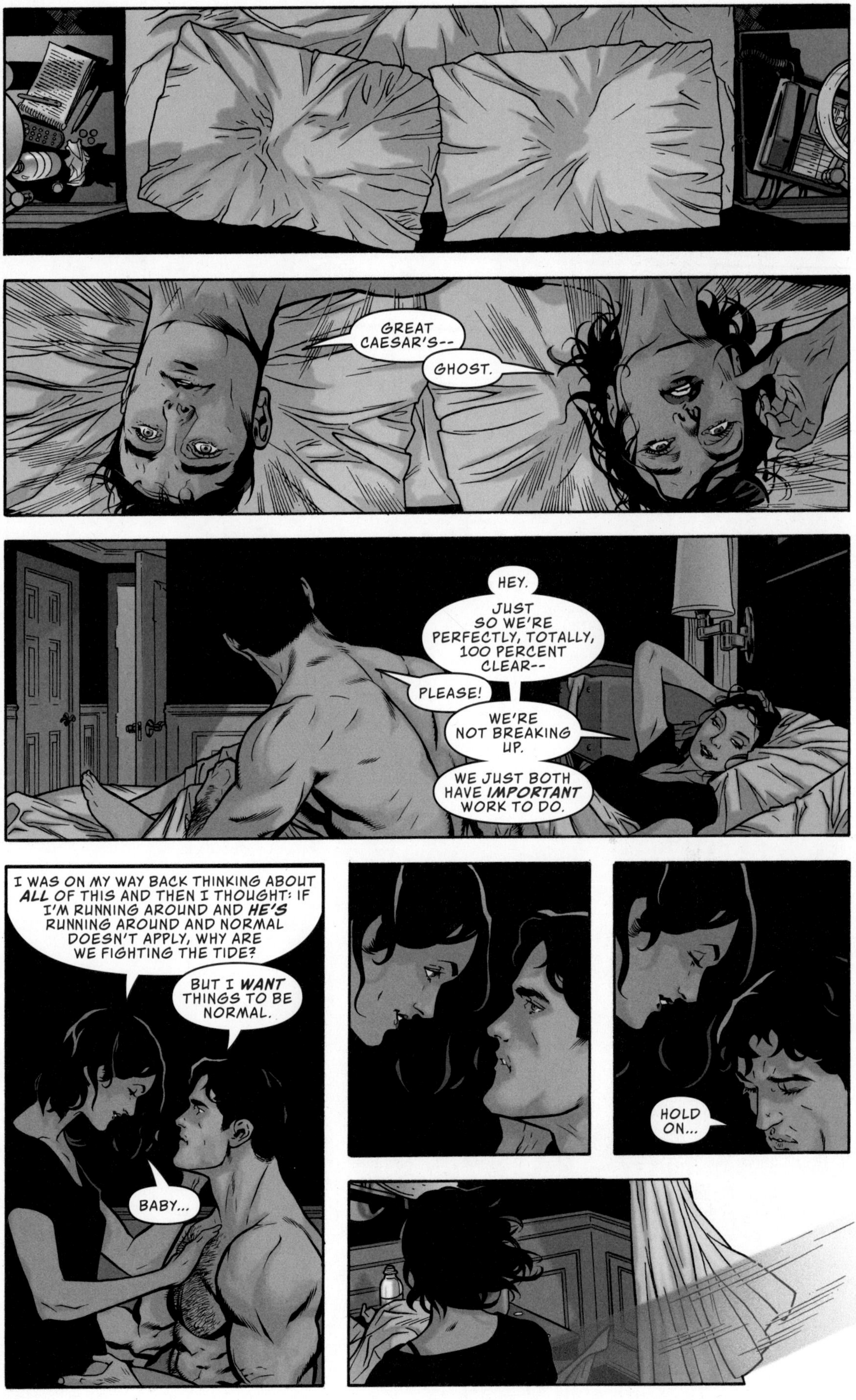
GREAT CAESAR'S--
GHOST.
HEY.
JUST SO WE'RE PERFECTLY, TOTALLY, 100 PERCENT CLEAR--
PLEASE!
WE'RE NOT BREAKING UP.
WE JUST BOTH HAVE IMPORTANT WORK TO DO.
I WAS ON MY WAY BACK THINKING ABOUT ALL OF THIS AND THEN I THOUGHT: IF I'M RUNNING AROUND AND HE'S RUNNING AROUND AND NORMAL DOESN'T APPLY, WHY ARE WE FIGHTING THE TIDE?
BUT I WANT THINGS TO BE NORMAL.
BABY...
HOLD ON...

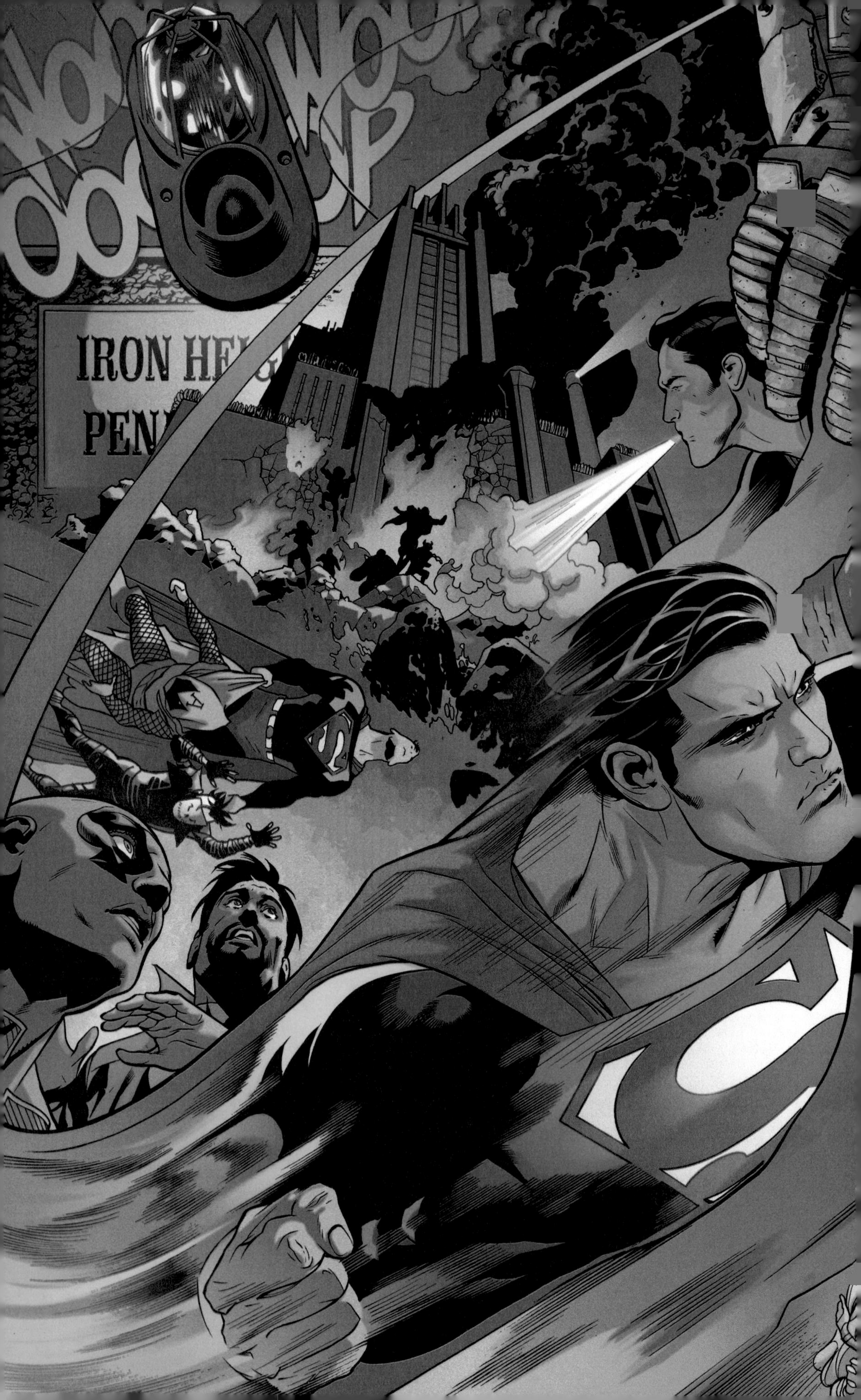
IRON HE
PEN

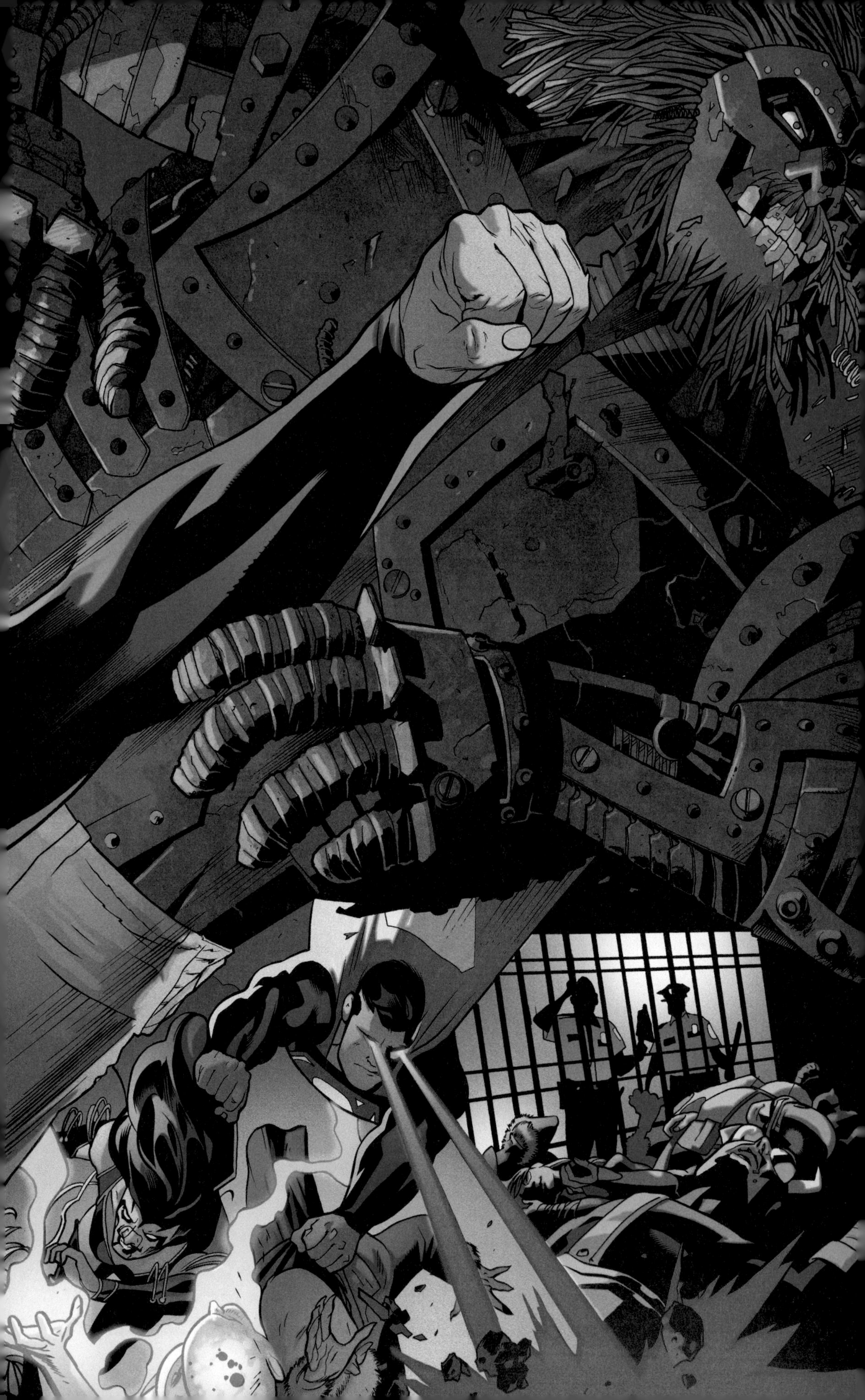

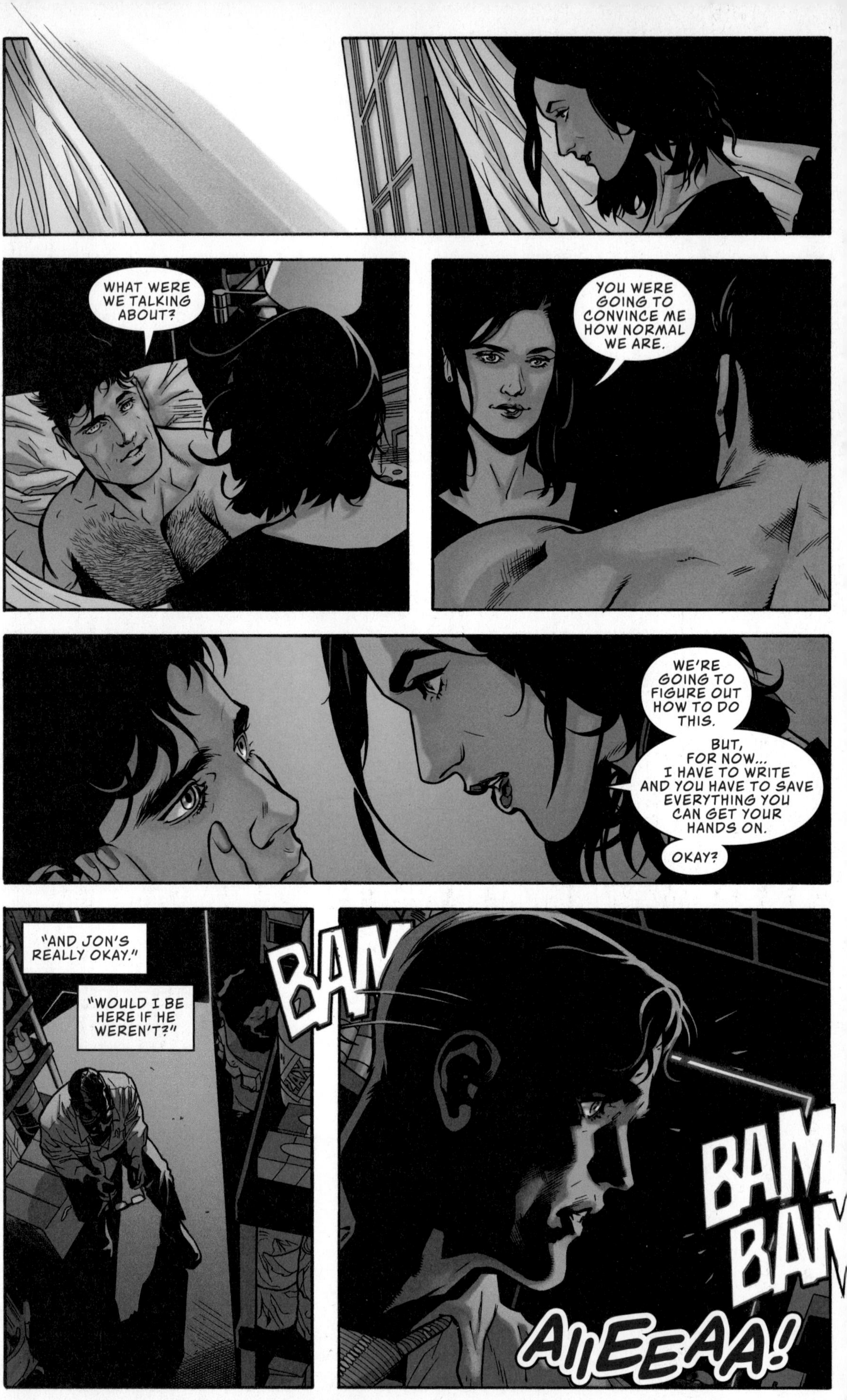
WHAT WERE WE TALKING ABOUT?
YOU WERE GOING TO CONVINCE ME HOW NORMAL WE ARE.
WE'RE GOING TO FIGURE OUT HOW TO DO THIS.
BUT, FOR NOW... I HAVE TO WRITE AND YOU HAVE TO SAVE EVERYTHING YOU CAN GET YOUR HANDS ON.
OKAY?
"AND JON'S REALLY OKAY."
"WOULD I BE HERE IF HE WEREN'T?"
BAM
BAM
BAM
AIIEEAA!

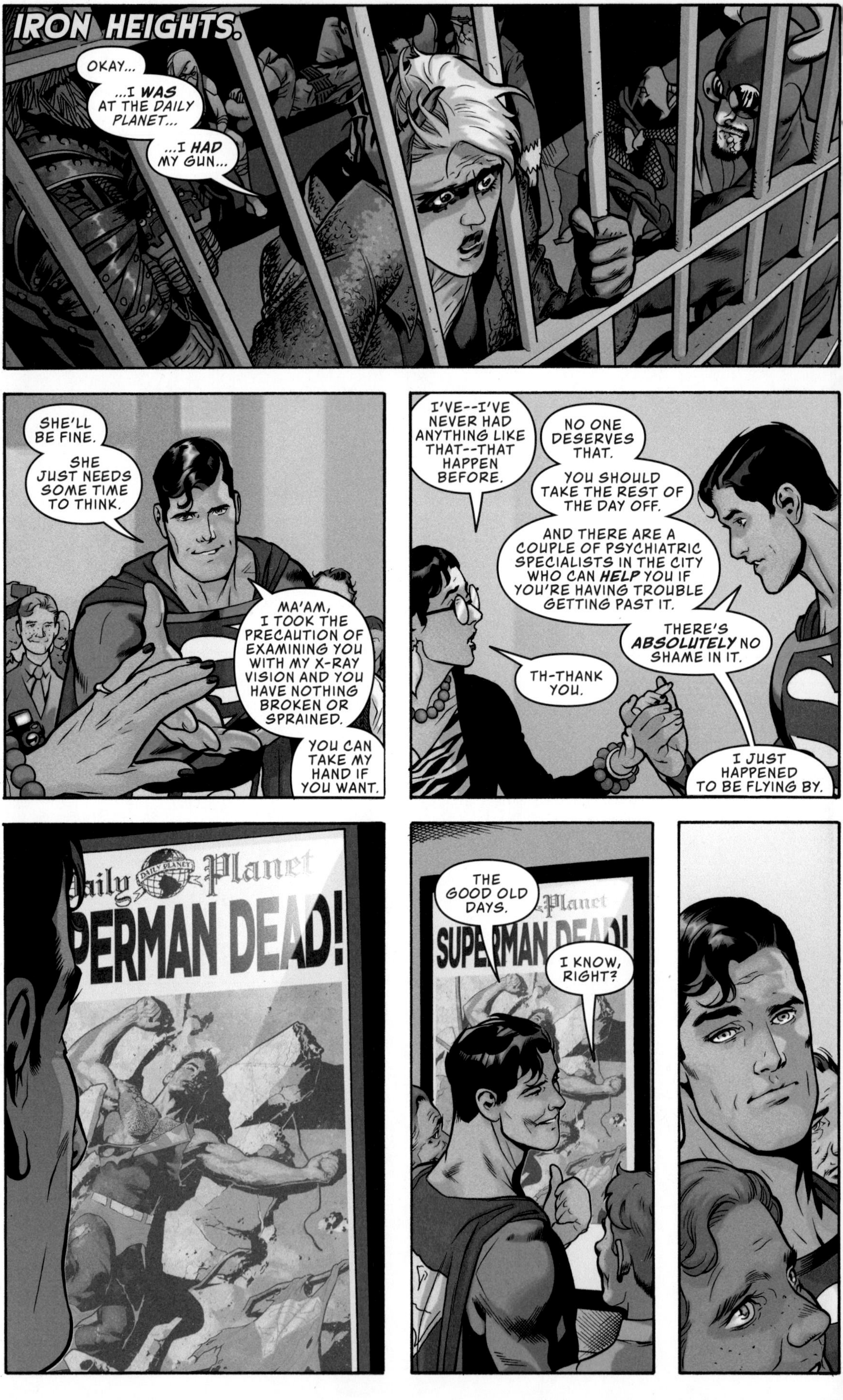
IRON HEIGHTS.
OKAY...
...I WAS AT THE DAILY PLANET...
...I HAD MY GUN...
SHE'LL BE FINE.
SHE JUST NEEDS SOME TIME TO THINK.
MA'AM, I TOOK THE PRECAUTION OF EXAMINING YOU WITH MY X-RAY VISION AND YOU HAVE NOTHING BROKEN OR SPRAINED.
YOU CAN TAKE MY HAND IF YOU WANT.
I'VE--I'VE NEVER HAD ANYTHING LIKE THAT--THAT HAPPEN BEFORE.
NO ONE DESERVES THAT.
YOU SHOULD TAKE THE REST OF THE DAY OFF.
AND THERE ARE A COUPLE OF PSYCHIATRIC SPECIALISTS IN THE CITY WHO CAN HELP YOU IF YOU'RE HAVING TROUBLE GETTING PAST IT.
THERE'S ABSOLUTELY NO SHAME IN IT.
TH-THANK YOU.
I JUST HAPPENED TO BE FLYING BY.
Daily Planet
DAILY PLANET
PERMAN DEAD!
THE GOOD OLD DAYS.
SUPERMAN DEAD!
I KNOW, RIGHT?

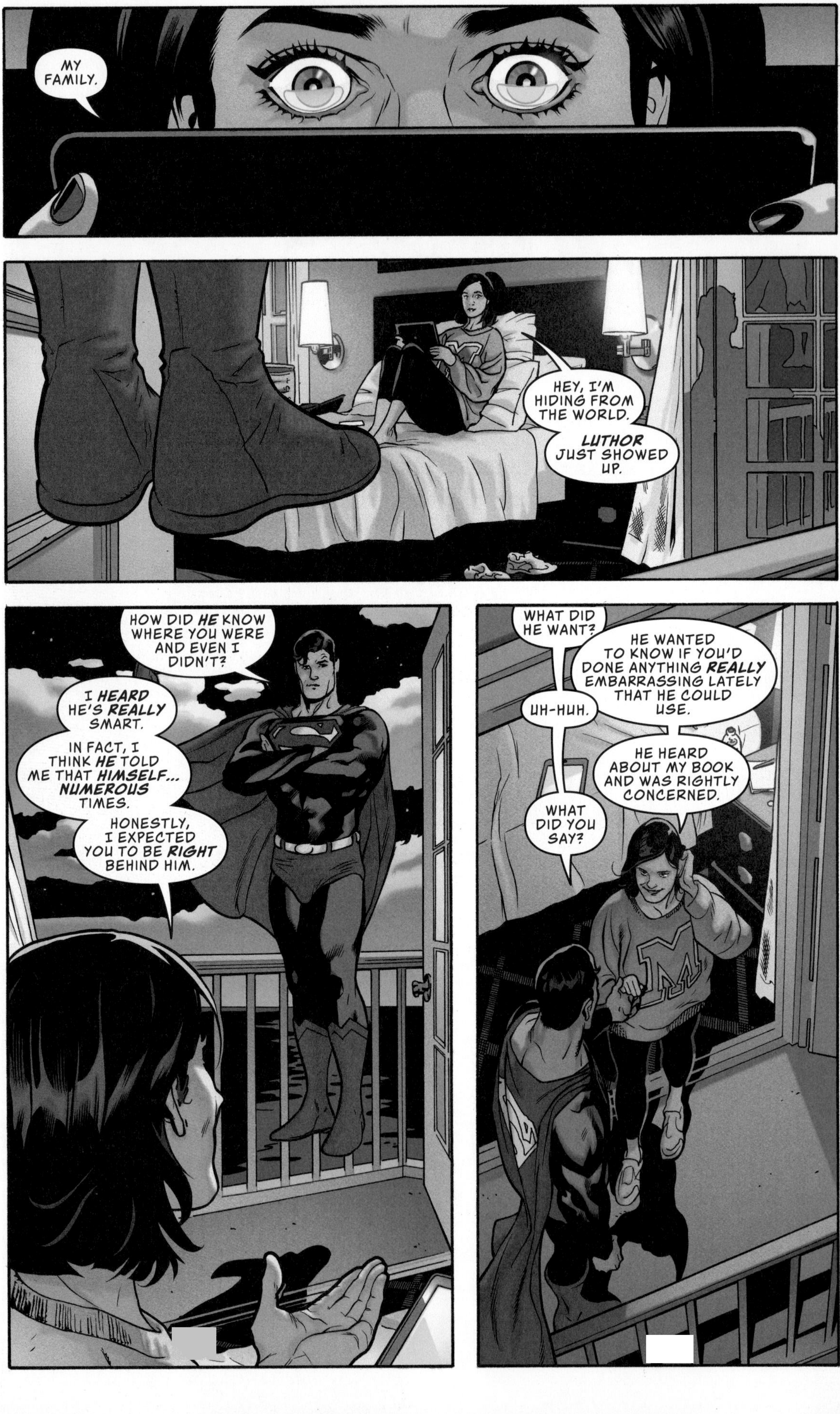

MY FAMILY.
HEY, I'M HIDING FROM THE WORLD.
LUTHOR JUST SHOWED UP.
HOW DID HE KNOW WHERE YOU WERE AND EVEN I DIDN'T?
I HEARD HE'S REALLY SMART.
IN FACT, I THINK HE TOLD ME THAT HIMSELF... NUMEROUS TIMES.
HONESTLY, I EXPECTED YOU TO BE RIGHT BEHIND HIM.
WHAT DID HE WANT?
HE WANTED TO KNOW IF YOU'D DONE ANYTHING REALLY EMBARRASSING LATELY THAT HE COULD USE.
UH-HUH.
HE HEARD ABOUT MY BOOK AND WAS RIGHTLY CONCERNED.
WHAT DID YOU SAY?

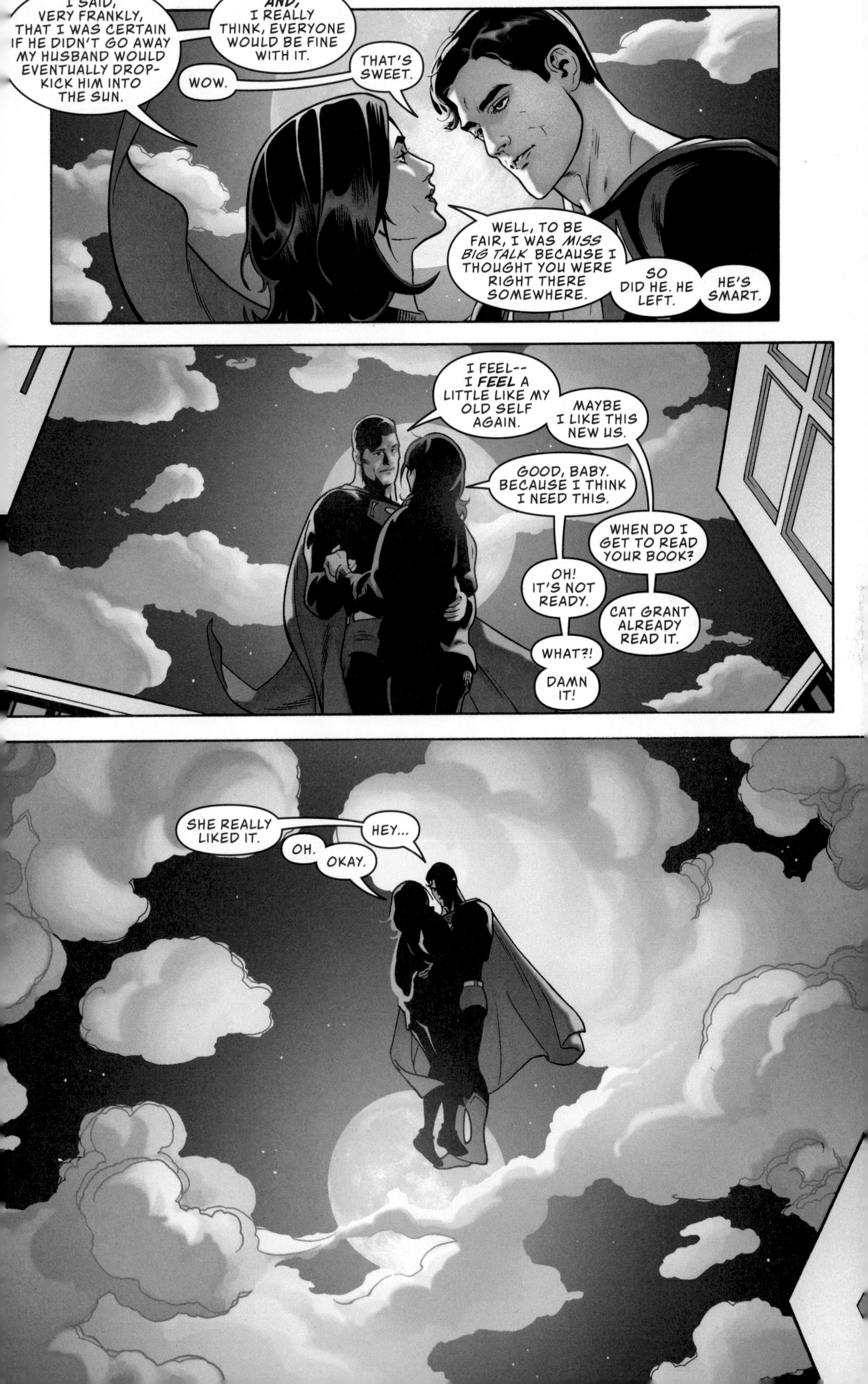

I SAID, VERY FRANKLY, THAT I WAS CERTAIN IF HE DIDN'T GO AWAY MY HUSBAND WOULD EVENTUALLY DROP-KICK HIM INTO THE SUN.
AND, I REALLY THINK, EVERYONE WOULD BE FINE WITH IT.
WOW.
THAT'S SWEET.
WELL, TO BE FAIR, I WAS MISS BIG TALK BECAUSE I THOUGHT YOU WERE RIGHT THERE SOMEWHERE.
SO DID HE. HE LEFT.
HE'S SMART.
I FEEL-- I FEEL A LITTLE LIKE MY OLD SELF AGAIN.
MAYBE I LIKE THIS NEW US.
GOOD, BABY. BECAUSE I THINK I NEED THIS.
WHEN DO I GET TO READ YOUR BOOK?
OH! IT'S NOT READY.
CAT GRANT ALREADY READ IT.
WHAT?!
DAMN IT!
SHE REALLY LIKED IT.
HEY...
OH.
OKAY.

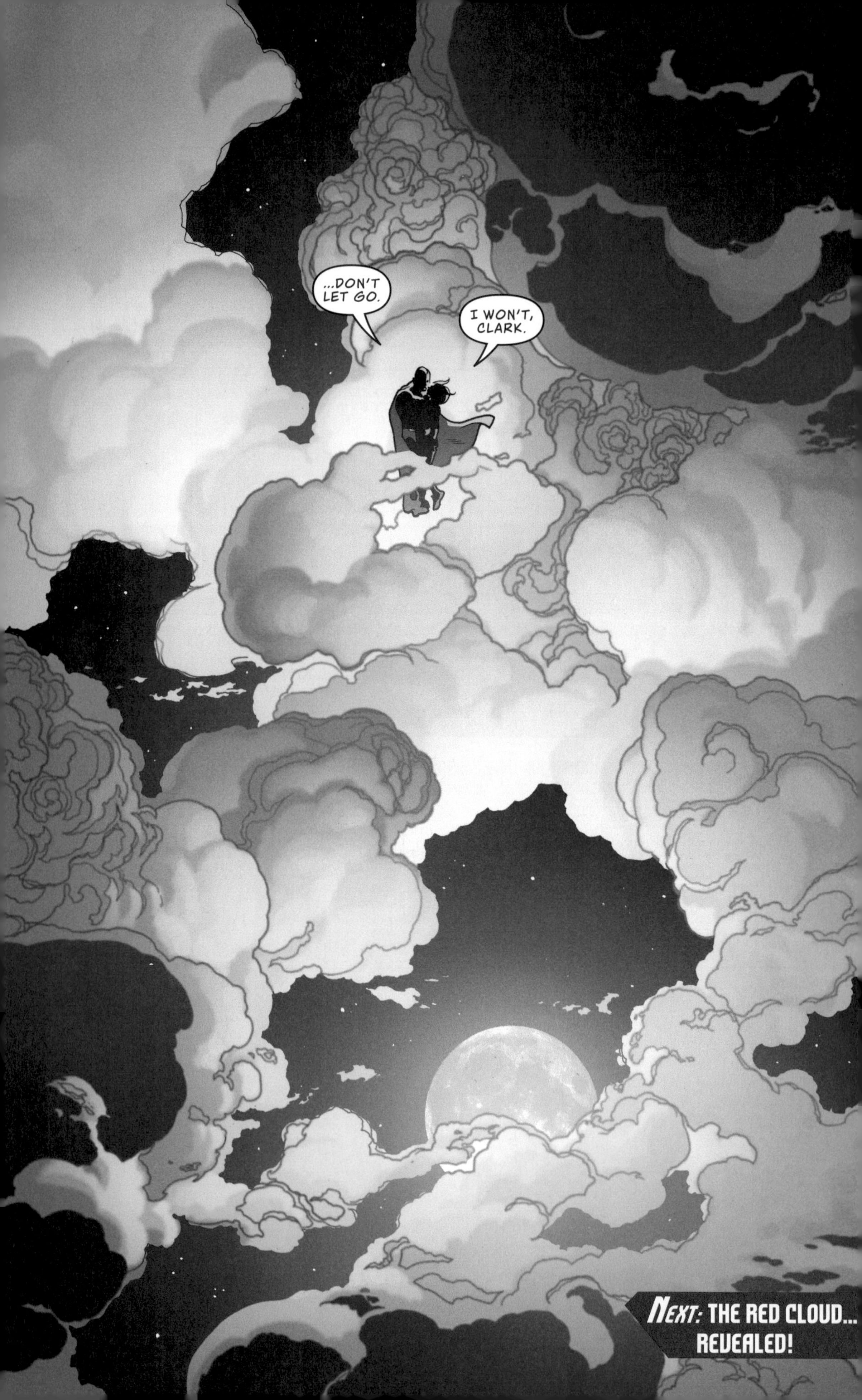
...DON'T LET GO.
I WON'T, CLARK.
NEXT: THE RED CLOUD... REVEALED!

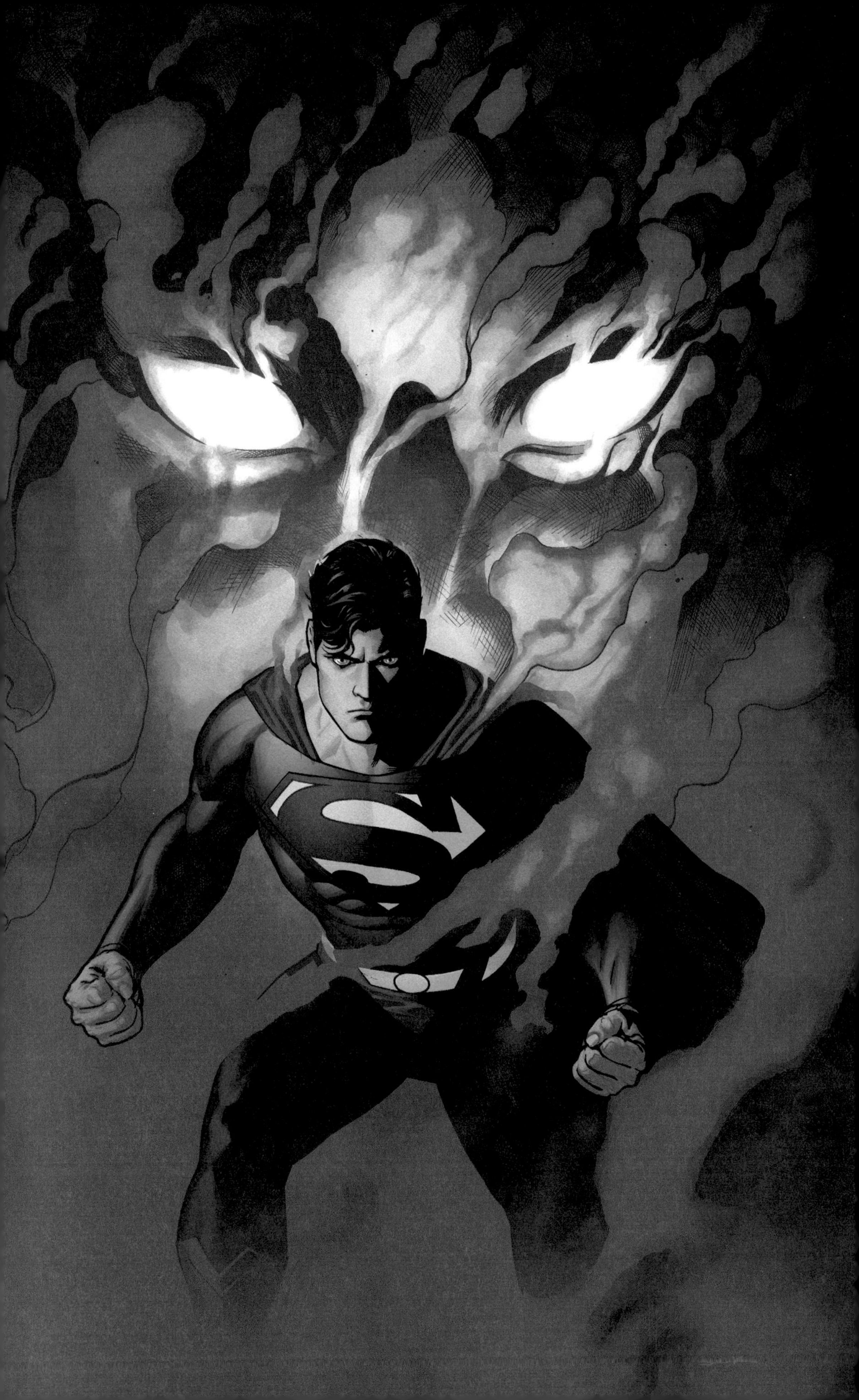

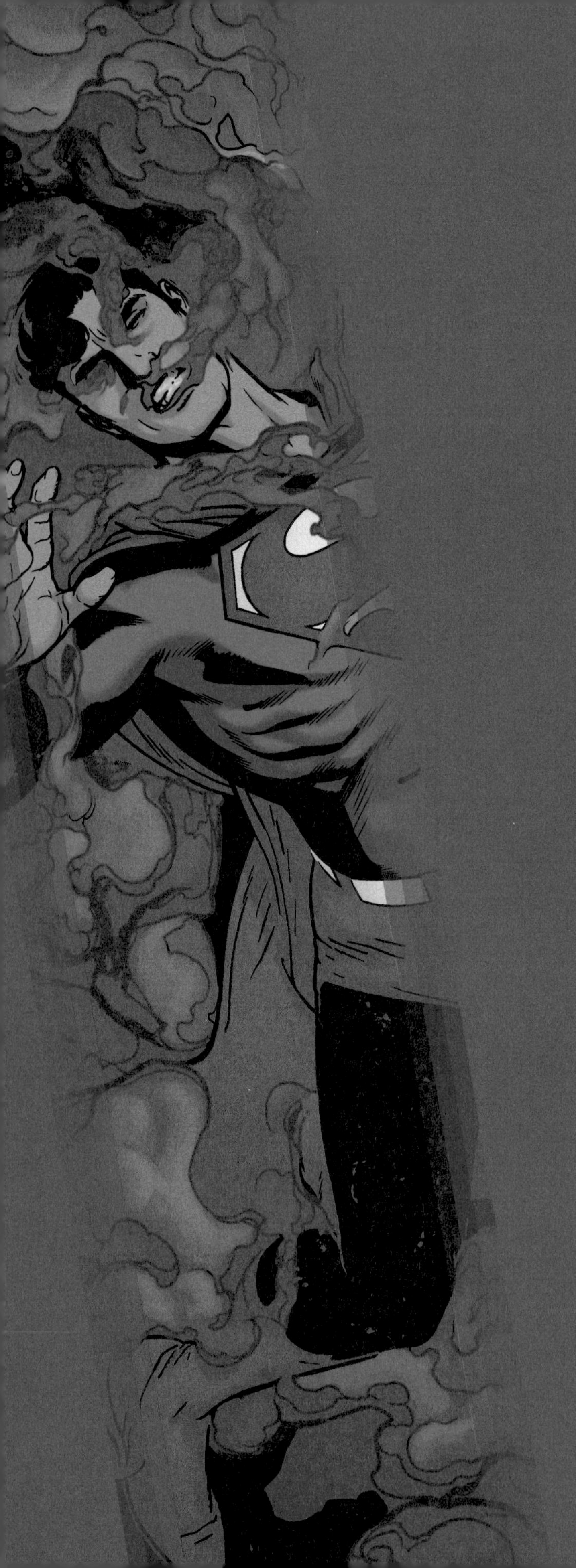

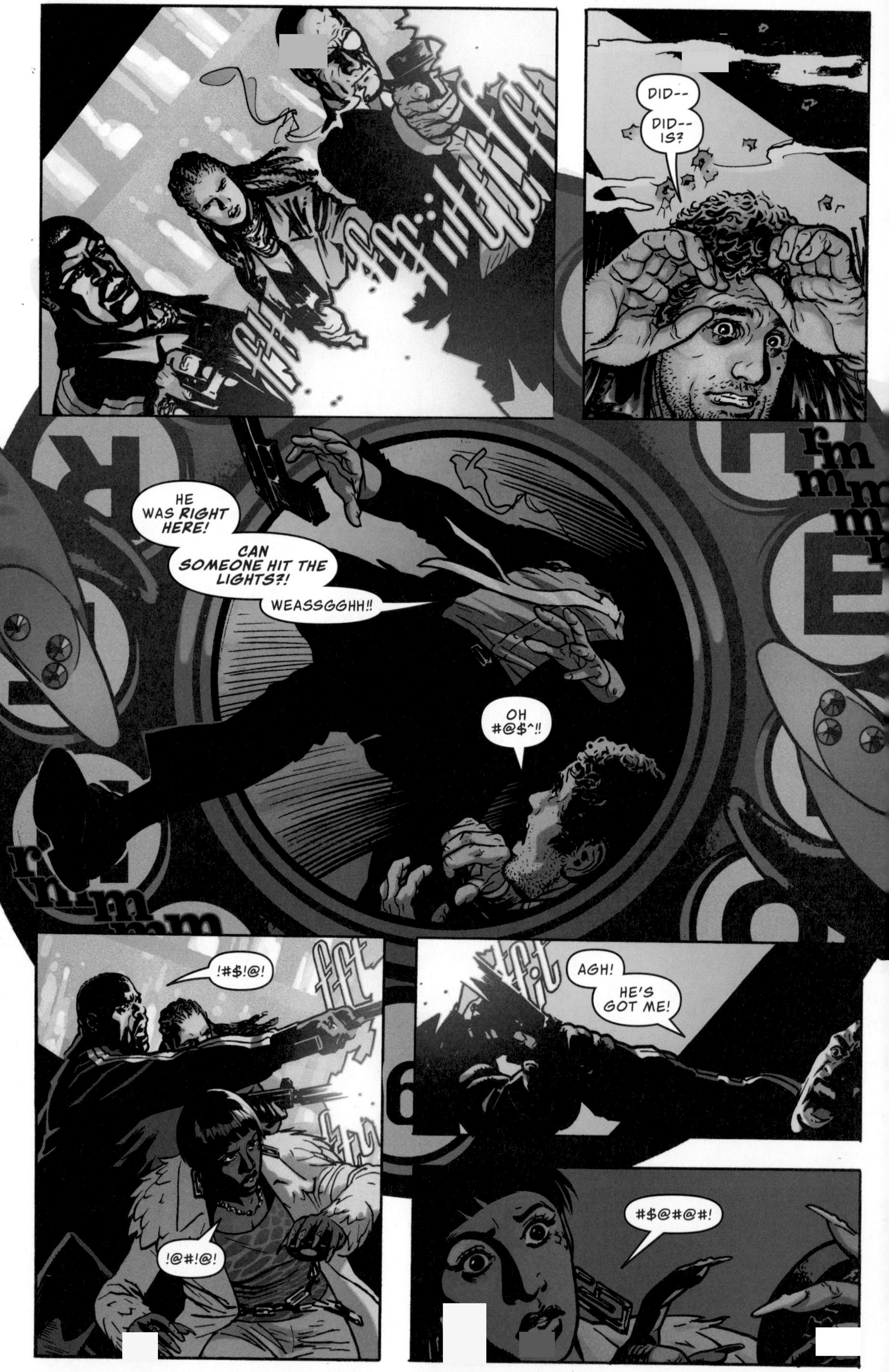
DID--
DID-- IS?
HE WAS RIGHT HERE!
CAN SOMEONE HIT THE LIGHTS?!
WEASSGGHH!!
OH #@$^!!
!#$!@!
fft
!@#!@!
AGH! HE'S GOT ME!
#$@#@#!

THE DAILY PLANET.

"WHO IS THE RED CLOUD?

"IN A WORLD OVERRUN WITH ALIENS, MUTATIONS AND COLORFUL CHARACTERS OF EVERY WALK OF LIFE...

"...THE LATEST QUESTION WHISPERED IN THE SHADOWS OF THE TEEMING STREETS OF METROPOL--"

"TEEMING STREETS OF METROPOLIS?"

YOU NEVER, CLARK KENT, IN ALL YOUR DAYS, WROTE THE WORDS "TEEMING STREETS OF METROPOLIS"?

MY PEERS HERE WERE GOOD ENOUGH TO STOP ME, MISS GOODE.

I THINK GETTING THE PUBLIC'S ATTENTION ON THIS SUBJECT TAKES A LITTLE SALESMANSHIP.

THERE IS A MYSTERY RED CLOUD MURDERING MOBSTERS.

YOU'RE SAYING IT SELLS ITSELF.

STICK TO THE FACTS.

BUT WE DON'T HAVE MANY FACTS.

AH! YOU'RE SAYING THAT'S WHY I WAS WRITING FLOWERY COPY.

TO COVER FOR THE FACT THAT I DON'T HAVE THE FACTS.

WE'VE ALL DONE IT. YOU CAUGHT IT.

NO HARM DONE.

OF THE FIVE TIMES I HAVE SEEN YOU IN MY LIFE, I HAVE NEVER SEEN YOU SO... CHIPPER.

DO PEOPLE STILL SAY CHIPPER?

SALE AT THE OPTOMETRIST?

UH, I SAW MY WIFE LAST NIGHT.

THE ELUSIVE LOIS LANE?

ELUSIVE?

YOU SAW THE ACTUAL LOIS LANE?

SHE'S NOT ELUSIVE. SHE'S--

OH, YOU STOP IT.

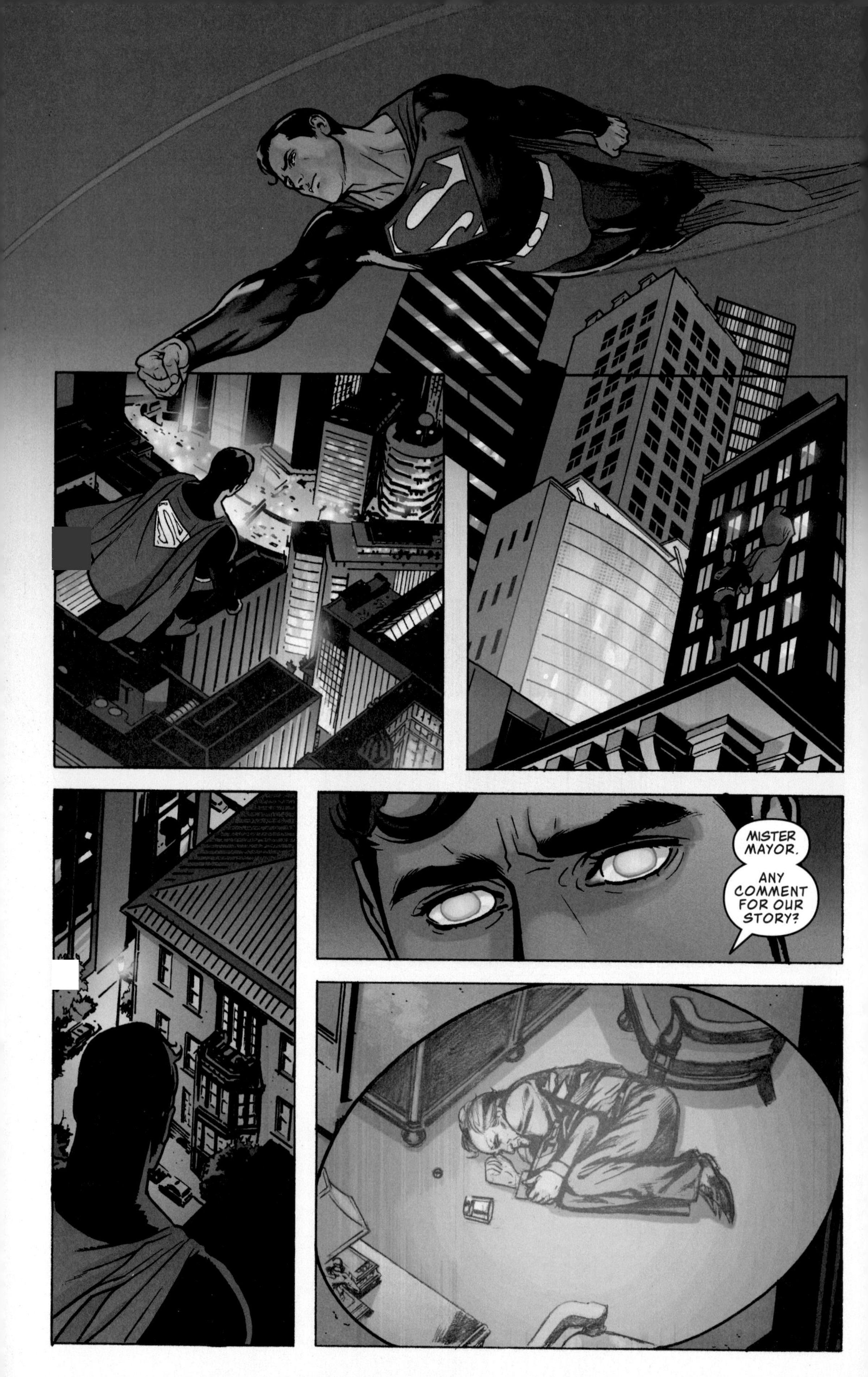
MISTER MAYOR. ANY COMMENT FOR OUR STORY?

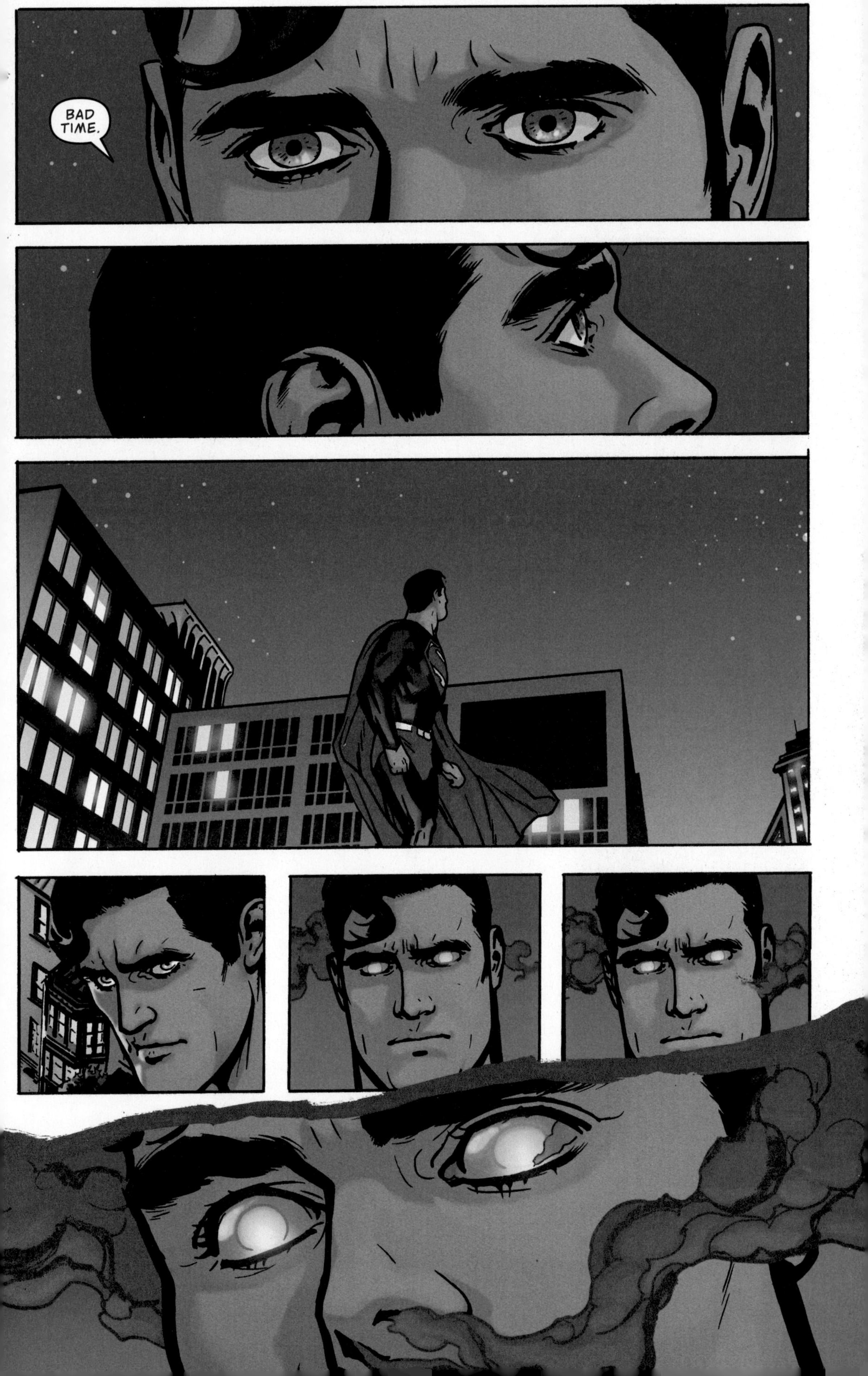
BAD TIME.

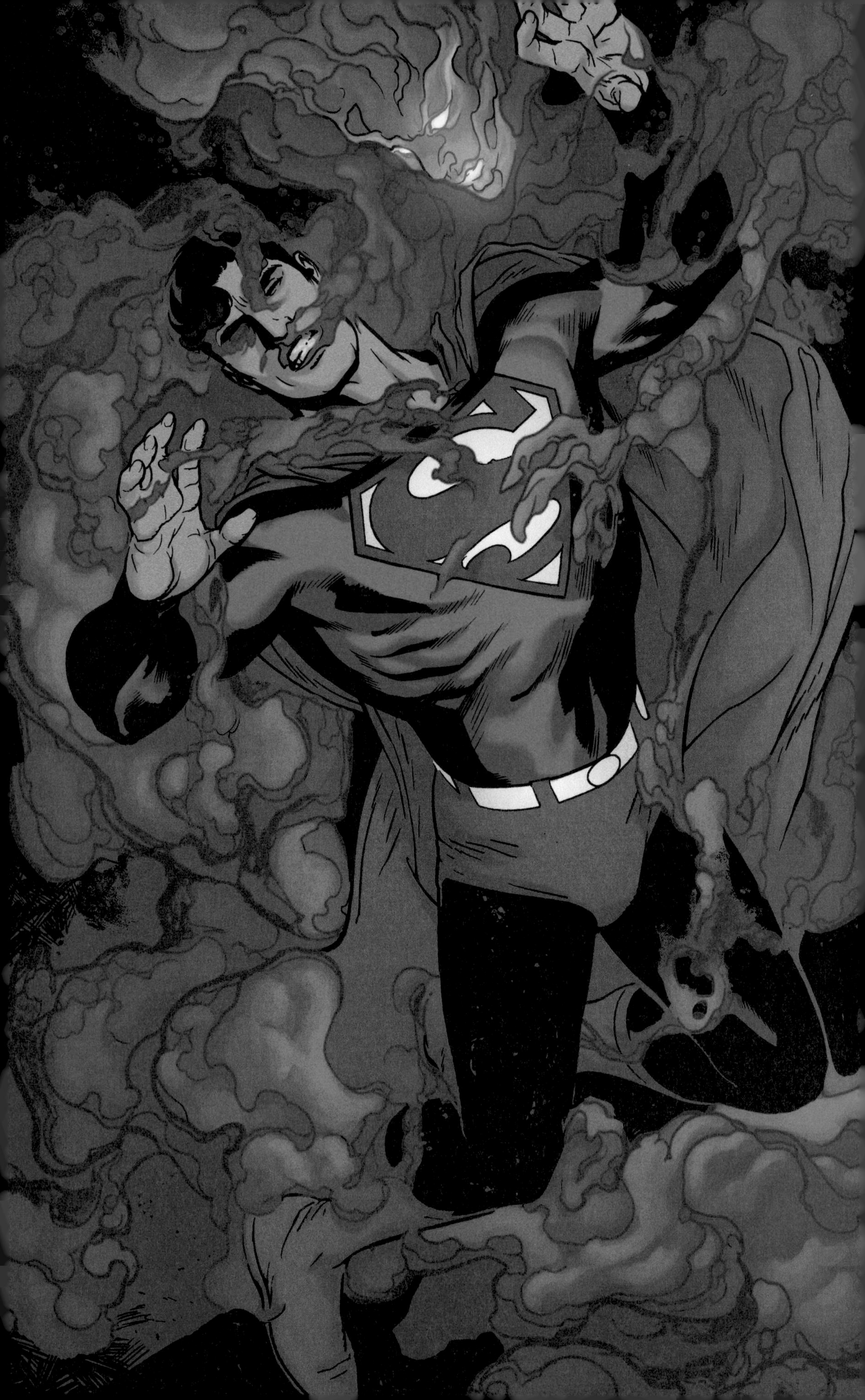

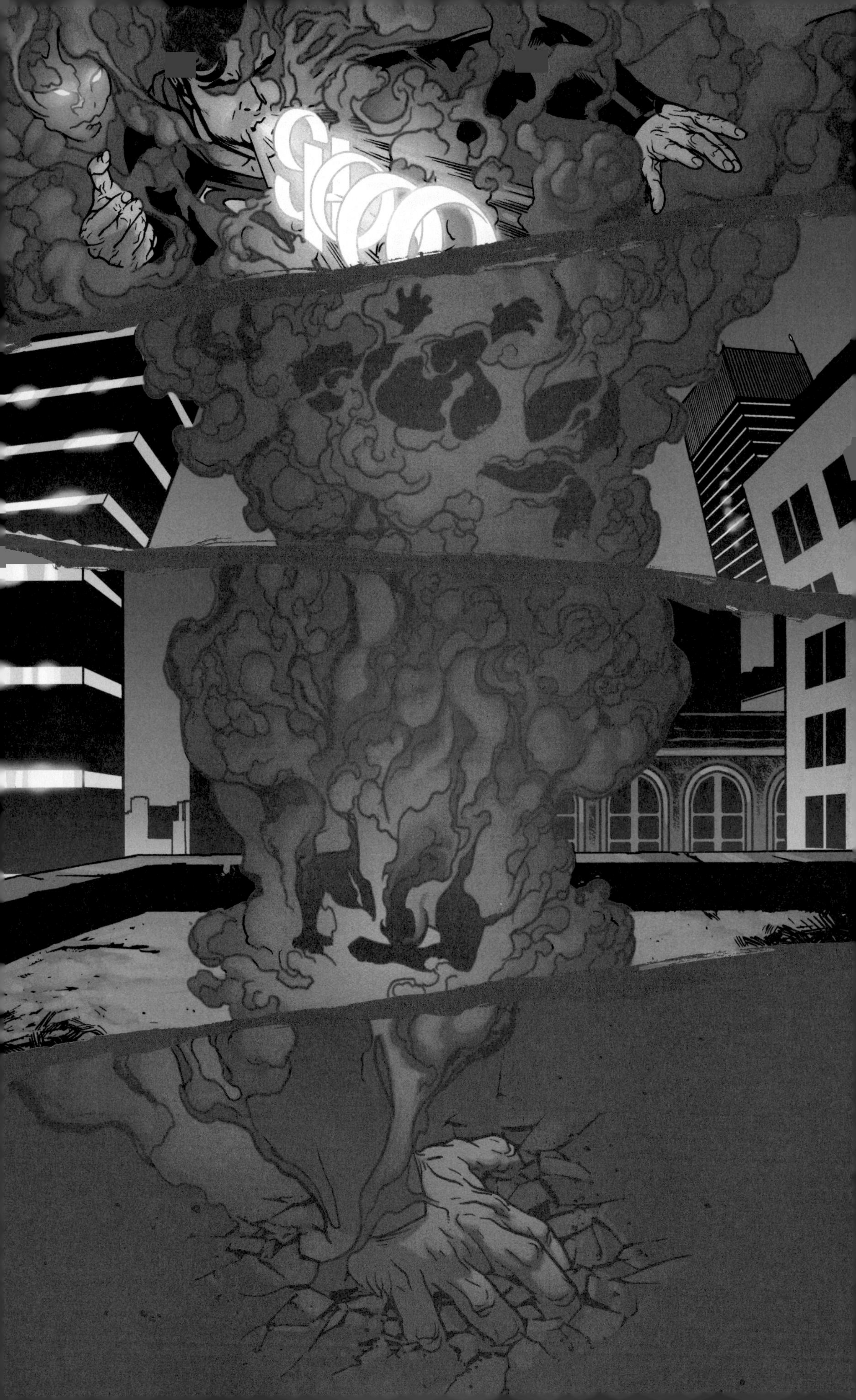
SHOOO

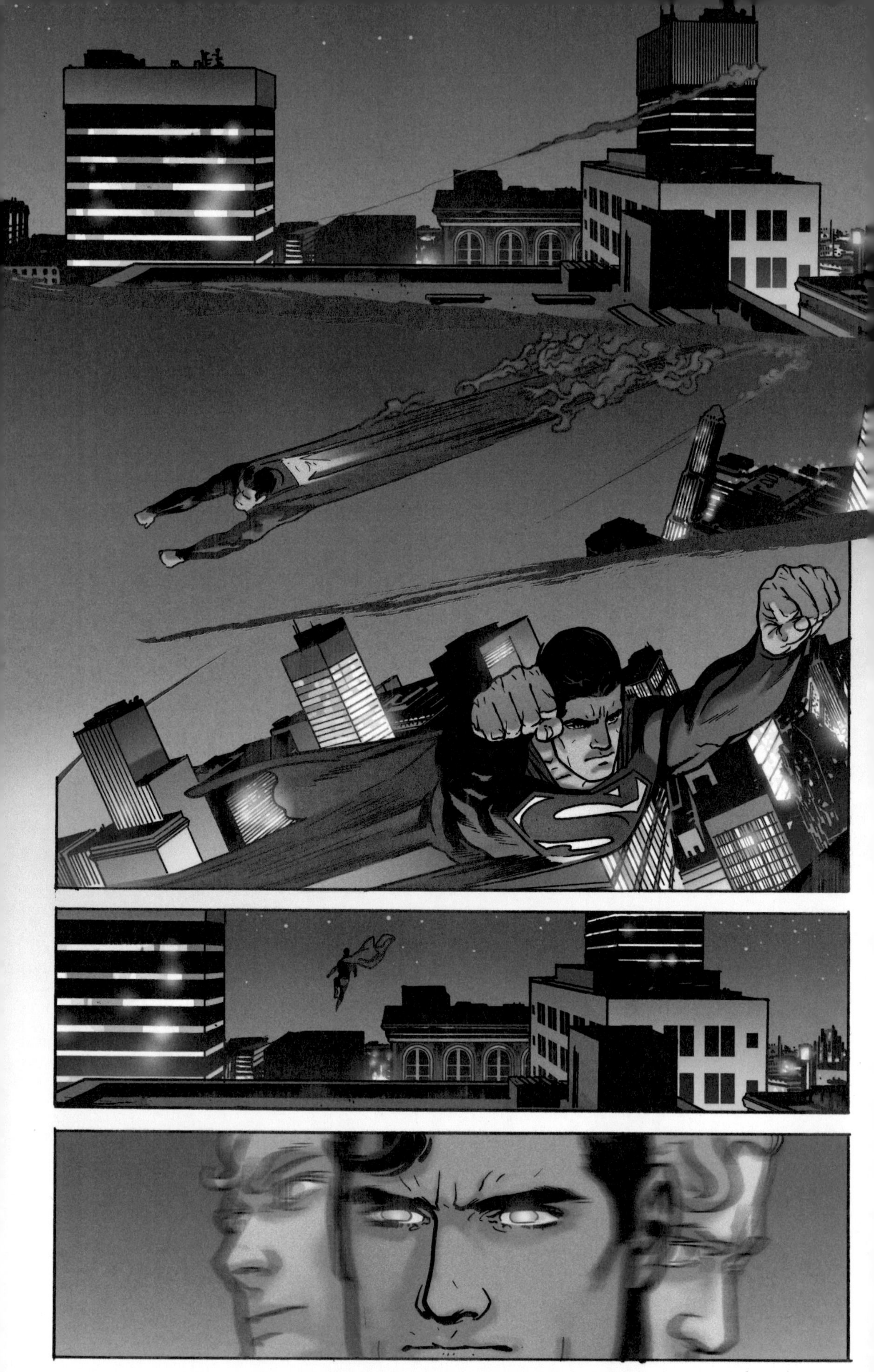

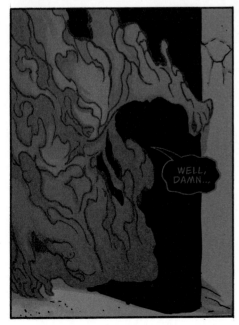

WELL, DAMN...

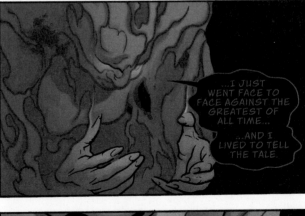

...I JUST WENT FACE TO FACE AGAINST THE GREATEST OF ALL TIME...

...AND I LIVED TO TELL THE TALE.

I CAN CHASE OFF SUPERMAN...

NEXT: THE DAILY PLANET, SOLD!

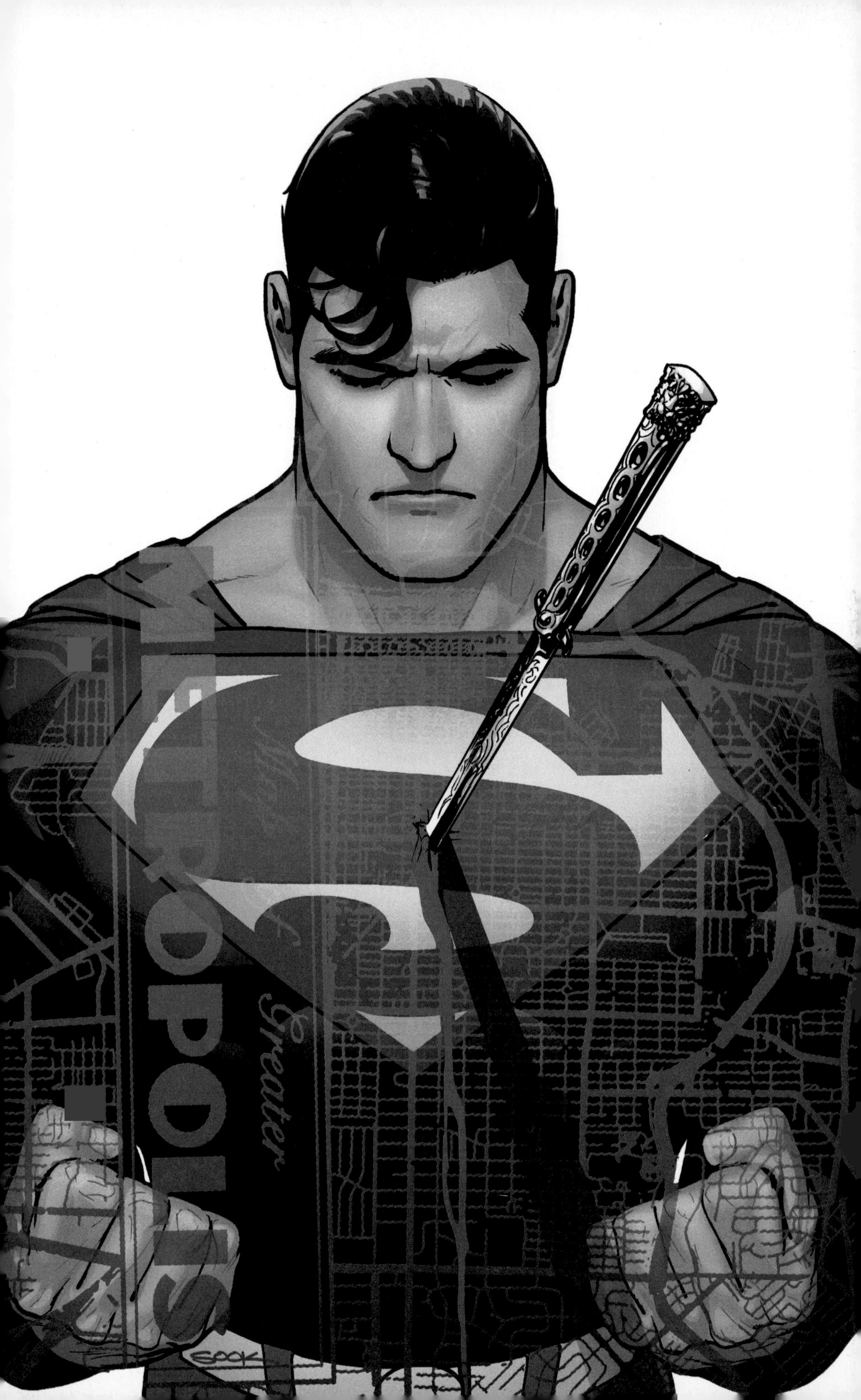
Greater
SOOK

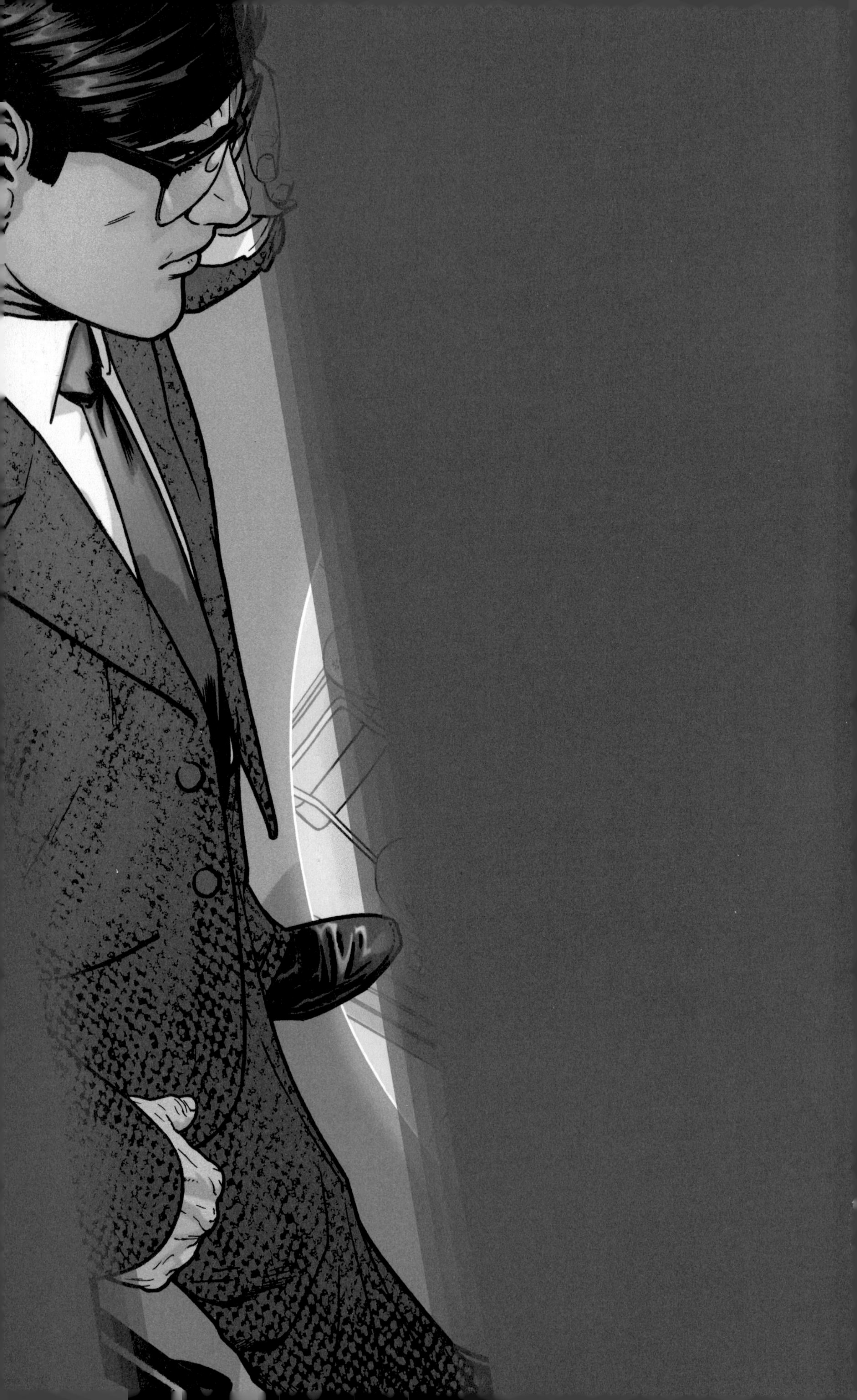

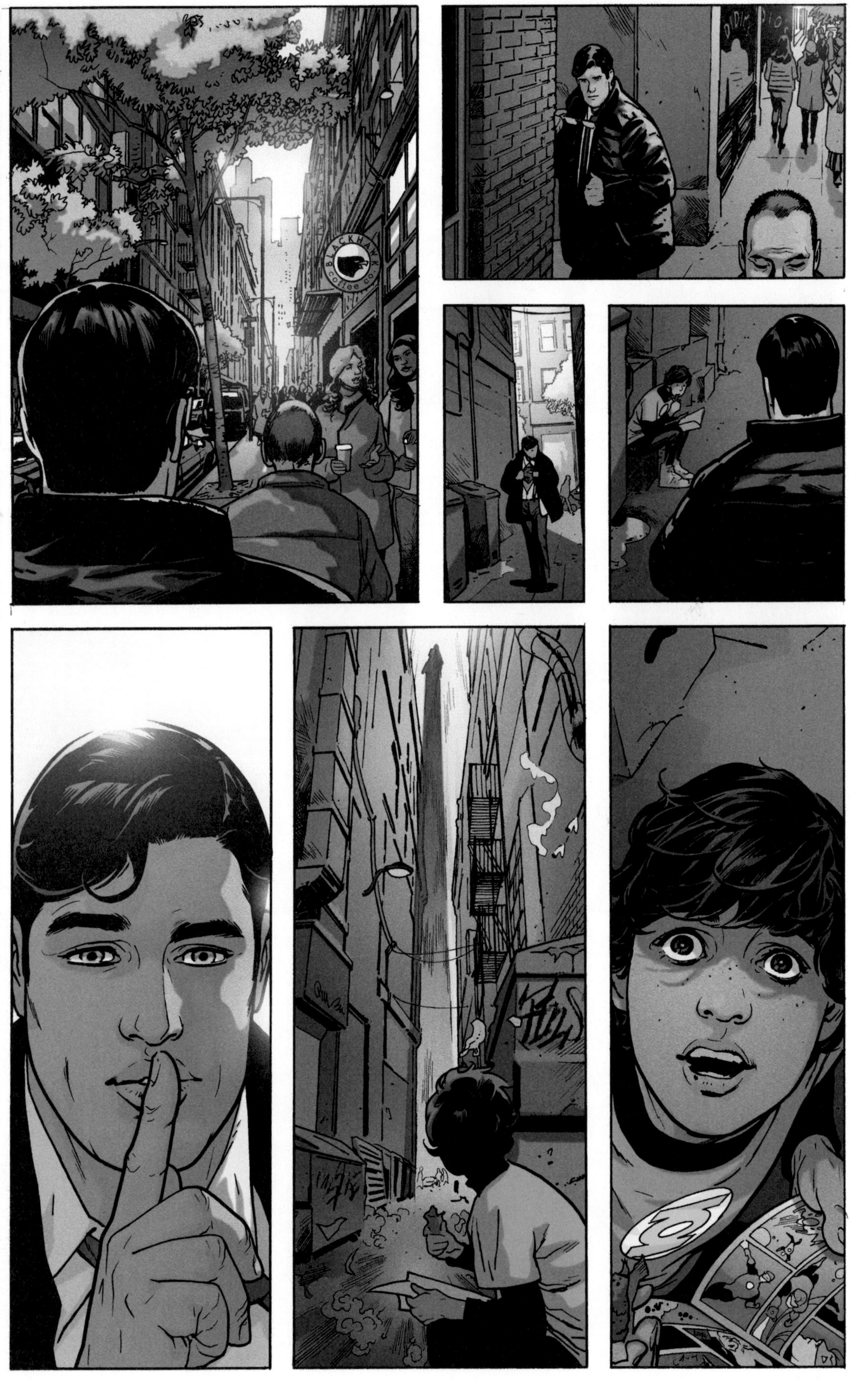
BLACKHAWK
coffee co.

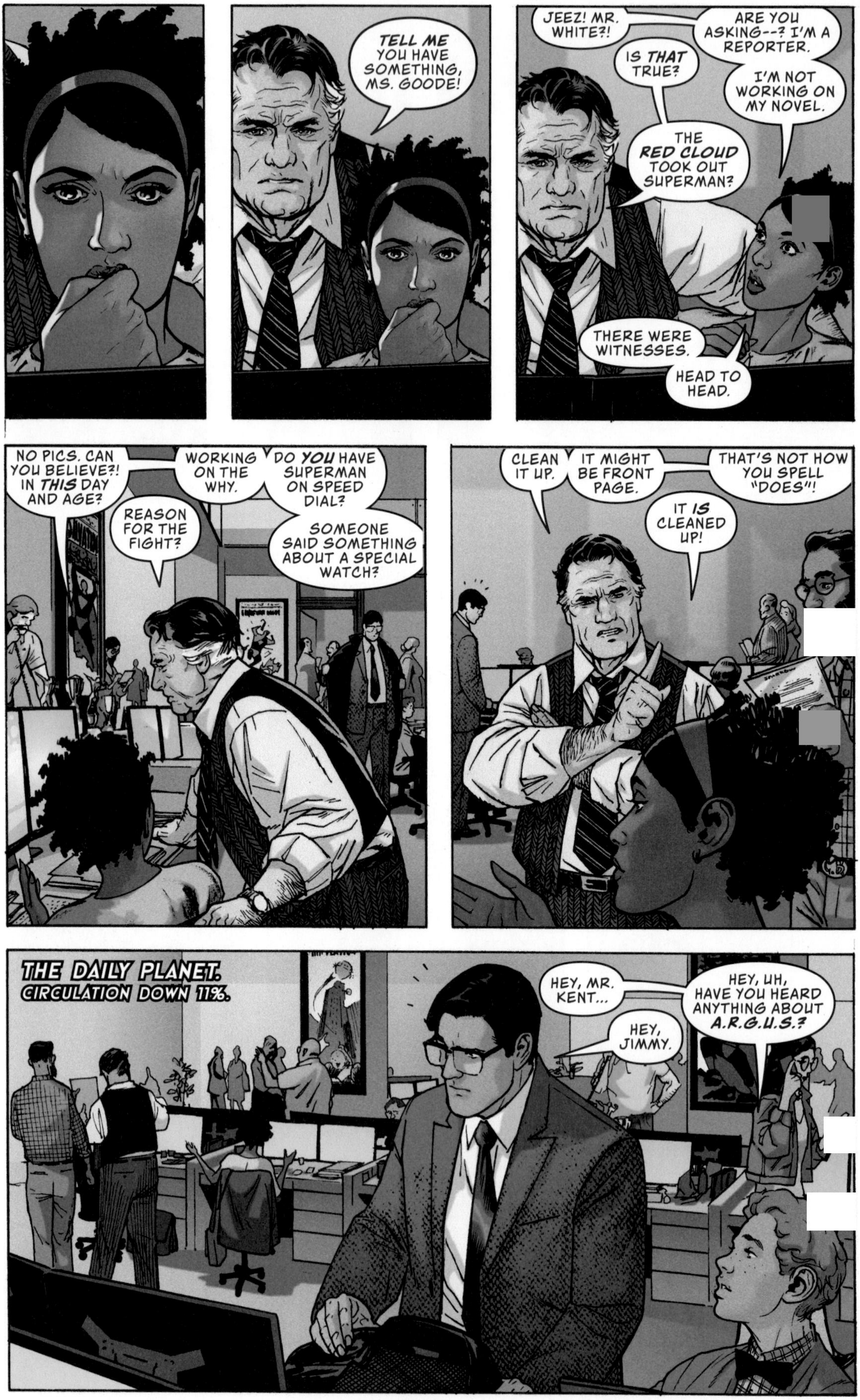
TELL ME YOU HAVE SOMETHING, MS. GOODE!
JEEZ! MR. WHITE?!
IS THAT TRUE?
THE RED CLOUD TOOK OUT SUPERMAN?
ARE YOU ASKING--? I'M A REPORTER.
I'M NOT WORKING ON MY NOVEL.
THERE WERE WITNESSES.
HEAD TO HEAD.
NO PICS. CAN YOU BELIEVE?! IN THIS DAY AND AGE?
REASON FOR THE FIGHT?
WORKING ON THE WHY.
DO YOU HAVE SUPERMAN ON SPEED DIAL?
SOMEONE SAID SOMETHING ABOUT A SPECIAL WATCH?
CLEAN IT UP.
IT MIGHT BE FRONT PAGE.
THAT'S NOT HOW YOU SPELL "DOES"!
IT IS CLEANED UP!
THE DAILY PLANET.
CIRCULATION DOWN 11%.
HEY, MR. KENT...
HEY, JIMMY.
HEY, UH, HAVE YOU HEARD ANYTHING ABOUT A.R.G.U.S.?

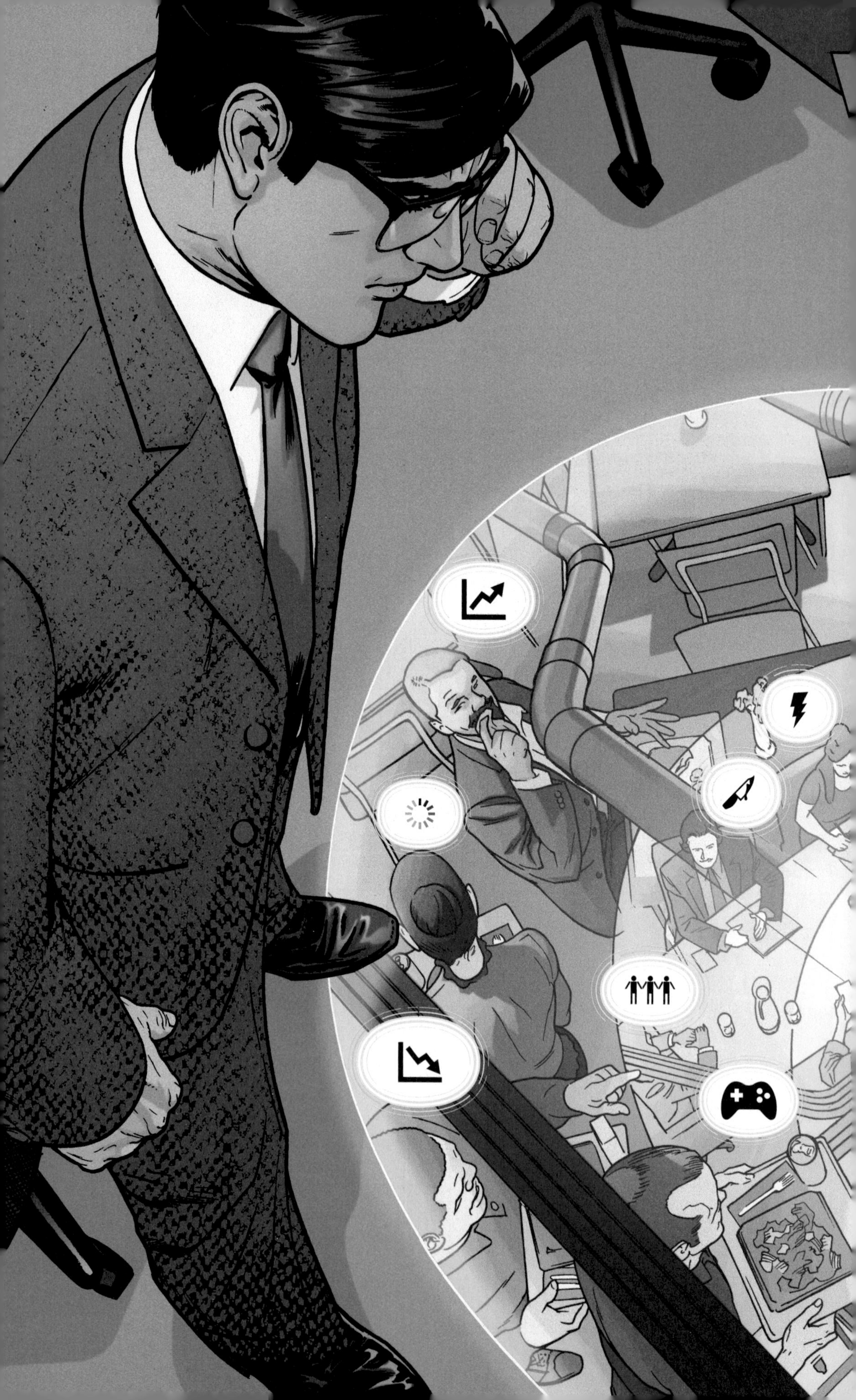

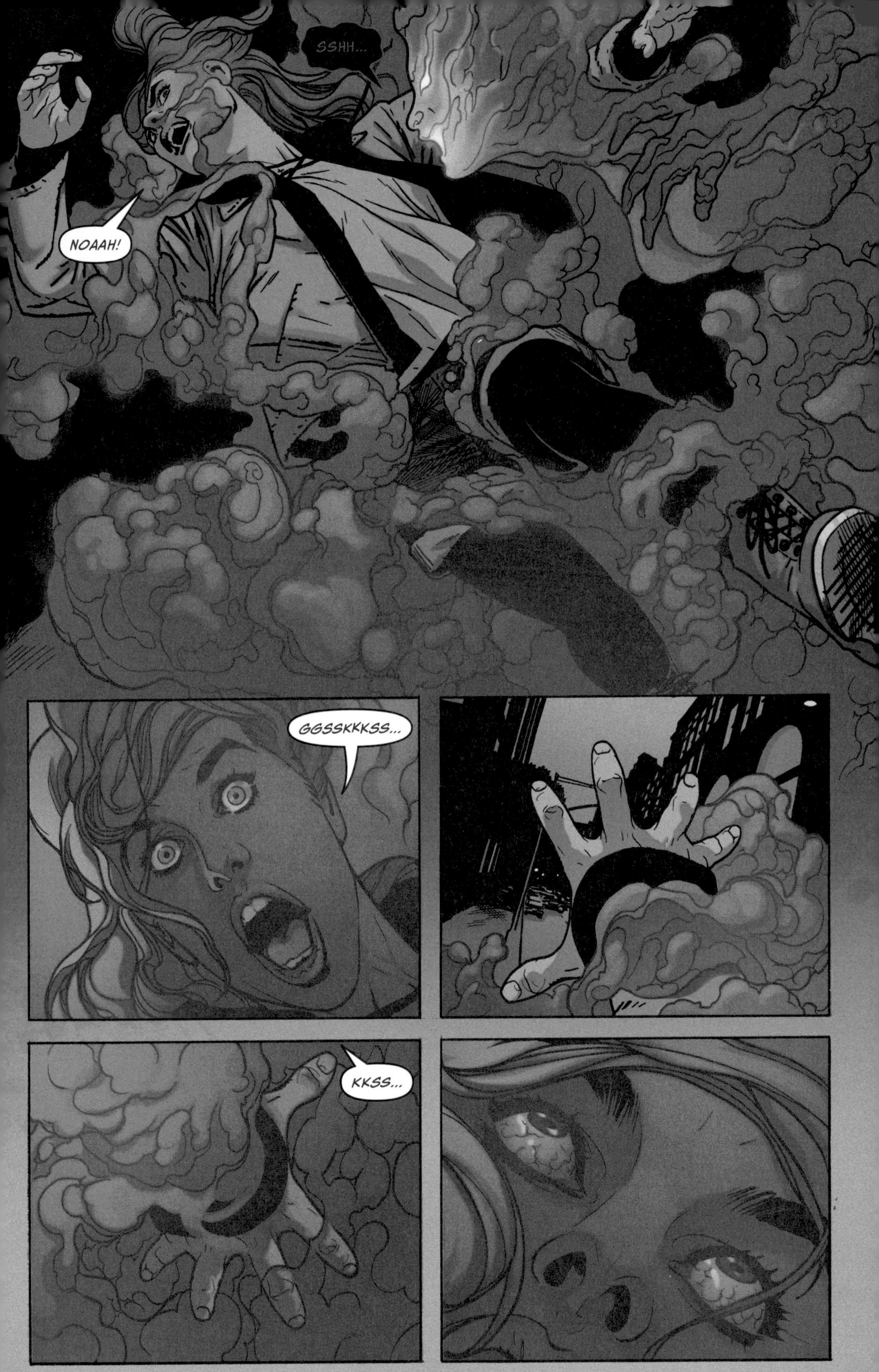
SSHH...
NOAAH!
GGSSKKKSS...
KKSS...

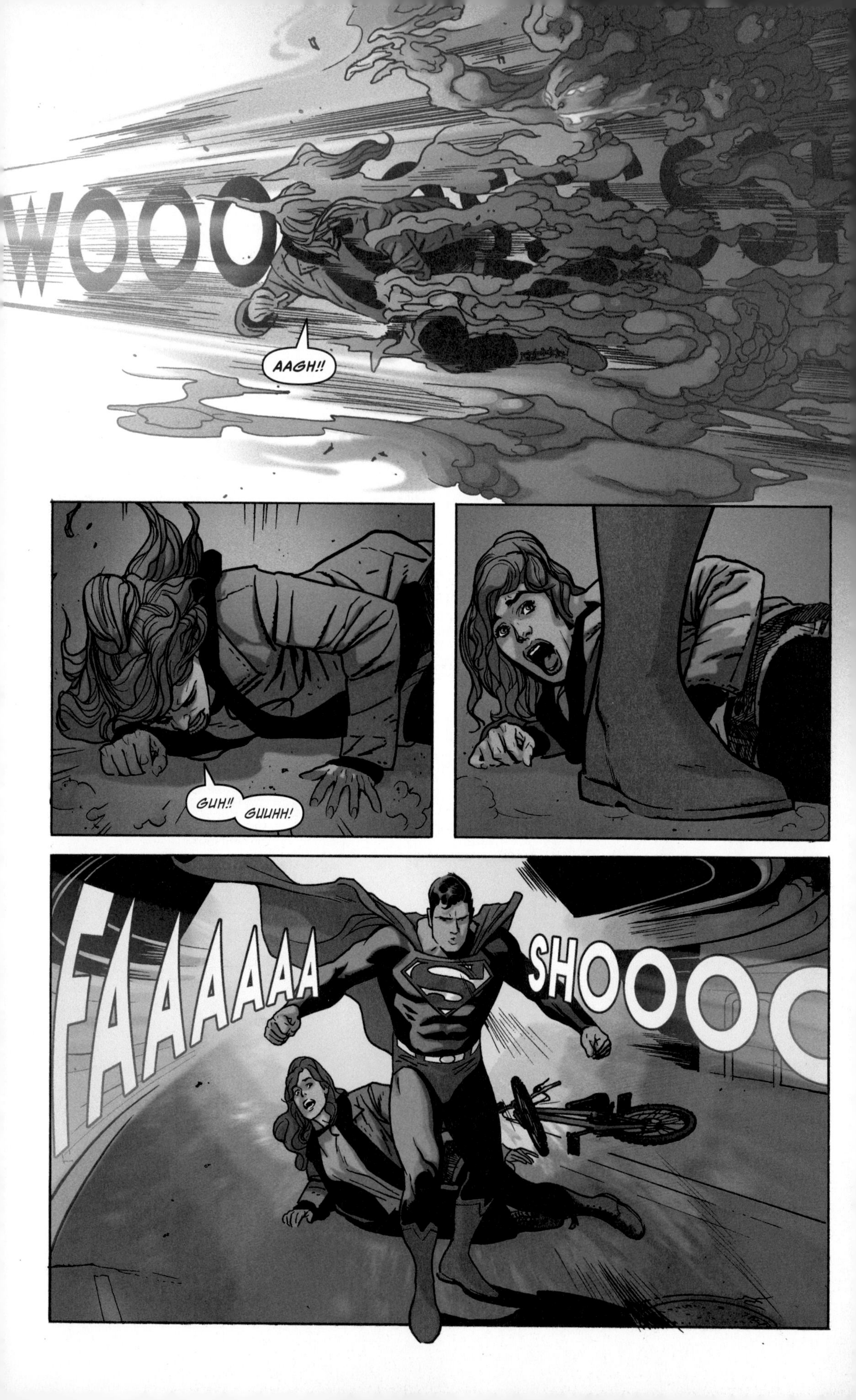
WOOOSH
AAGH!!
GUH!!
GUUHH!
FAAAAAA
SHOOOO

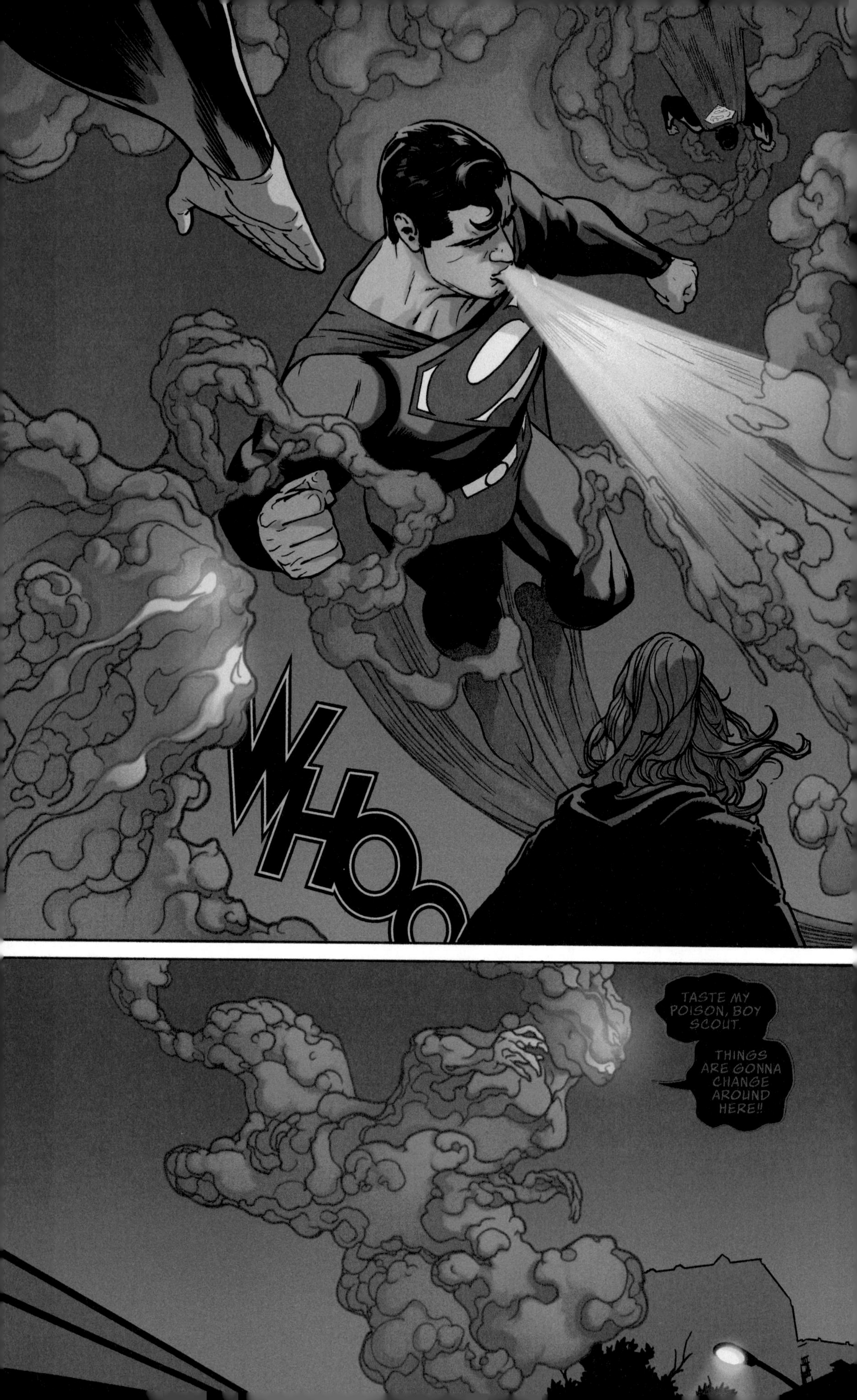
WHOO
TASTE MY POISON, BOY SCOUT.
THINGS ARE GONNA CHANGE AROUND HERE!!

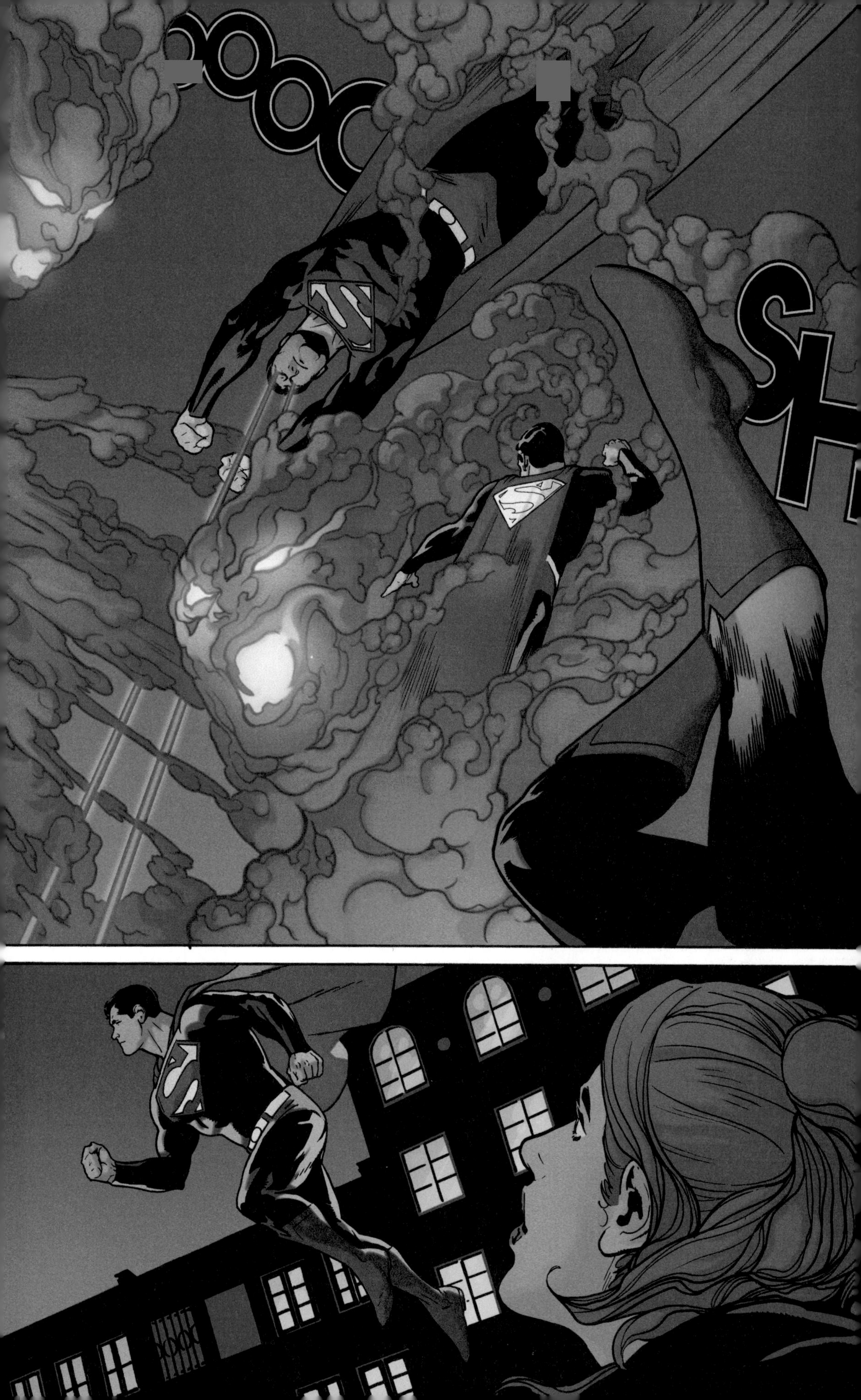
OOOO
SH

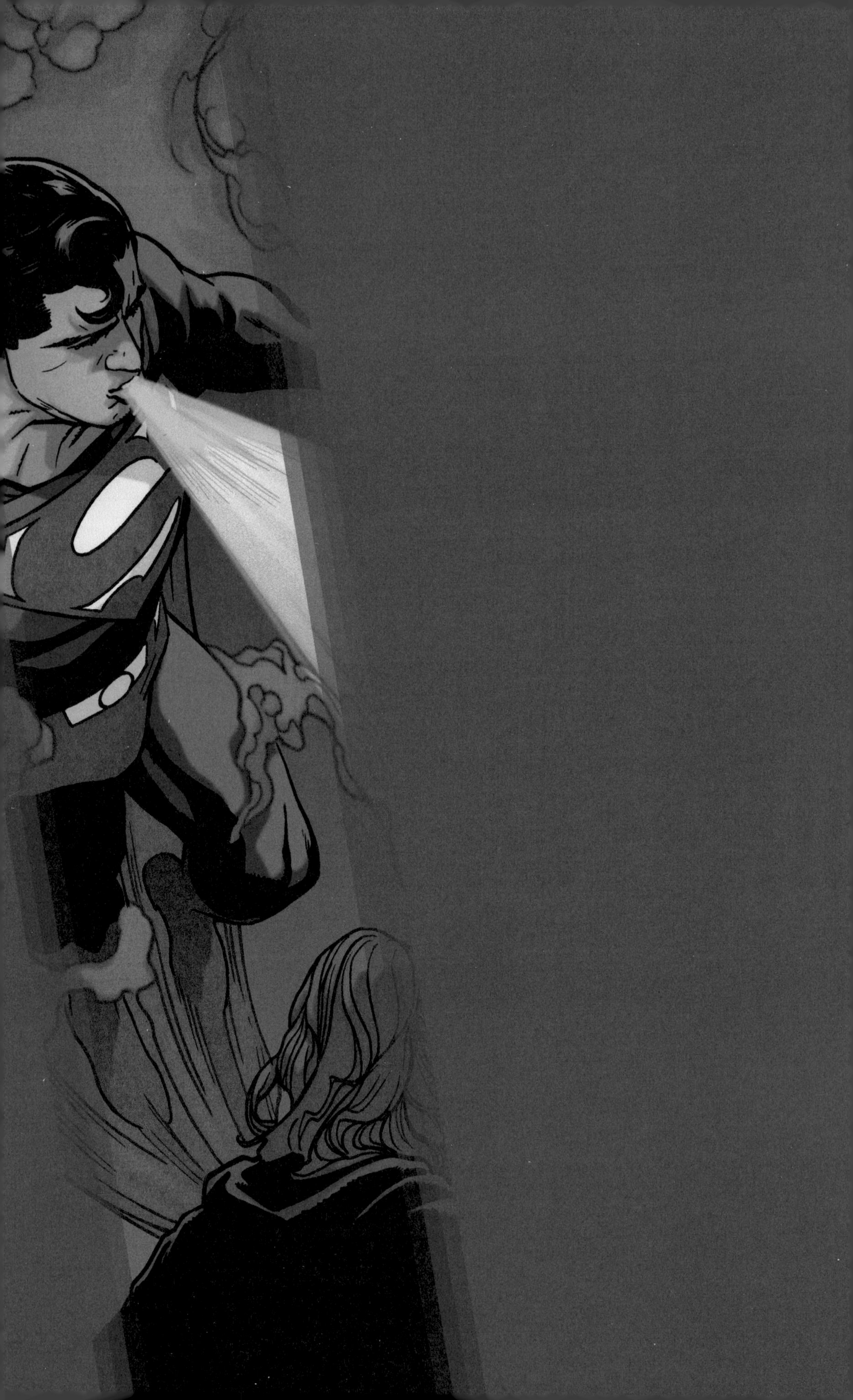

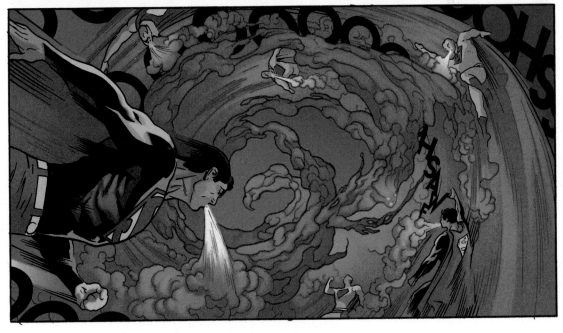

YES. BUT I CHEATED A LITTLE.

IT IS VERY NICE TO MEET YOU FACE TO FACE, ROBINSON.

WHAT I LOVE ABOUT YOU, BEYOND THE OBVIOUS...

...IS YOU SEEM TO INHERENTLY UNDERSTAND AND RESPECT THE PHILOSOPHY BEHIND THE ORGANIZATION.

EVEN PEOPLE WHO WORK FOR ME, AFTER A WHILE, THEY GET--

IT'S LIKE THEY FORGET THE MOST IMPORTANT THING.

I HAVE EXPERTS.

SCIENTISTS WORKING POWER-SET ALGORITHMS TO KEEP AN EYE ON THESE THINGS.

MY NAME IS LEONE. ADD THAT TO THE LIST OF THINGS WE NEVER SAY.

LOOKING FOR NEW PEOPLE I MIGHT HIRE, RECRUIT OR HEADHUNT.

AND YOU'RE RIGHT, WHAT HAPPENED TODAY...THIS DOES CHANGE THINGS.

THEY GET GREEDY.

ARROGANT.

LAZY.

THAT'S WHAT INSPIRED ME TO INSTALL YOU BEFOREHAND.

KLINK

ONE DAY, THE BOY SCOUT, HE CAME HERE AND CHANGED THE RULES AND DIDN'T ASK ANYBODY'S PERMISSION.

BABY, I WAS BORN IN A BASEMENT TENEMENT IN SUICIDE SLUM AND BUILT MYSELF INTO SOMETHING.

AND THIS BLUE BASTARD...

...I HAVE TO GET IT INTO MY SYSTEM, WE'RE NEVER GOING TO KILL HIM.

WE ARE NEVER GOING TO BEAT HIM.

BUT WE'VE BEEN ABLE TO RUN THIS CITY WITHOUT HIM EVEN KNOWING ABOUT IT FOR YEARS...

...AND WE NEED TO GET BACK TO THAT VERY SIMPLE CORPORATE PHILOSOPHY.

I HAVE AN IDEA IN THAT REGARD.

IT'S A BACK-TO-BASICS APPROACH.

IT SENDS A BOLD MESSAGE WITHOUT...

...WITHOUT MAKING THE SAME MISTAKE SO MANY OTHERS HAVE.

OOOOOH...

...I LOVE A NEW PLAN.

AND IT'S GOOD TIMING, TOO, BECAUSE WHILE YOU WERE BUSY DOING YOUR THING...

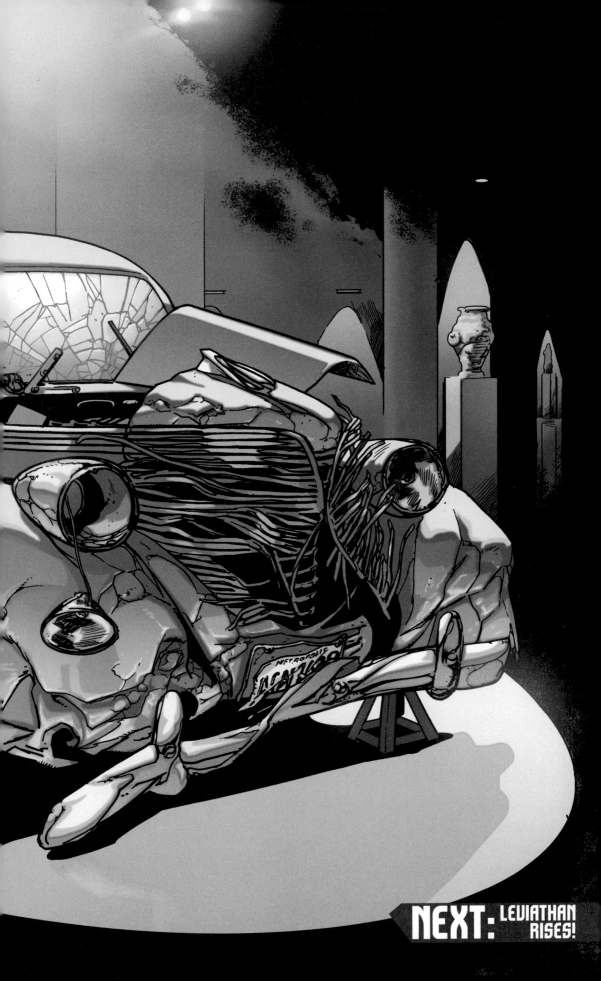

NEXT: LEVIATHAN RISES!

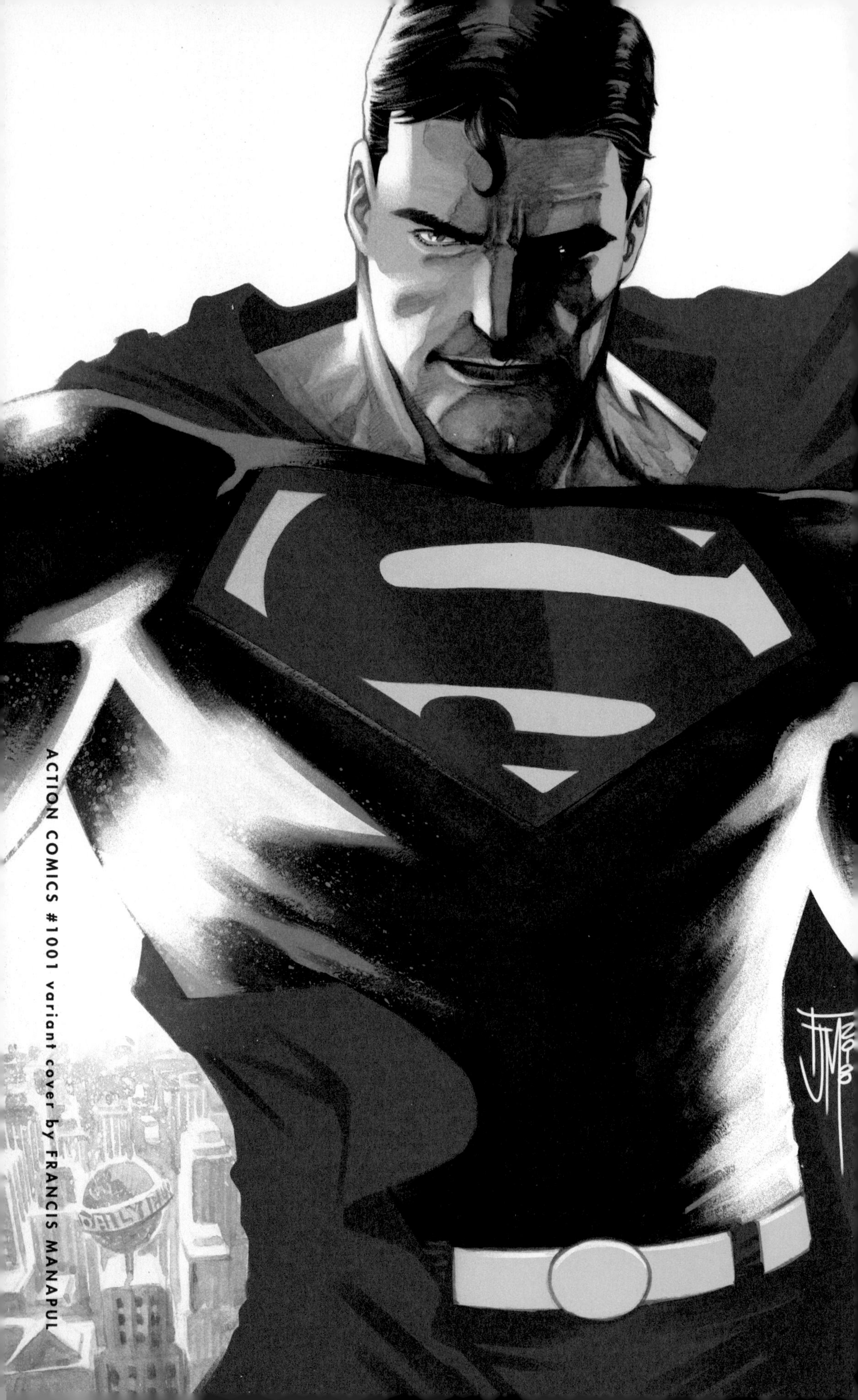

ACTION COMICS #1001 variant cover by FRANCIS MANAPUL

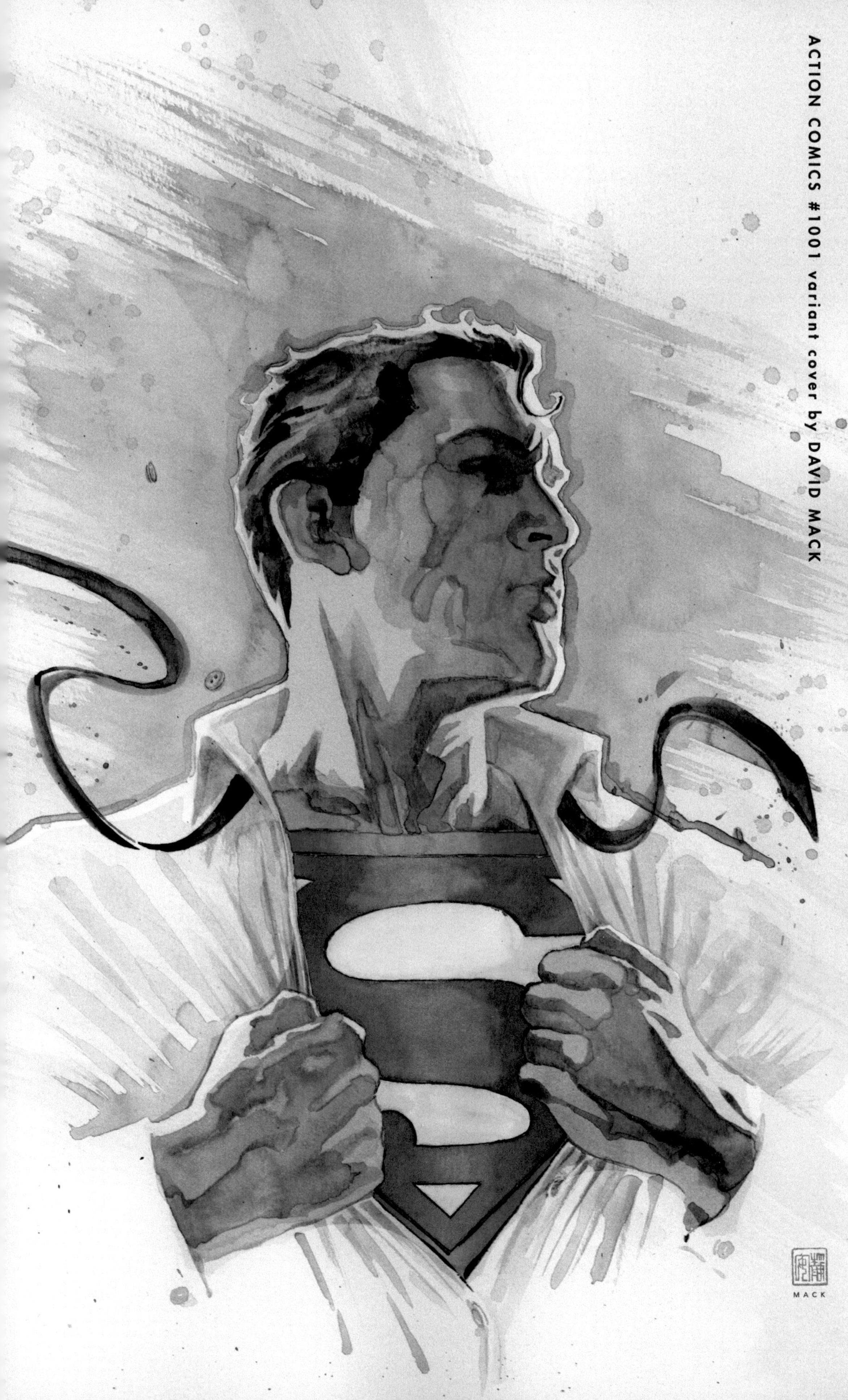
MACK

ACTION COMICS #1001 variant cover by DAVID MACK

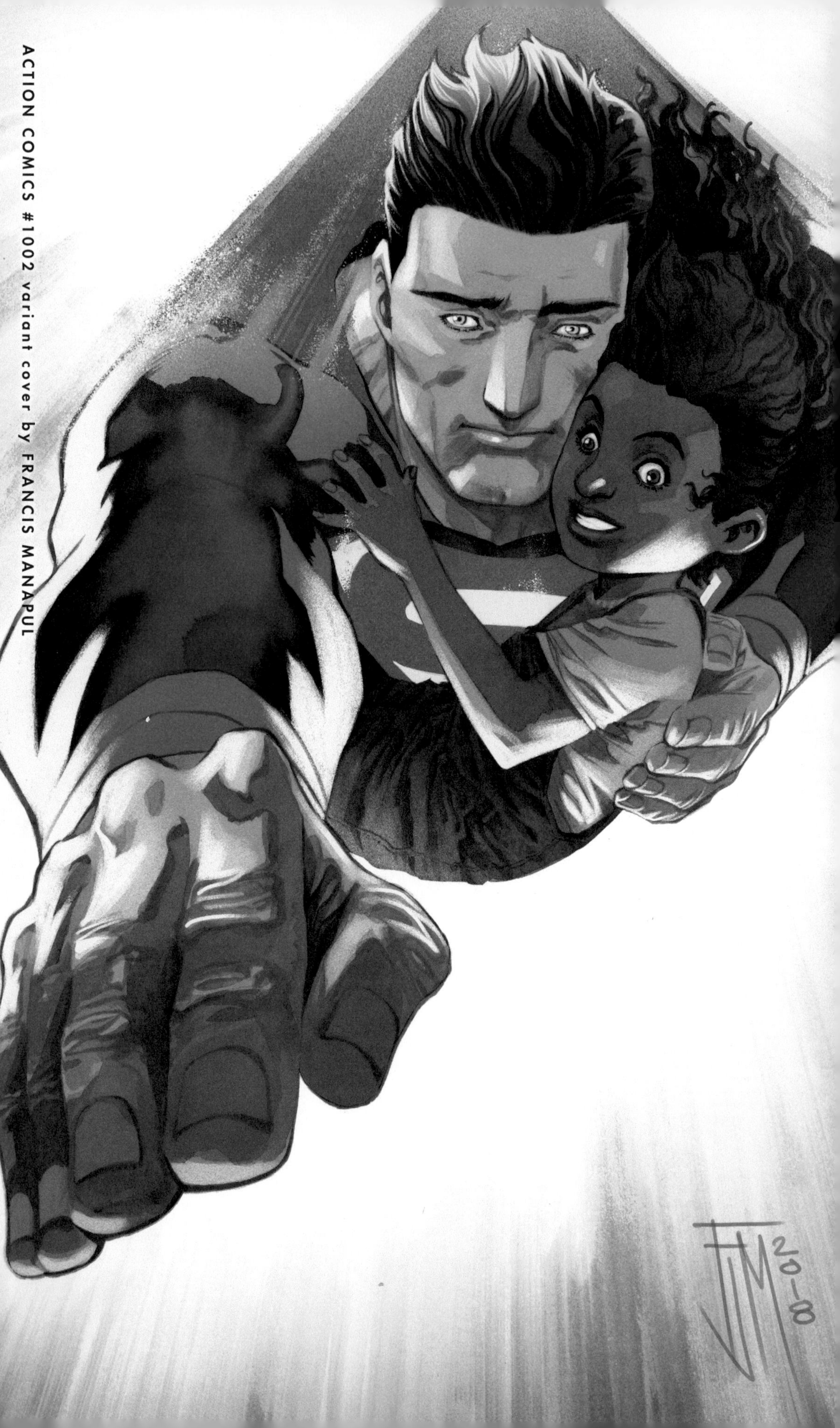

ACTION COMICS #1002 variant cover by FRANCIS MANAPUL

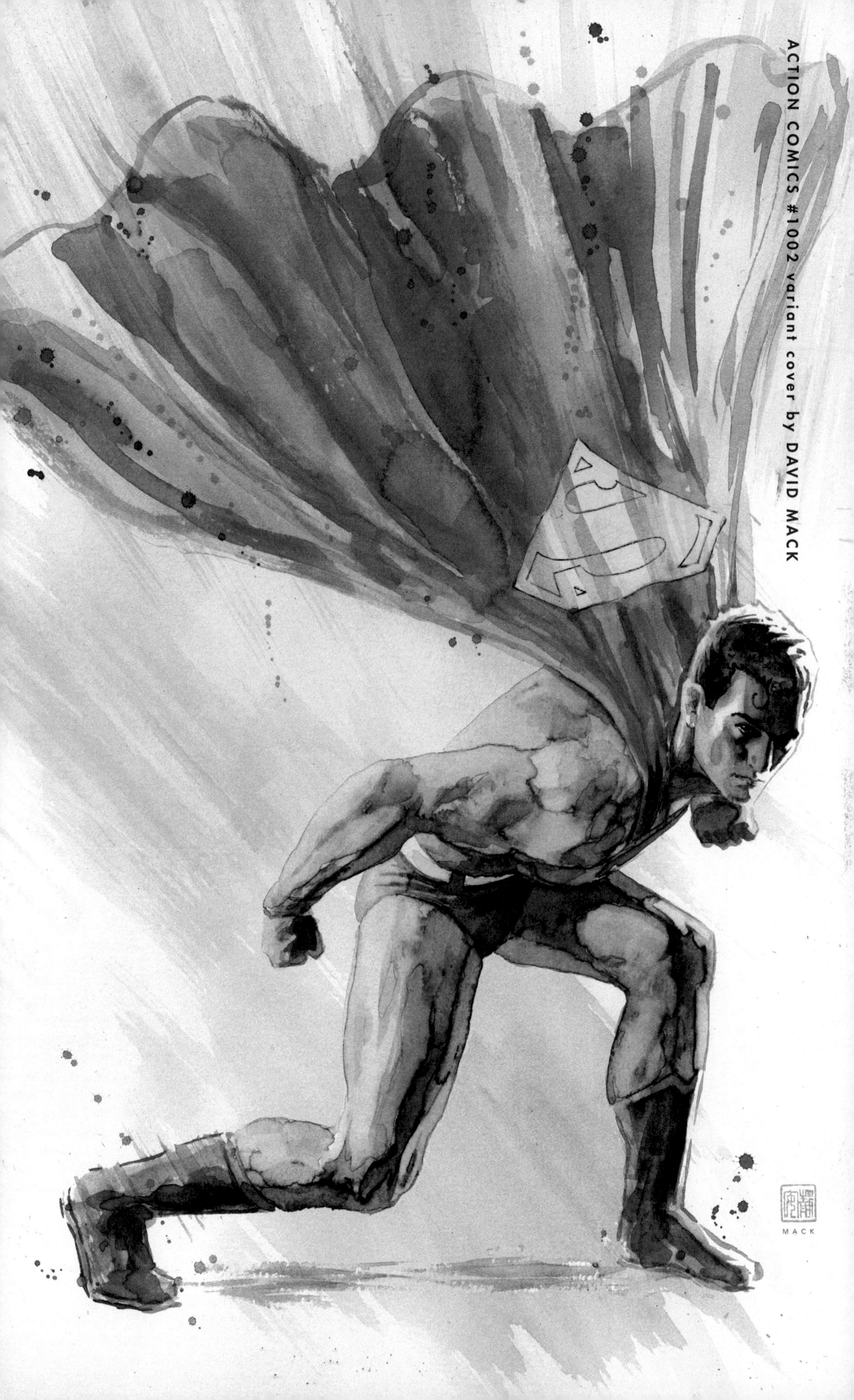
MACK

ACTION COMICS #1002 variant cover by DAVID MACK

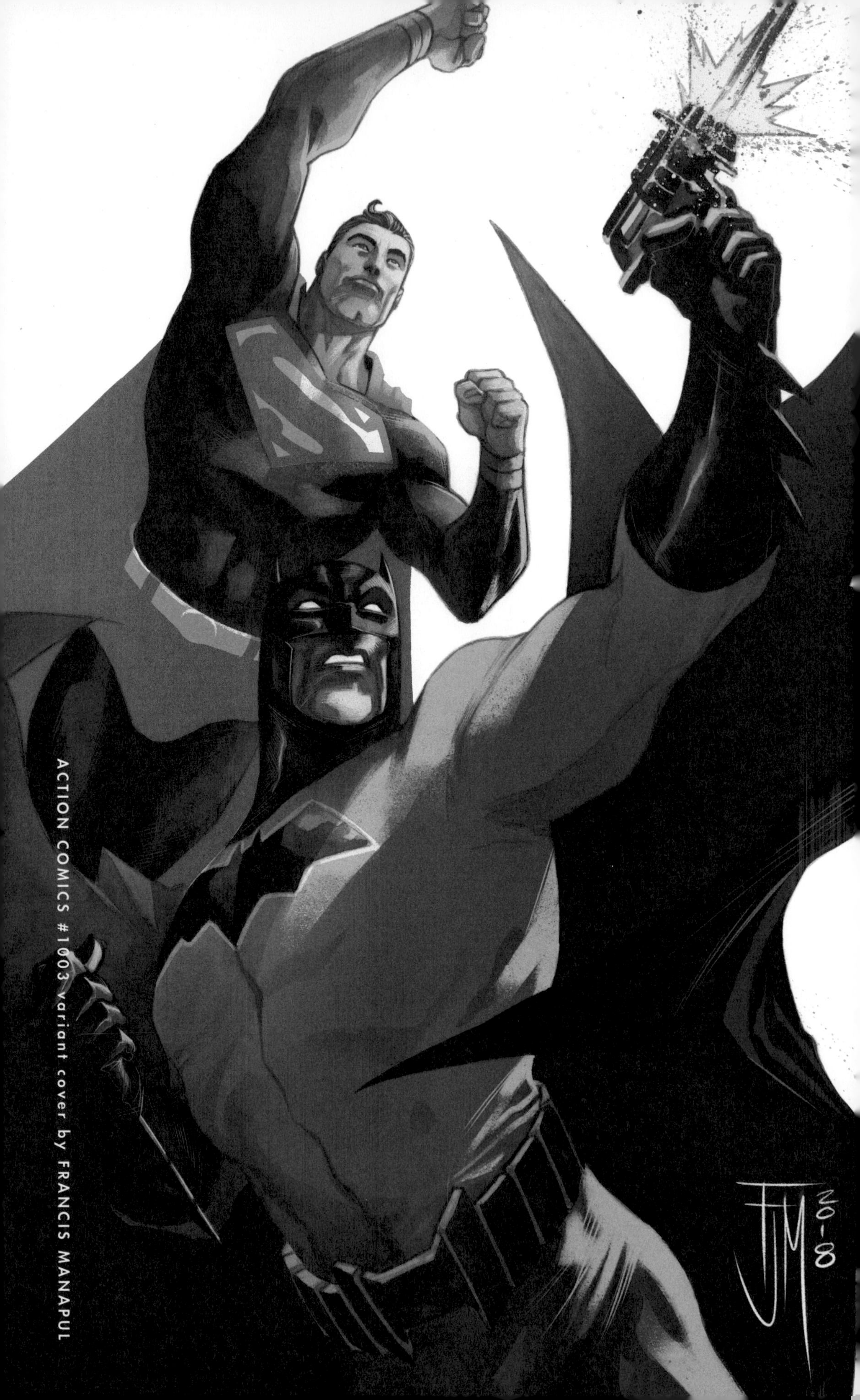

ACTION COMICS #1003 variant cover by FRANCIS MANAPUL

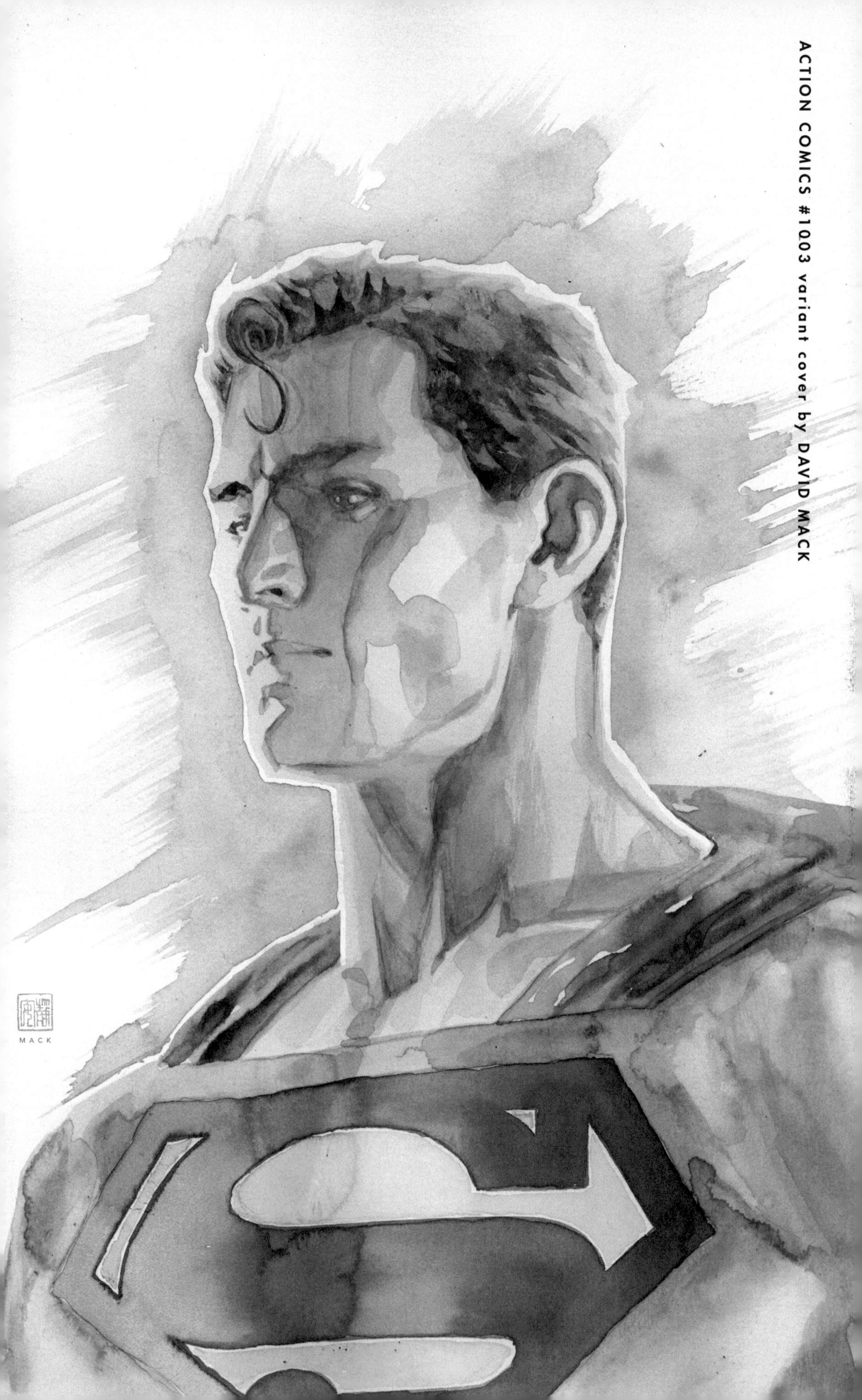
MACK

ACTION COMICS #1003 variant cover by DAVID MACK

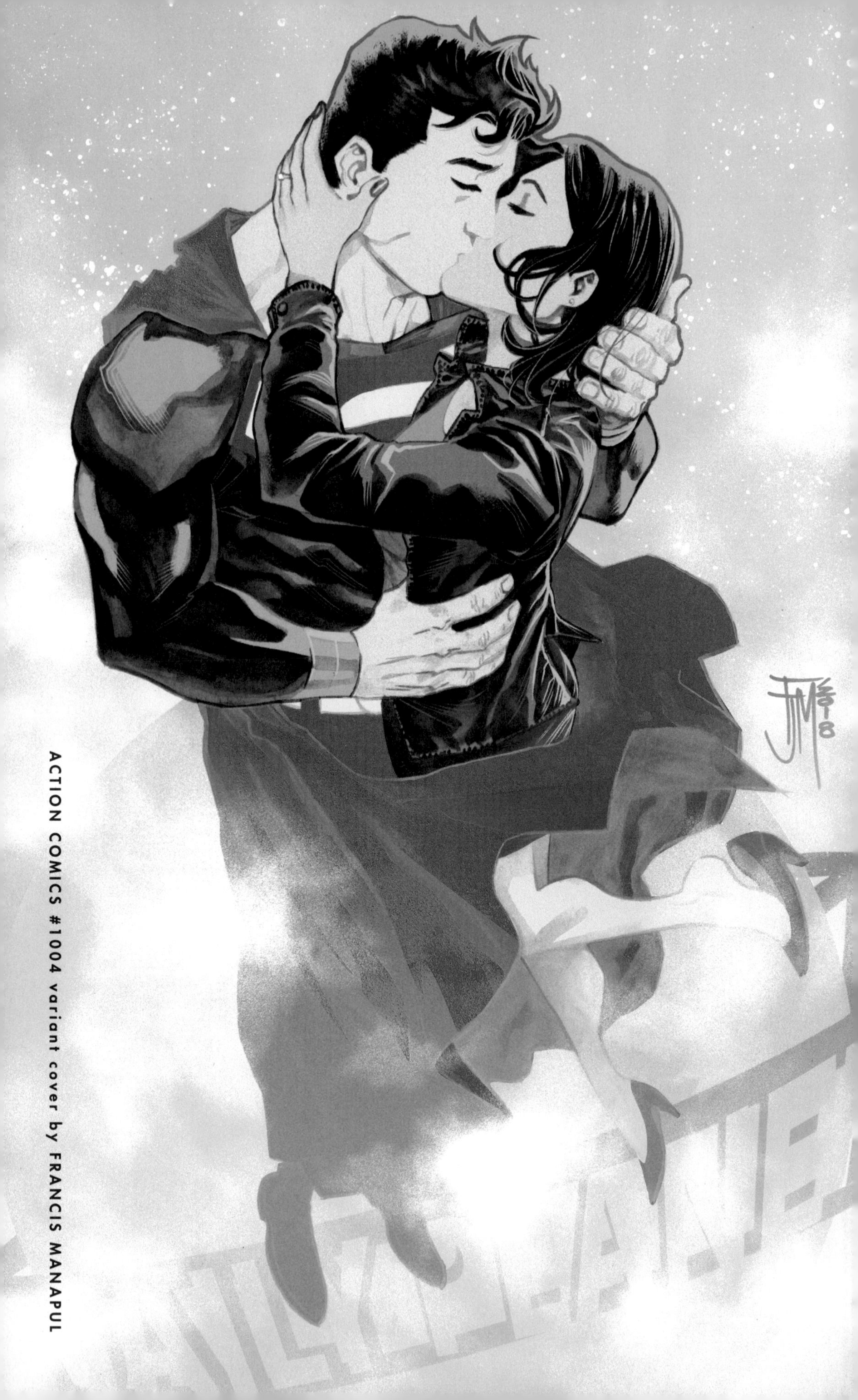

ACTION COMICS #1004 variant cover by FRANCIS MANAPUL

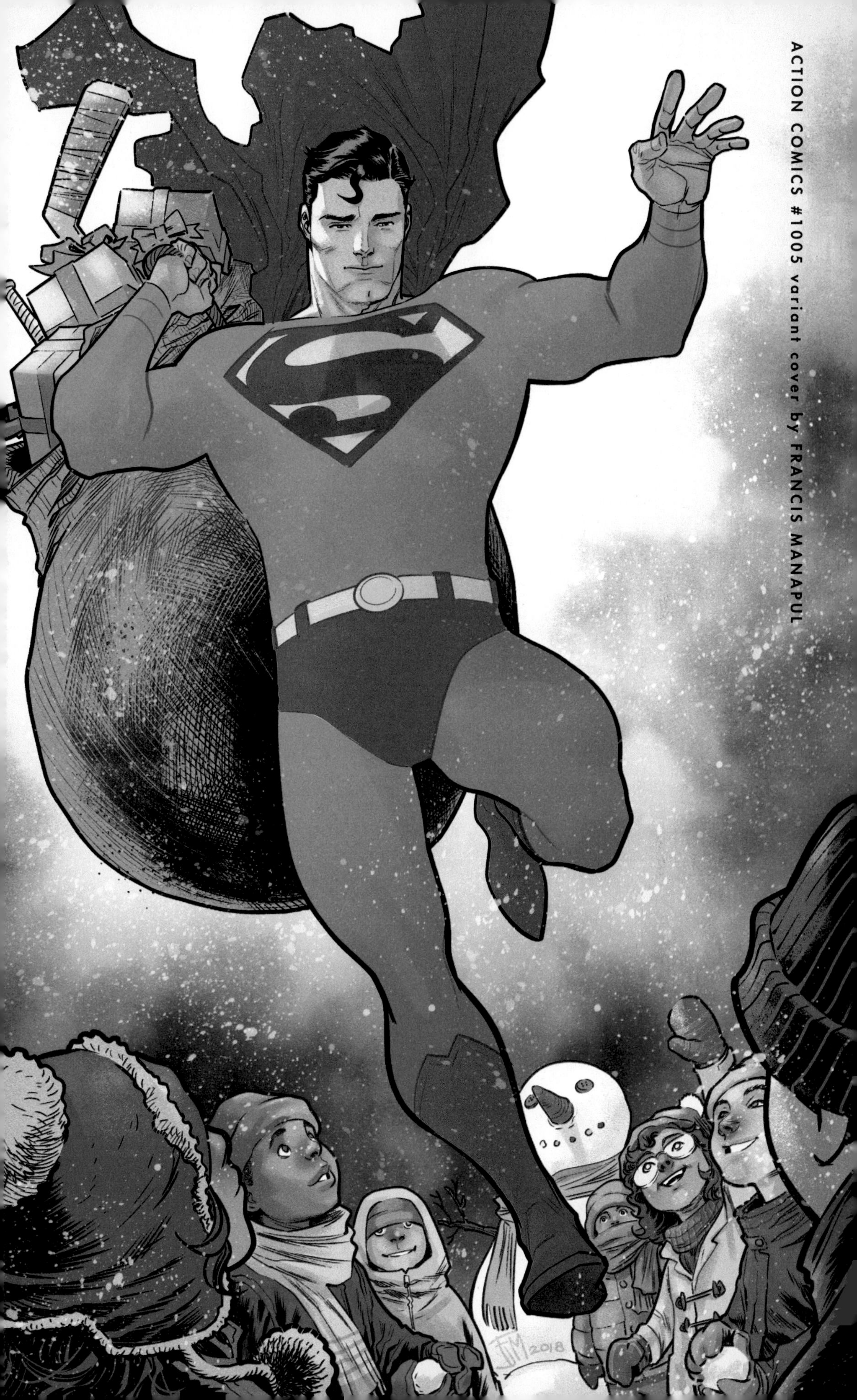

ACTION COMICS #1005 variant cover by FRANCIS MANAPUL

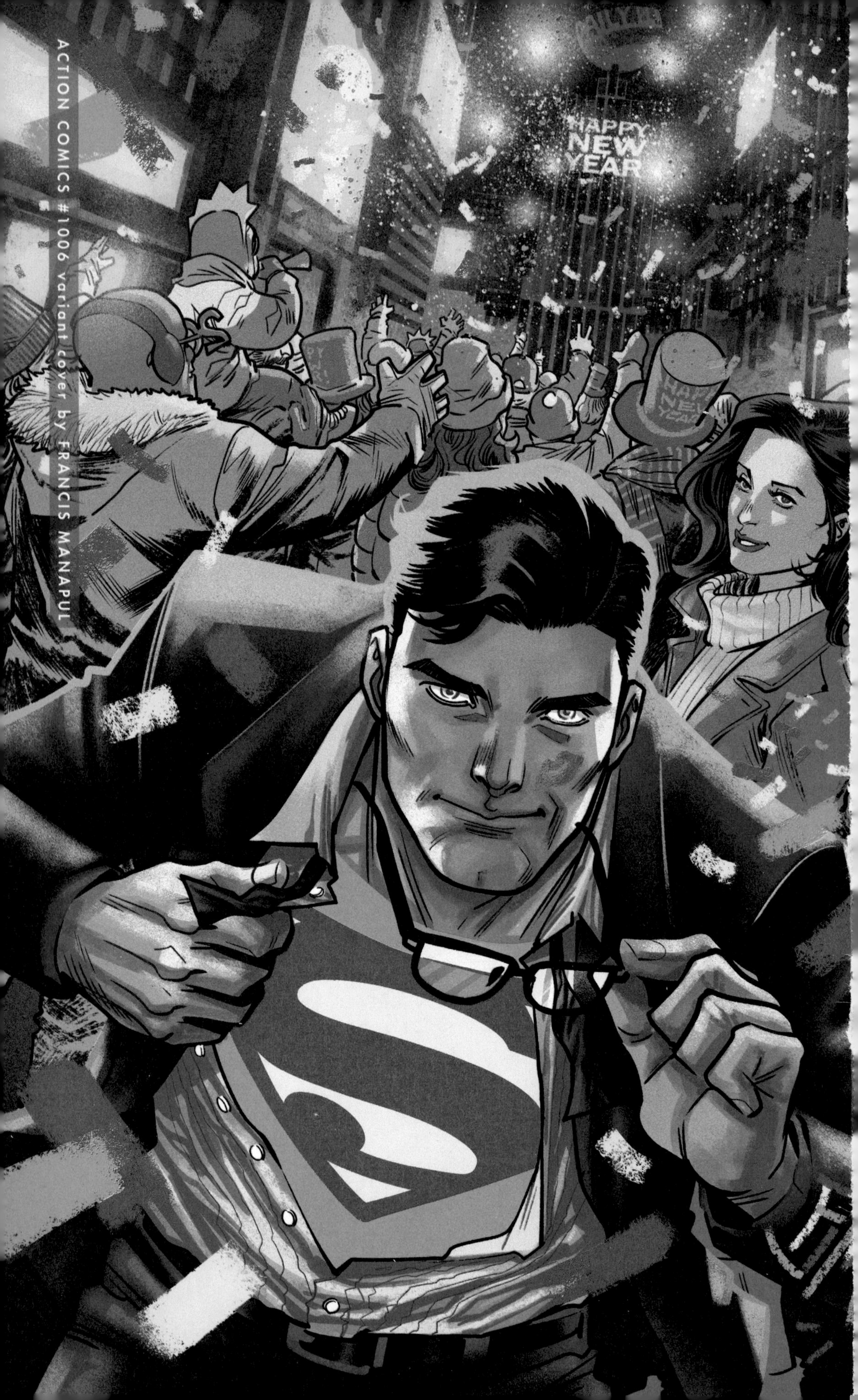
HAPPY NEW YEAR
ACTION COMICS #1006 variant cover by FRANCIS MANAPUL